Anglo-Norman England
1066–1166

Anglo-Norman England
1066–1166

Marjorie Chibnall

Basil Blackwell

© Marjorie Chibnall 1986

First published 1986
Reprinted 1986
First published in paperback 1987

Basil Blackwell Ltd
108 Cowley Road, Oxford OX4 1JF, UK

Basil Blackwell Inc.
432 Park Avenue South, Suite 1503,
New York, NY 10016, USA

British Library Cataloguing in Publication Data

Chibnall, Marjorie
Anglo-Norman England 1066–1166.
1. Great Britain——History——Norman period, 1066–1154
I. Title
942.02   DA195

ISBN 0-631-13234-1
ISBN 0-631-15439-6 Pbk

Library of Congress Cataloging in Publication Data

Chibnall, Marjorie.
Anglo-Norman England, 1066–1166.

Bibliography: p.
Includes index.
1. Great Britain——History——Norman period, 1066–1154. I. Title.
DA195.C47   1986   SOUTH 942.02   85-11255
ISBN 0-631-13234-1
ISBN 0-631-15439-6 (pbk)

Typeset by Freeman Graphic, Tonbridge, Kent
Printed in Great Britain by The Bath Press, Bath

Contents

Maps

Preface

While studying Anglo-Norman history over a long period I have incurred many debts to both colleagues and pupils. In particular I would like to acknowledge with gratitude the stimulus of the Cambridge seminars in medieval history held by Professor J. C. Holt and Dr John Hatcher, and the annual Battle Conferences organized indefatigably by Professor R. Allen Brown. Professor Holt has put me further in his debt by reading a draft of Part II and making valuable suggestions for its improvement. Dr Ann Williams kindly gave me permission to cite her forthcoming paper on the knights of Shaftesbury Abbey; and Dr Martin Brett provided me with a fully collated text of Henry I's coronation charter. My daughter Joan has given me valuable assistance with the proofs. Finally, I am grateful to Mr John Davey of Basil Blackwell for inviting me to write this book, and to the editorial staff and cartographer for their practical helpfulness in guiding it through the press.

Marjorie Chibnall
Clare Hall
Cambridge

Introduction

For some centuries the history of the Norman conquest and its aftermath has been rewritten in every generation. It is one of the events that have been constantly reinterpreted in terms of the political conflicts and social problems of the moment, and so have found a place – often an impassioned place – in literature, oratory, and legal controversy no less than in academic history. In the seventeenth century Henry Spelman and Robert Cotton traced the feudal customs that had become legal abuses in their day back to the Norman conquest.[1] They and their fellow antiquaries helped to foster the myth of the 'Norman yoke' imposed by an alien king and landlords on free and equal Englishmen:[2] a myth elaborated by reformers and revolutionaries in their day, cherished by romantic nineteenth-century writers like Charles Kingsley and George Borrow, and strong enough to colour the work of some academic historians in the rising history faculties. E. A. Freeman's exaggerated and uncritical championing of English freedom helped to provoke the equally exaggerated though more critical attacks of J. H. Round. The controversies of these two learned men – for Freeman was as thoroughly versed in chronicles as Round was in charters and administrative records – have left so deep a mark on a century of historical study that, as late as 1972, two Belgian historians could divide the English writers of works on military organization into 'neo-Freemanians' and 'neo-Roundians'.[3]

Yet in fact the intense historical activity of the past half-century has achieved a much greater measure of critical detachment than this jesting comment implies. Studies of the period, particularly numerous since the ninth centenary year of 1966, have led to a rephrasing of many important questions. There is a far keener appreciation of the relevance of European

[1] D. C. Douglas, *The Norman Conquest and British Historians* (David Murray Lecture, Glasgow, 1946).

[2] Christopher Hill, *Puritanism and Revolution* (London, 1958), pp. 57 ff.

[3] F. L. Ganshof and R. C. van Caenegem, *Les institutions féodo-vassaliques* (Introduction bibliographique à l'histoire du droit et à l'ethnologie juridique, Brussels, 1972), p. 20 n. 13.

social developments to changes taking place in England and Normandy both before and after the conquest. There is also a clearer understanding of the nature of the gradual assimilation of Norman and English institutions over several decades. Fewer serious historians continue to fight the old Freeman–Round battles, or to align themselves with the English or the Normans, and claim all the political, constitutional or artistic achievements for one side, even if some of the old illusions persist in works of popularization. When we talk about the question of the 'introduction of knight service into England' we know that we are quoting Round, not stating a historical fact; and that knight service, as it evolved in post-conquest England, had not existed in exactly that form in either the kingdom of Edward the Confessor or the earlier duchy of Normandy. Questions now need to be reformulated to take account of what happened. We must not push back conditions shown in mid twelfth-century records into the reign of William I. Fiefs took time to develop in a hereditary form; feudal obligations were only slowly defined.

So much has been written on 'feudalism' that some historians now shy away from the word altogether. This is too drastic; one might more usefully adapt Voltaire's aphorism, 'if feudalism did not exist, we would need to invent it.' For though historical discussion of feudalism has sometimes become a question of semantics, long before the word was coined in the seventeenth century the legal, social and military organization it expressed was a reality in many parts of western Europe. The basic territorial units, however, were not the fiefs or fees (*feuda*), the units of knightly tenure owing more or less standardized services from which later theorists derived the name. They were the extensive estates or honours of the great barons, centred on a principal residence (caput) which was often a castle, with their nerve centre in the honour court. These courts were places for military training, social life and the transaction of business. In them the military dependants of the great tenants-in-chief bound themselves to their lord in the ceremony of homage and became his vassals, undertaking whatever military or other service was customary at the time. There too some received rewards in land and were granted tenure (technically seised) of it in a visible ceremony of enfeoffment; and there they were punished if they failed in their duty to their lord. Courts were frequented too by many household knights, particularly younger sons, who were paid wages and held no land, but served in hope.

When the Normans came to England the honour court was a reality in Normandy; mounted knights and castles (whether ducal or private) were realities too. Contemporaries did not think in terms of knights' fees; these emerged slowly as enfeoffment reacted on older customs of patri-

monial inheritance and fiscal needs required the assessment in terms of
cash of services that might no longer be demanded. When in 1166 Henry
II enquired of his tenants-in-chief how many knights they had enfeoffed
before 1135 and how many since, how many fiefs these knights held and
how many knights were still serving in their households without land, the
barons sent back the returns known as the *cartae baronum,* which show
a widespread network of knights' fees.[4] A hundred years earlier the
relationship between lord and vassal had been more personal, but all the
seeds of feudal development were already in it. This was, however, only
one side of the picture. In the English kingdom as the Normans found it
there was always much that was not feudal, in the powers and traditions
of kingship and in the ancient courts and customs of the land, as well as
in the law and organization that was common to the whole of the
western church.

In writing this book my object has been to ask new questions rather
than to rehearse arguments for and against the ancient theories; and to
try to relate the recent findings of historians in specialized fields to the
general course of English development. Unpublished charters have come
to light, and old law books and chronicles have been re-evaluated
in new editions. Domesday studies have profited from the work of
V. H. Galbraith and others; fundamental work has been published on
law by S. F. C. Milsom and R. C. van Caenegem, on inheritance customs
by John Le Patourel and J. C. Holt, on military service and castles by
J. O. Prestwich and the authors of *The King's Works,* on literacy by
M. C. Clanchy, and on individual reigns by David Douglas, C. Warren
Hollister, Frank Barlow and R. H. C. Davis, to name but a few. Archae-
ology, numismatics and language studies have all added to our appreciation of the interplay of different cultures. The work of the giants –
particularly F. M. Stenton and F. W. Maitland – remains fundamental;
some revision of their work has inevitably become necessary, yet the
penetration with which they evaluated the material they knew and
anticipated later discoveries based on sources hidden from them remains
a constant source of wonder and admiration. My debt to them, as well as
to more recent writers, will be apparent on every page.

My chosen dates, 1066 to 1166, are open to objections, as any dates
must be; yet they have great advantages. The first century of English
feudalism, as Stenton called it, opened with the battle of Hastings and
closed with Henry II's inquest into military service that produced the
cartae baronum of 1166. The relevance of this particular century to
feudal change is apparent; but it marks a stage of English historical
development in other ways as well. Before 1066 there had been relations

[4] See Stenton, *English Feudalism,* pp. 137–9.

of various kinds between England and Normandy; the marriage of Duke Richard II's sister, Emma, to King Aethelred in 1002, and Edward the Confessor's upbringing in exile at the Norman court brought a number of Norman knights and churchmen to England, and prepared the way for a Norman claim to the crown. There were cultural and trading exchanges; yet the contact was 'normal and neighbourly, and it did not involve the kind of interpenetration that took place after 1066'.[5] Time was necessary for the nature and effects of that interpenetration to begin to show clearly, and there are objections to attempting to assess them from the standpoint of 1087, or 1135, or 1154, rather than 1166.

At first the most visible results of the conquest were depopulation in certain regions through fighting and castle building, the violent dispossession of the greater part of the English aristocracy and their replacement by Normans (with a sprinkling of Bretons and Flemings), and the slightly slower taking over of church appointments by continental bishops and abbots. But an assessment made in 1087 would be misleading; the long-term changes only became apparent later. The reigns of William I's sons were of immense importance in administrative and financial development, as well as being the time when the Normans became fully integrated in English society without weakening their cross-Channel ties.

Yet much was still experimental; from the standpoint of 1135 or 1154 one might well ask how far the changes of the early twelfth century would be permanent, what difference was made by the anarchical interlude of Stephen's reign, and how far Henry II was building on earlier achievements, how far moving in a different direction. By 1166 Henry had restored the boundaries of his father's realm, abandoned some undesirable judicial expedients, issued his first great assizes, instituted the first general eyres,[6] and attempted in a new way to define the limits of secular and ecclesiastical jurisdiction. Danegeld, though not formally abandoned, had been collected for the last time; the *cartae* of 1166 provided information for a more comprehensive system of assessing aids on the knight's fee. The social changes that followed the conquest were beginning to show, but had not yet been distorted by the rapid inflation of the late twelfth century. And something approaching a common law was emerging, even though the attempt of Glanvill towards the end of the reign to describe some general rules was in places no more than an assertion of the rules some of the royal justices thought desirable, and in others (particularly on freedom and villeinage) hopelessly confused. I have had to look at some of the treatises and some evidence later than

---

[5] Le Patourel, *Feudal Empires*, ch. 18.
[6] See below, p. 179.

1166 to illustrate trends; but by concentrating on the period before that date rather than including the whole reign of Henry II it has been easier to avoid implying too rapid a systematization, or too inevitable a process of change. For the study of far more than feudal history in England, Stenton chose his century wisely.

One further objection may be raised. To devote a book to Anglo-Norman England may seem retrograde, even if it extends a little beyond the bounds of England to include some Norman settlement in Wales and on the moving Scottish border. The work of recent scholars has placed the Anglo-Norman realm in its European setting. Le Patourel in particular has shown the influence of the cross-Channel estates in shaping Norman institutions and policy, and the reality of the Norman *imperium* or empire. The most recent German book by K.-U. Jäschke sees the Anglo-Normans in relation to the whole of Europe; and a similar reorientation of study has been undertaken by a number of historians, including James Campbell for Anglo-Saxon England and David Bates for Normandy. But it is not necessary to repeat what Le Patourel has done so well; and though this book is about England, I have tried to keep the wider context always in mind, and to show in what ways it affected changes in England. During the century after the Norman conquest, law and society changed as a result of the interaction of peoples and cultures; there was no question of English interests being sacrificed in foreign adventures, as is still sometimes asserted. By the mid-twelfth century the Normans in England were appropriating English history as part of their own tradition, alongside the annals and legends of their own people.[7] Intermarriage was taking place at all levels from the king downwards. The two cultures became increasingly intermingled during an age of rapid change, and were always open to influence by new European movements. By the reign of Henry II an Anglo-Norman culture and society had emerged and was to survive. This book is concerned with what it was, and how it came into being.

---

[7] Southern, *Medieval Humanism*, pp. 154–5.

PART I

Conquest and Settlement

1

The First Phases of Conquest

The first phase of the conquest of England began on 16 October 1066, after the armies of Duke William of Normandy and King Harold met, in the words of the *Anglo-Saxon Chronicle*, 'at the hoary apple-tree', and after bitter fighting and heavy casualties on both sides, 'King Harold was killed and Earl Leofwine his brother and Earl Gyrth his brother . . . and the French remained masters of the field.' Even so decisive a victory was only a beginning. The English hesitated to submit; only after William's army, reinforced by fresh knights from overseas, advanced towards London, were the chief magnates, led by the earls Edwin and Morcar, with Archbishop Ealdred of York and the Londoners persuaded of the hopelessness of rallying round Edgar Atheling as a rival claimant. They made their submission, and William's coronation in Edward the Confessor's new church at Westminster set the seal of legitimacy on his rule.[1] It did not bring peace or security to the Normans. For the next four or five years of uneasy co-operation with the half-conquered English they were, even in the southern part of the kingdom, in the position of an army of occupation. In the north they faced the particularly difficult problem of subduing a province with a long tradition of independence; the western frontier was open to attack from the Welsh princes, recently defeated by Harold, and to raids from dispossessed English who had fled to Ireland. The most pressing need during the first phase of conquest and settlement was to maintain a strong military force in a country of doubtful loyalty. It was a need that left an indelible stamp on the Norman settlement.

The army William led to conquer England was a formidable, highly

[1] *ASC* (CDE) 1066; William of Poitiers, pp. 184–223. *The Anglo-Saxon Chronicle* is the name given to a number of annalistic compilations written in Old English in various English monasteries. The two most important versions for the period after C (compiled at Abingdon) ends in 1066 are D, a northern compilation, and E, written first at St Augustine's, Canterbury, and from 1121 at Peterborough. See *The Anglo-Saxon Chronicle*, ed. Whitelock, Douglas and Tucker.

trained force of mounted knights, made up of various elements. Of prime importance were the leading vassals whom he had consulted in an assembly at Bonneville-sur-Touques before embarking on the enterprise: men such as Robert, count of Eu, Richard fitz Gilbert, William, count of Evreux, William fitz Osbern and William of Warenne, who were related to the ducal family. They brought their vassals and dependents, who fought under their leadership in closely-knit units.[2] Similar groups of knights were brought from Brittany, Boulogne and other territories by men who were not William's vassals, but who joined the enterprise in the hope of gain. Another large element consisted of the stipendiary knights in the duke's household troops: men drawn to a great extent from landed families, who had undergone the same training as the landed vassals, but had not yet inherited or acquired substantial estates. The core of the army was a force of fighting men, seasoned in the many wars Duke William had fought to establish himself in his duchy, resist invasion from France and Anjou, establish a new southern outpost in the fortress town of Domfront, and most recently to conquer and hold Maine.

The mailed knights were trained to fight on horseback or on foot, singly or in groups, with lance and sword; to charge an enemy line and, if necessary, carry out the most difficult manoevre of retreating, reforming, and charging again: the so-called feigned flight. They were supported by skilled archers, and possibly also at Hastings by some crossbow men. Equally experienced in sustaining long sieges, they could construct small siege castles and motte and bailey castles at high speed with the aid of requisitioned local labour. This knowledge enabled them to establish firm bases as they advanced into hostile country, and use them as spring-boards for further advance. The nature of the army, with organized vassal groups under their own leaders, and stipendiaries in the household troops trained under their captains (known as *magistri militum*), made it possible for William to assemble a large force from provinces as diverse as Maine, Brittany, Picardy, Poitou, Burgundy, Anjou and Normandy, and weld it into an efficient fighting body in a matter of weeks. The final training was carried out in the weeks between mid-August and late September, when the army waited on the coast of Normandy for a favourable moment to launch the attack. They may have been waiting for a favourable wind, as the Norman sources, eager to stress the piety and prayers of their duke and point to the hand of God in his victory, liked to maintain. But a change of wind in response to the prayer of a man of God was a favourite theme in miracle stories, and the *Anglo-Saxon Chronicle* said nothing of any wind.[3] Instead it recorded that King Harold and his

---

[2] William of Poitiers, pp. 148–51; Le Patourel, 'The Norman colonization of Britain', pp. 420–38; Le Patourel, *Norman Empire*, ch. 2.

[3] Cf. *Vita Herluini*, pp. 100–1.

land force waited in the Isle of Wight 'until the provisions of the people were gone and nobody could keep them there any longer'. The delay may have been a deliberate tactic of William, who had ensured the adequate provisioning of his army, to outwit Harold and complete the training of his own followers. As little as possible was left to chance. Planning and military skill made the hard-won victory at Hastings just possible. To complete the conquest and establish firm foundations for his rule it was essential to keep a substantial part of his army in England on a war footing.

Minor changes in the army took place both in the lull between the victory at Hastings and the march on London and in the months immediately after William's coronation. Some of the ablest of his vassals, notably Roger of Montgomery, vicomte of the Hiémois and husband of the Bellême heiress, Mabel, had been left behind to help the duchess Matilda to administer Normandy. They could now be brought over. Some leaders were unwilling to remain in England, possibly because they considered the enterprise too risky and were satisfied with the extent of their continental patrimonies, although chroniclers suggested that they either had no taste for plunder or were lured home by their unfaithful wives. Both Gilbert of Auffay and the Poitevin, Aimery of Thouars, were among those who went home early; Humphrey of Tilleul remained less than two years.[4] Besides these defections, the heavy casualties at Hastings made some replacements necessary. These changes did not affect the nature of the army. William was able to make some limited use during his early campaigns of any Englishmen who wished to serve him; but they had different methods of fighting and, until a new generation could be trained in Norman-Frankish warfare, they could not become an integral part of the army, even when their loyalty could be trusted.

So practical considerations underlay his early provisions for the defence of the country and the reward of his followers. His immediate task was to secure the south coast ports that guarded his lines of communication. The establishment of his men in Sussex, Kent and Hampshire was made easier by the great extent of the royal demesne and the lands of the house of Godwin in these counties, and the fact that many English thegns from the region had fought against him at Hastings and thereby forfeited their lands. The first need was to construct and man castles; some of these were rapidly run up within a few weeks of the Norman landing. Immediately on landing the Normans constructed a rough fortification at Pevensey within the Roman fortress, followed by a second motte at the better base of Hastings. After the battle they secured and fortified Dover. Humphrey of Tilleul was put in charge of the garrison at Hastings. When William returned to Normandy after a

[4] Orderic, ii. 194–7, 220–1; iii. 254–7; Le Patourel, *Norman Empire*, p. 29.

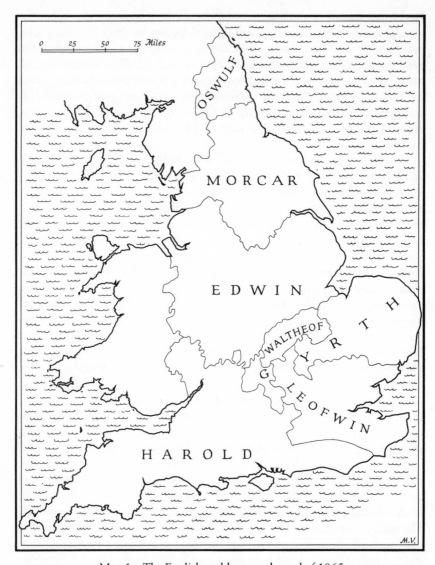

MAP 1   The English earldoms at the end of 1065
(after E. A. Freeman, *The History of the Norman Conquest of England*, 6 vols,
Oxford, 1867–79)

triumphal progress in March, 1067, he made further provisions for the
control of the southern counties. His half-brother, Odo, bishop of
Bayeux, was entrusted with Dover and the greater part of Kent; William
fitz Osbern, already charged with the defence of the Isle of Wight, was
given a base at Winchester, where work began on the castle. By the end of

that year, when the king returned from Normandy, the defensive arrangements in Sussex were completed. His half-brother Robert, count of Mortain, had probably already been based in Pevensey, and his kinsman William of Warenne received Lewes at an early date. Roger of Montgomery, who accompanied William on his return, was then given Arundel, so that the castles manned by loyal Normans guarded almost all the river estuaries of Sussex. The one exception was the river Adur; but within a few years a fifth castellany had been established in Bramber, just by Steyning, under William of Braose, one of the new men who rose through the opportunities offered by the conquest. The grant of land in the five districts, which took the old name of rape for a new territorial division, followed very rapidly.[5]

Recent studies have recognized that lands in vulnerable regions were kept to some extent in compact blocks focused on castles. The older view that William at first normally granted the scattered lands of individual Englishmen to his followers as they were forfeited, and changed policy in certain regions after the first rebellions, has given way to the recognition of an important strategic element in his planning from the beginning. Studies of honours in Sussex, the Welsh marches and the north of England have shown that the regrouping of lands after enfeoffmen often extended to subtenants.[6] Besides this, initial grants might be changed, as the later formation of William of Braose's rape of Bramber and the compensation of William of Warenne, from whose lands the new rape had been carved, with lands in Norfolk demonstrates. The conquest was progressive; castles were bases for further advance, and William's actions in Normandy show that he regarded castellanships as offices, not hereditary fees, whenever circumstances allowed this. So the building and manning of castles, in which the king frequently retained some right, went on simultaneously with the granting of lands to reward vassals and ensure that the army did not melt away. We cannot always be certain exactly what was implied when a later chronicler makes the sweeping statement that the king gave a vassal a particular county or castle; it has often been assumed prematurely that he granted an earldom or a private castle, or that land given to a knight could immediately be regarded as a knight's fee. The first phase of conquest established spheres of interest, some of which became hereditary earldoms, strongholds which could be

[5] Mason, *Sussex Rapes*; R. A. Brown, 'The Norman conquest', *TRHS* (1967), 109–30; Brown, Colvin and Taylor, *The King's Works*, pp. 20–5. There is an admirable account of the status and duties of the thegn in H. R. Loyn, *Anglo-Saxon England and the Norman Conquest* (London, 1962), pp. 211–19.

[6] Kathleen Thompson, 'The Cross-Channel Estates of the Montgommery-Bellême Family c.1050–1112' (unpublished MA dissertation, University of Wales, Cardiff, 1983); Wightman, *Lacy Family*; *VCH Staffs*. iv. 25–30; Davies, *TRHS* (1979), 41–61.

manned, and the means of support for some of the knights. The next stage secured enfeoffments, and converted many acquisitions into the patrimonies of the second generation. But the process was far from complete even in 1086.

The practical considerations that dominated the first phase of conquest included the need to pick up the threads of administration and restore law and order under legitimate rule. To do this while supporting a large army, suppressing internal revolt, and warding off invasion from abroad was no easy task. Entries in the *Anglo-Saxon Chronicle* are a barometer for the first period of stress. Monk chroniclers were as familiar as lay magnates with the motives that underlay the ravaging of armies. Some were strategic; to gain victory by demonstrating the inability of an opponent to protect his men, or to discourage further rebellion by punishing the peasants who had supported him. Some were predatory; ever since the payment of geld had been devised to ward off Viking attacks the English had been familiar with invasions backed by a demand for all the tribute that could be extorted by terror. The laments of the .chroniclers suggest the stages by which William gained control of the realm he wished to rule as a legitimate king. After the submission of the leaders at Berkhamsted, when they gave hostages and promised to be his liege men, the chronicle expressed surprise that still 'in the meantime they ravaged all that they overran.' When William had been crowned on Christmas Day and promised to rule well, 'all the same he laid taxes on people very severely.' In the spring he went overseas to Normandy, leaving behind Bishop Odo of Bayeux and Earl William fitz Osbern, who 'built castles far and wide throughout the country, and distressed the wretched folk'.[7]

Fifty years previously, when Cnut had won the kingdom, part of the pattern of brutal conquest had been the same. The men of Cnut's army had ravaged all the land, slaying and burning wherever they went, and seizing provisions for themselves. But after Cnut had come to terms with Edmund Ironside, and the Londoners had bought peace and agreed to pay tribute, his ships sailed to London bringing all the produce they had captured, and the army took up winter quarters there.[8] Tribute continued to be exacted, but we hear no more of ravaging. William's problem was a different one; he needed his ships in the Channel to keep open his lines of communication with Normandy, and even though he invaded just after the harvest, when supplies of corn must have been plentiful, he had not the same opportunities as Cnut's men to build up supplies of provisions in any safe base; indeed he had first to establish

---

[7] Stenton, *Anglo-Saxon England*, p. 597; ASC (CD), 1066, 1067.
[8] *ASC* (CDE), 1016.

safe bases. Even when the imposition of a geld after his coronation had given him a legitimate revenue, the money had to be collected. This is where the castles played an additional role; they were from the first collecting points for both money and produce. In spite of the lament that William's deputies oppressed the people, the chronicle makes only two further complaints of unreasonable plundering by William's men. In the winter of 1068 William returned from Normandy to face rebellions on the Welsh borders and at Exeter; he imposed another geld, and nevertheless his men ravaged all they overran.[9] Possibly his action was punitive then, as it was to be in the north a year later, since there had been rebel risings. But possibly in 1067–8 the castles, though adequate for local defence, had not yet had time to accumulate adequate supplies for the large army brought into the region. In William's later large-scale expeditions into the north of England in 1071–2 he was able to bring up a force of ships, which was capable of provisioning the army as it advanced towards Scotland; there were then no complaints of ravaging. And once he had brought the English administration under firm control, so that sheriff and castellan worked together, order and discipline could be maintained. The journey of Edgar Atheling from Scotland under safe conduct, after his submission in 1074, showed in miniature how the problem of supply was overcome.[10] The sheriff of York met Edgar and his retinue at Durham, and went all the way with them and had them provided with food and fodder at every castle they came to, until they got overseas to the king in Normandy.

The levying of geld was essential for more than the purchase of provisions; much of the army was paid. The king's military household provided a hard core of elite fighting knights throughout the reigns of the Conqueror and his sons.[11] There were both feudal and stipendiary elements in the household. Anselm in a famous passage described how some men who already held lands from their lord fought out of loyalty; others fought for wages; a third group fought in the hope of recovering a lost patrimony.[12] The stipendiaries hoped for a reward in land; after the conquest many received it, but others had to wait. In the households of the greatest vassals also, such as those of William fitz Osbern or Richard fitz Gilbert of Brionne, there were many stipendiary knights. The speed with which some magnates, like Richard fitz Gilbert or Ernulf of Hesdin, developed the cash resources of the estates granted to them may have been partly due to a wish to pay their knights in preference to enfeoffing

[9] *ASC* (D), 1067 (for 1068).
[10] *ASC* (D), 1074.
[11] Prestwich, *EHR* (1981).
[12] Eadmer, *Vita Anselmi*, pp. 94–5.

all of them.[13] Even when lands were granted, they might be very small estates in the neighbourhood of castles, given as a reward for service, to enable a knight to support a wife in England and live at home when not actually following his lord on campaigns or manning a castle garrison. They were the first step towards a landed settlement; but wages did not necessarily cease when the gift that came as a bonus for good service took the form of a few acres of land and not cash. The holdings of knights in the Conqueror's reign were not the institutionalized knights' fees of later feudal theory. Feudal society was still very fluid, and feudal custom did not cover all the obligations of knights. Many surplus sons remained landless stipendiaries to the end of their lives; and they made up a substantial part of the king's permanent household troops.

For the first five years the danger of rebellion backed by external enemies was never absent. In 1068 troubles began in the west, when the men of Exeter rose. Once William had captured the city he began building a castle and established Baldwin of Meules, the brother of Richard fitz Gilbert, as castellan there, while he himself advanced further into Cornwall. Judhael, a Breton lord who in 1086 held a significant concentration of lands round the castle of Totnes, may have been placed in charge of a new castellany at the same time. The Breton count, Brian, was left to defend Cornwall.[14] It was important for the king to hold the shores of the Bristol Channel as firmly as possible, because of the danger of invasion from Ireland, where some English exiles, including two of the sons of Harold, had taken refuge. His measures succeeded, and two later raids by Harold's sons were easily scotched by the forces on the spot.[15]

Raiding from Ireland or Brittany into one of the deep inlets of the Cornish or Devon coast was relatively easy; but full-scale invasion was different. One resolute punitive expedition by King William was enough; thereafter he was able to leave the defence to the forces on the spot. Other frontiers, both sea and land, were more exposed to full-scale invasion; and the northern parts of the country were barely pacified. The English earls, Edwin of Mercia and Morcar of Northumbria, made their submission and swore allegiance; but even though Edwin at least re-covered his earldom Morcar's position was more uncertain, and the loyalty of both was doubtful. Beyond Tees Northumbria was resolutely separatist, with its own native line of earls; and both Scotland in the north and the Welsh principalities to the west provided a refuge for rebels and a breeding-ground for hostile alliances.[16] Scandinavian invaders

[13] See below, ch. 5.

[14] Orderic, ii. 212–15; Stenton, *Anglo-Saxon England*, p. 629; *VCH Devon*, i. 467–79, 558; *EYC*, iv. 16, 84–5.

[15] *ASC* (D) 1069; Orderic, ii. 224–5. The definitive work on homage in the marches is Lemarignier, *L'hommage en marche*.

[16] Kapelle, pp. 106–19.

MAP 2   Attempted invasions 1068–1071

might attempt a landing at any of the east coast harbours or inlets; the Humber estuary was particularly vulnerable. From 1068 to 1070 these were the regions that demanded William's constant attention.

He knew too little of the internal feuds of Northumbria, and his first choices of men to govern the province proved ill advised, even when his agents were themselves northerners. One was murdered in a local rising, and another himself took part in a rebellion. In 1068 a rebellion led by Edwin and Morcar, and the threat of a Danish invasion of Yorkshire, brought the king and his army to the north as soon as he had settled the west country. His campaign, accompanied by the building and garrison-ing of castles at Warwick, Nottingham, York, Lincoln, Huntingdon and

Cambridge, was swift and effective. The Danish invasion never materialized. Edwin and Morcar were received back into allegiance, at least as far
as outward appearances went; but there were now Norman garrisons in
royal castles in the territories of both men, as well as in that of the
Englishman Waltheof, earl of Huntingdon.[17]

A year later Edwin and Morcar were again active in the most dangerous rebellion of the reign. There were risings in the north of England, the
Welsh marches, and the west country, stirred up by English exiles who
had taken refuge in Scotland, Wales and Ireland. Most serious of all, a
Danish invasion was launched all along the east coast. Repulsed from the
Kentish ports by strong Norman garrisons at Dover and Sandwich, the
Danes turned their attention to East Anglia; here local forces repelled
them from Ipswich, and knights from Norwich under Ralph of Gael
effectively drove them away. But the Humber estuary was more vulnerable; they reached York, slaughtered the Norman garrison, and went
into hiding in the marshes of Lindsey. William's reaction was as swift and
decisive as in the previous year, though the magnitude of the rising
prolonged his campaign right through the winter. By Christmas he had
crushed rebels at Stafford and in Yorkshire and had destroyed the Danish
forces; he then took terrible punitive measures by ravaging large areas of
the north. This was a deliberate scorched earth policy; seed corn was
destroyed, houses burnt, and animals slaughtered. It was an act of cruelty
that was never forgiven, and whose consequences were felt far beyond
Yorkshire; the Evesham chronicler remembered destitute and uprooted
fugitives seeking alms at his monastery some years later.[18] William then
turned his attention to rebels in Chester and Shrewsbury, where the
English outlaw, Edric the Wild, had enlisted the support of men from
Wales. A rising in Devon and Cornwall was suppressed by Count Brian
and William fitz Osbern; one in Somerset by forces from Winchester,
London and Salisbury, commanded by Geoffrey, bishop of Coutances.
These did not call for the king's presence. By Easter 1070 he was back in
Winchester; and the suppression of a last rising in the Fens, where Edwin
and Morcar held out for a time with the support of Hereward the Wake,
did not take long. Morcar perished in the fighting, possibly through
treachery. Edwin was captured and imprisoned for life. Edgar Atheling,
on whom the English legitimists pinned their hopes, withdrew to Scotland where his sister Margaret was the wife of King Malcolm.[19] With all
the charm and talent for courting disaster that later proved fatal to the
plans of Bonnie Prince Charlie, his lack of any quality of leadership made

[17] Orderic, ii. 216–23; ASC (D) 1067 (for 1068).

[18] Orderic, ii. 224–33; ASC (DE) 1069); Chron. Evesham pp. 90–1.

[19] Orderic, ii. 234–37, 256–9; Simeon of Durham, ii. 188; ASC (DE) 1072 (for 1071);
FW, ii. 9.

him an even more ineffectual claimant. William could safely pardon him as often as he rebelled; he was more dangerous to his own side than to his enemies.

The first phase of conquest was over by the summer of 1070, and the more permanent pattern of Norman settlement began to emerge. It is not always possible to date the changes in tenure that Domesday Book registered between 1066 and 1086; and even in 1086 Norman settlement was far from being completed. But after 1070 it moved decisively into Mercia and the lands beyond Humber and Ribble, and the frontier castles were pushed northwards and further into Welsh territory.

The whole of William's reign was a period of experiment, the first five years most of all. He was taking over the distribution of the land of England, and learning how it was governed. When his officials translated Anglo-Saxon writs into Latin, and Norman chroniclers described the events of his reign in the same language, they had to find words to express the English offices, institutions and government. There was no Norman equivalent of the Anglo-Saxon shire or sheriff; the absence of local, popular institutions was the most striking difference between Normandy and both England and the Scandinavian homeland of the Viking settlers who had forged the duchy of Normandy.[20] Normandy was familiar with a local unit of government, the *pagus*, which had survived, greatly transformed, from Carolingian and even earlier administration. The duke had his local officials, the vicomtes, who exercised authority in regions very roughly based on the *pagi*; they were essentially his agents. Some, like Roger of Montgomery, vicomte of the Hiémois, or Hugh, vicomte of the Avranchin, were dominant lords in the regions they administered. The duke also had his counts, all closely related to him by blood; sometimes their designation was territorial, but it was as likely to be derived, like the title of Count Gilbert of Brionne, from a patrimony of their own as from an administrative district. It implied honour as much as office, and had been transformed since the days of the Carolingians. In Carolingian terms there was one count only; the count of Rouen, who had become the count or duke of Normandy.[21]

English earldoms too were being transformed; the English earls of 1066 have been described with justice as approximating to regional viceroys.[22] But they still had an area of responsibility and a defined relationship with the shire-reeve or sheriff, who was the earl's deputy in the shire court. In spite of fundamental differences there were some superficial resemblances which led to earls being given the Latin name

---

[20] Musset, 'Gouvernés et gouvernants', pp. 439–68.

[21] Bates, *Normandy*, pp. 155–8; D. C. Douglas, 'The earliest Norman counts', *EHR*, 61 (1946), 129–56.

[22] Le Patourel, *Norman Empire*, p. 257.

(*comes*) of the Norman counts, and sheriffs like vicomtes emerging as *vicecomites*. Counties were more difficult; to chroniclers at least a county might be either *pagus* or *comitatus*. And here there is a source of confusion, for *comitatus* could also mean the office of a count or earl. The confusion arose partly from the failure of language to adapt quickly enough to changing institutions, but also possibly from a certain over-lapping of function in the early years of the conquest. It is not easy to determine exactly what authority the Norman lords believed they were exercising in each new region as the conquest moved forwards. It seems certain that in places there were a number of rapid changes of sheriffs, and that many of the early and some of the later sheriffs were English.[23] There were also, for personal no less than strategic reasons, changes among the Norman counts, earls and leading castellans. And there was a subtle change too in William's attitude to his position in the kingdom he had conquered.

The Norman narrative sources for the conquest were all written slightly later, and expressed, with some individual variations, the fully developed Norman theory of Harold's perjury and William's right to the crown. William, a monk of Jumièges, completed his *Gesta Norman-norum ducum* a little after 1070, probably about 1071–2. William of Poitiers, a secular clerk in the king's service, wrote his *Gesta Guillelmi* slightly later. Both were determined to justify and exalt King William. The unique pictorial record, the Bayeux Tapestry, made in England for Bishop Odo, tells a story broadly in line with these, though recognizing Harold's title of king. It has moreover been suggested by Nicholas Brooks that some of the pictures have a double meaning, and can be interpreted as an expression of some of the English traditions, more sympathetic to Harold, that were fostered in Canterbury and also appear in the *Historia Novorum* of Eadmer.[24] In spite of the rhetorical conven-tions and poetic language that make the *Carmen de Hastingae Proelio* attributed to Guy of Amiens an extremely unreliable source (whatever the date of its composition) for the course of the battle and much besides, the strongest argument for an early date is its attitude to both Harold and Archbishop Stigand. In the *Carmen* Harold is treated as a king and allowed honourable burial, and Stigand, who was deposed in 1070 and blotted out of all later Norman accounts of William's coronation, is given a part alongside Archbishop Ealdred of York in the ceremony.[25]

[23] J. Green, 'The sheriffs of William the Conqueror', *Anglo-Norman Studies*, 5 (1983 for 1982), 129–45.

[24] N. P. Brooks and H. E. Walker, 'The authority and interpretation of the Bayeux Tapestry', *Anglo-Norman Studies*, 1 (1979 for 1978), 1–34.

[25] R. H. C. Davies and L. J. Engels, 'The *Carmen de Hastingae Proelio*', *Anglo-Norman Studies*, 2 (1980 for 1979); *Carmen*, pp. 36–9, 50–1.

Some early records support the view that for a few years, while William was using English clerks in his writing office and leaving some provinces in the charge of their English earls, he was more conciliatory to the English tradition also. In particular one charter, issued early in the year 1067 and written in English, grants to Regenbald, his first chancellor, land at Eisey in Wiltshire as freely as it had belonged to 'Harald kinge'. Addressed to Count Eustace of Boulogne (before his temporary disgrace in the summer of 1067) the English bishops Hereman of Ramsbury and Sherborne and Wulfstan of Worcester, the English magnates Eadrich and Brihtric, and all the king's thegns in Wiltshire and Gloucestershire, it belongs to the period before Norman officials had been appointed in the west country, and shows that Harold's legitimacy was not then questioned.[26] Within five years the Norman chroniclers, no doubt under direction from the court, had perfected a story of Harold's perfidy and treachery, and his coronation by the schismatic Stigand, who was allowed no part in the record of William's coronation. Domesday Book denied Harold the royal title; he was to be remembered as 'Count Harold' and referred to as a usurper. His nine months' rule was nullified; legitimate tenure dated from the last day of King Edward's reign. Yet government had remained active under Harold, the royal secretariat continued to issue charters, and coins were minted all over the country.[27] The government that William took over was Harold's government, and he was crowned, not like earlier kings at Winchester, but like Harold at Westminster. It was only after he had tightened the Norman grip on the country that he developed the theory of his direct succession from Edward the Confesor, after the interlude of Harold's usurpation.

A few traces of early administrative expedients remained in some regions. Herefordshire was one; just when William fitz Osbern was given the county in addition to the Isle of Wight is uncertain, but in view of the inroads he had made into Gwent by the beginning of 1071 it must have been early in 1067. The account of Orderic Vitalis is revealing; he wrote that the king gave William fitz Osbern the county of Hereford 'and set him up in the marches with Walter of Lacy and other powerful warriors to fight the bellicose Welsh'. Recent work by Christopher Lewis has shown that he never had complete control of the whole county of Hereford, as Hugh of Avranches had in Cheshire, and that Walter of Lacy and Roger Mortimer held some lands directly of the king from the first, as indeed they did in parts of south-west Shropshire.[28] Fitz Osbern

[26] Round, *Feudal England*, pp. 421–30; *Regesta*, i. 9; Galbraith, *Domesday Book*, pp. 176–9.

[27] Dolley, *English Coinage*, pp. 11–12; Harmer, *Writs*, pp. 18–19, 270.

[28] Orderic, ii. 260–1; C. Lewis, 'The Norman settlement of Herefordshire under William I', forthcoming in *Anglo-Norman Studies*, 7 (1985 for 1984).

took over some of the authority of his predecessor, Earl Harold, in Worcestershire and Gloucestershire as well as Herefordshire, to which was added the authority of a Norman castellan in a frontier region; and he was called earl by both Anglo-Saxon and Norman chroniclers. His brief but active rule in the marches belongs to the experimental period of the Norman conquest, and does not fit exactly into any pattern of power.

In January, 1071, he returned to Normandy on the duke's business, led a small contingent of Norman knights in a French army fighting over the Flemish succession, and was killed at the battle of Cassel. His son Roger, who succeeded him in the title of earl, held Hereford until his rebellion and forfeiture in 1075. Hugh de Port, sheriff of Hampshire, emerged as the most powerful and wealthy baron in Hampshire and the Isle of Wight after William's death. Edwin's forfeiture left a vacuum on the Welsh border, and the Conqueror's first earl of Chester, Gherbod the Fleming, did not remain long in that most perilous outpost. By 1071 he had returned to Flanders, and William replaced him with Hugh, vicomte of the Avranchin, a man who throve on warfare and went about, in the words of Orderic Vitalis, with an army rather than a household.[29] Hugh had first been planted in the castle of Tutbury; this was now entrusted to Henry of Ferrers. Shrewsbury was given to King William's most trust-worthy vassal, Roger of Montgomery, vicomte of the Hiémois, who had held Arundel since 1067 and continued to hold it. For a few years some survivors from the pre-conquest aristocracy held the east Midlands and East Anglia; Ralph of Gael, the Breton who had served Edward the Confessor as staller or steward, was granted Norfolk and Suffolk. Waltheof, last and most favoured of the old English earls, was restored to Huntingdon and married to Judith, a kinswoman of the Conqueror. In 1075, however, he was drawn into rebellion with the earls Ralph of Norfolk and Roger of Hereford, and all three suffered forfeiture. Judith transmitted the earldom of Huntingdon to her daughter's husband, Simon of Senlis; but King William established no new earl in either Hereford or East Anglia. The men next in power to the disinherited earls rose to prominence. Roger Bigod, sheriff of Norfolk and Suffolk, who appears to have been a younger and more or less portionless son of a good Norman family, enjoyed the king's trust, and continued to build up his wealth and power. Richard fitz Gilbert consolidated his estates around Clare on the borders of Suffolk and Essex. He was already castellan of Tonbridge, and held a compact territory called the lowy around the castle; there is some evidence that he may have consolidated his power first in Kent and later in Suffolk.[30] In Herefordshire Walter of

[29] Orderic, ii. 260–7.

[30] R. Mortimer, 'The beginnings of the Honour of Clare', *Anglo-Norman Studies*, 3 (1981 for 1980), 119–41.

Lacy and the Mortimers emerged to even greater prominence. The Lacy honour of Weobley was thereafter held in chief of the crown, and both families took a leading part in the defence of the region.[31]

Further north, apart from a series of unfortunate experiments in Northumberland, William established no earls. But one of his Breton followers, Count Alan, received the honour of Richmond; and a Fleming, Drogo of La Beuvrière, was set up in Holderness and given one of the king's cousins as his wife. After the death of the lady in mysterious circumstances embellished by the chroniclers, Drogo withdrew hastily to Flanders, and Holderness was given to Odo of Champagne, another of the king's kinsmen by marriage.[32] Both Holderness and Richmond remained tightly-knit honours; and William encouraged settlement north of the Ribble under Roger 'the Poitevin', a younger son of Roger of Montgomery. William Malet, sheriff of York, took a prominent part in the defence of the region during the earlier period of rebellion and invasion.

The process of granting land, and the terms on which it was granted, can be pieced together only tentatively and partially from chronicles, lawsuits, the Domesday record and a very few charters. The E version of the *Anglo-Saxon Chronicle*, written at Canterbury at the time, states baldly that when the king returned from his first visit to Normandy, at Christmas 1067, he 'gave away every man's land'. This implies a major distribution of the lands that had been forfeited by those who had fought against him at Hastings, and perhaps too a confirmation of the tenures of those who had submitted and done homage to him. Some of the greater churches had already begun the process of securing confirmation of their estates. Brand, abbot of Peterborough, certainly lost no time; shortly after William's coronation he offered forty marks in gold (worth about £250) for the confirmation of the estates claimed by the abbey. These included some fifty-two carucates of land in Lincolnshire which had been given by Brand's own family, according to the abbey's traditions 'in the doubtful time between the death of Harold and William's own coronation'. The charter confirming them, one of the first issued by the new king, refers to all the lands held by free and hereditary right in the time of King Edward; they may have been promised then and hastily transferred after the disaster at Hastings, as the only means of keeping them out of Norman hands.[33] Churches secured their endowments as best they might, by submission, gifts, and a readiness to accept Norman knights as

[31] Wightman, *Lacy Family*, pp. 123–6, 165–6.

[32] J. F. A. Mason, 'The Honour of Richmond in 1086', *EHR*, 78 (1963), 703–4; English, *Holderness*, pp. 6–10.

[33] *Regesta*, i. 8; *ASC* (E), 1066, 1067; King, *Peterborough*, pp. 9–10.

subtenants. The land hunger of the invading army was satisfied gradually, over a number of years, and mostly by oral transfer. But however the transfer was made, the normal place for detailed land transactions was the shire court, either by verbal declaration by the king's envoy, or by the reading aloud of a royal writ; this had been customary in the time of King Edward and continued after the conquest.[34] It is likely, however, that King William made broad allocations in one or other of his great courts, and made some particularly extensive grants in the Christmas court of 1067 that caught the attention of the Anglo-Saxon chronicler.

Distribution of some estates may have taken the form initially of a grant to a particular magnate of the land of a dead or disinherited Englishman. This gave rise to a number of land pleas, for some earls and thegns were holding church lands at farm, or had annexed them unlawfully; the family of Earl Godwin had been particularly predatory. At times when Odo of Bayeux, as earl of Kent, was attacked by Christ Church or St Augustine's, Canterbury, for withholding land that was theirs, he had merely taken over land unlawfully held by Harold at the time of his death. The Ely land pleas involved some estates previously held at farm by thegns whose properties had passed to Normans. The king gave orders that in such cases the abbot should come to an agreement with the thegns' successors about the terms of tenure.[35] Comparison of great estates in 1086 with those of various Saxons in 1066 reveals a rough correspondence in some places, but this is rarely more than approximate. In Bedfordshire Hugh de Beauchamp acquired the greatest fee, partly by marriage with the Taillebois heiress, Azelina. His honour included ten estates of the king's thegn Aschil and five of Aschil's men; but he had fourteen more that had been held by various men of King Edward, Queen Edith, Godric the sheriff, Earl Waltheof, Earl Tostig and even the abbey of St Albans, as well as the lands of nearly a hundred small sokemen. In Devon the Breton Judhael of Totnes held an honour concentrated round his castle of Totnes, made up of the estates of thirty-nine previous Saxon owners. It was deliberately created as a centre of power, irrespective of previous tenures. Henry of Ferrers likewise received a tightly-knit honour made up of the lands of numerous thegns round his castle of Tutbury.[36] Domesday Book records numerous exchanges of land, which were particularly necessary round the main castles or on estates where the lords had moved on with the advance of conquest.

[34] Bishop and Chaplais, p. xi; DB, i. 32a, 36b, 208a; Harmer, Writs, p. 545.
[35] Bates, BIHR (1978), 1–19; Le Patourel, 'Penenden Heath', pp. 15–26; Liber Eliensis, p. 203.
[36] Fowler, Bedfordshire in 1086, Map 3; VCH Devon, i. 558; see Map 4.

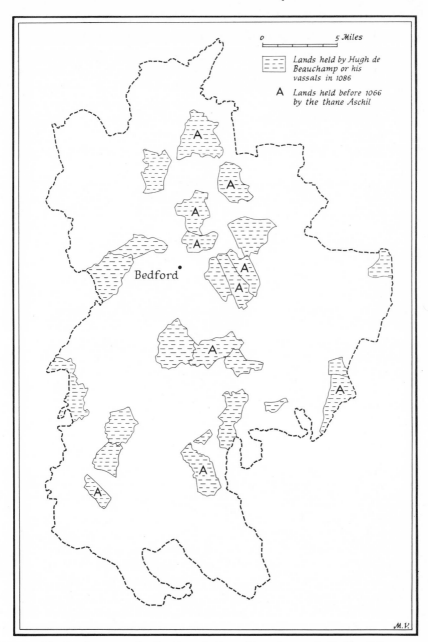

MAP 3   Patterns of settlement: the Beauchamp honour in Bedfordshire
(based on G. H. Fowler, *Bedfordshire in 1086*, Quarto memoirs of the Bedfordshire
Historical Record Society, 1922, Maps II and IV; and Joyce Godber, *History of
Bedfordshire*, Luton, 1969, Map 7)

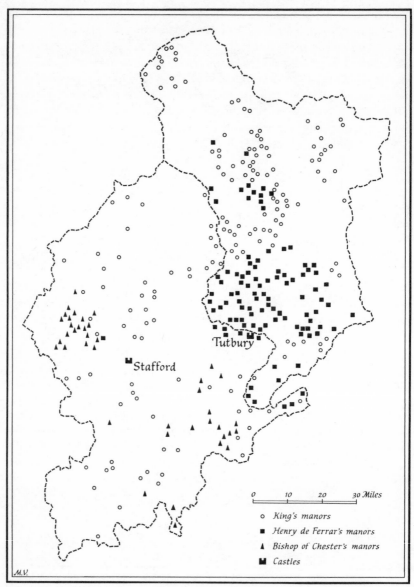

MAP 4   Patterns of settlement: the castles of Tutbury and Stafford

The transfer of power was not always smooth and legal, particularly in the half-subdued north and the marches of Wales. Words like those attributed by the Welsh *Chronicle of the Princes* to Henry I when he commissioned Gilbert fitz Richard to subdue Ceredigion must often have been spoken earlier: 'I will give you the land of Cadwgan ap Bleddyn. Go and take possession of it.'[37] Sometimes fighting was as necessary as finding out exactly what lands were included in a grant. The earls entrusted with pushing forward the frontiers were men experienced in the problems of the marches of Normandy. Roger of Montgomery may have been given a similar licence to occupy whatever he could claim and hold in the Bellême lands after his marriage to Mabel of Bellême.[38] From Shropshire he led his armies across Wales to the sea, and placed his son Arnulf in the castle of Pembroke. His powers, like those of Hugh of Avranches and William fitz Osbern, were great, as the task demanded. They have sometimes been described as 'palatine', a misleading term since they corresponded neither with those of later 'palatine earls' in Durham and Chester nor with those of contemporary counts palatine in France. There the term had come to be applied solely to the counts of Blois, as a more or less honorific court title. Roger held the former royal demesnes in Shropshire; he appointed his own sheriffs and had more control than the king normally allowed over the castles he and his men built in the course of their conquests.[39] Castles were an essential element in the control of the Welsh frontier and the conquest of the Welsh lands. Even in Edward the Confessor's reign a few Norman settlers had occupied the borders of Herefordshire, and built their mottes in the region of Richard's Castle. William fitz Osbern built castles at Clifford, Wigmore and Chepstow at the mouth of the Wye. Shrewsbury was a royal castle under Roger's control; he himself built Montgomery, named after his Norman patrimony. His vassal Rainald of Bailleul built Oswestry. Hugh of Chester's cousin Robert established his base at Rhuddlan. These, Rhuddlan apart, are among the 'castellaria' mentioned in Domesday Book; there were others along the disturbed frontiers.[40] Normally the king was as unwilling in England as he had been in Normandy to recognize hereditary right to castles, even though he frequently appointed the son of a castellan to his father's office; but in the marches of Wales as in those of Normandy exceptions had to be made.[41]

The English landholders who, as a group, might expect to have their patrimonies respected were the great churches, monastic and episcopal. Broadly speaking, once they had made their submission to the new king, these lands were respected at a price. There was, for example, no consolidation of the lands round the royal castle of Stafford, where the

[37] Brut-y-Tywysogyon, p. 34.
[38] Bates, Normandy, pp. 78–81.
[39] Orderic, i. 245; Mason, TRHS (1963), 8–13.
[40] DB, i. 183–4, 254; Eyton, Shropshire, x. 320–1.
[41] Bates, Normandy, pp. 114–62, 165–6; Davies, TRHS (1979), 41–62.

lands of the bishop of Chester were left in the hands of the church; this contrasts with the concentration of lands round the nearby castle of Tutbury. The position of the abbot of Fécamp in Sussex was even stronger; as a Norman abbot who had held Steyning and other lands in the valley of the river Adur before the conquest and had given conspicuous help to William through his knowledge of the local topography when the invaders first landed, he could confidently anticipate that his claims would be fully respected. When in the early 1070s William of Braose was established in the valley of the Adur with a castellany that became known as the rape of Bramber, his castle (the focal point of his control of the Sussex coast) was built, not at the ancient ecclesiastical and hundredal centre of Steyning, but at nearby Bramber. Steyning, briefly appropriated by Harold, was restored to Fécamp.[42] In some places the needs of defence were met by an exchange of properties or by arranging a subtenure from an ecclesiastical tenant-in-chief. And the church in England, like the church in Normandy (but far more systematically), was drawn into the system of defence.

In approaching the much debated question of knight service it must be clearly understood that there was no defined general service of quotas of knights before the conquest in Normandy. The publication of the pre-1066 charters of the dukes of Normandy provided evidence which was bound in time to undermine the previously dominant theory of Haskins, that quotas of knights had been imposed from above in early eleventh-century Normandy. The actual situation was that vassals were bound to serve their lords in the field; greater vassals with military obligations brought knights with them as part of their obligation. If any attempt was made to define the length of reasonable service, the number of men owed or the obligation to provide castle garrisons, this was done piecemeal by individual contracts. When a lord granted land to a household knight in return for homage some obligations were implicit. If duties were enumerated the service most likely to be specified was garrison duty in a castle. Increasing precision has been noted from about 1050 in Normandy; but it was very far from being a general system.[43]

Similarly in England the general obligations to assist with defence cannot be read as a first stage in the establishment of knight service, quite apart from the different technique of fighting and absence of castles. Assisting in the general upkeep of fortified towns and in the provision and

[42] VCH Staffs. iv. 30; see above, Map 4; Mason, Sussex Rapes, pp. 13–15.

[43] Fauroux, nos 113, 188, 197; Bates, Normandy, pp. 122–7; M. Chibnall, 'Military service in Normandy before 1066', Anglo-Norman Studies, 5 (1983 for 1982), 65–77; E. Z. Tabuteau, 'Definitions of feudal military obligations in eleventh-century Normandy', Essays in Honour of S. E. Thorne (Chapel Hill, 1981), pp. 18–59. For a recent reassessment of knight service in England see Holt, Anglo-Norman Studies, 6.

maintenance of men for the military force known as the fyrd was a general obligation falling on all free men, unless they had been exempted by special privilege. The Danish kings had their military households, composed of retainers called housecarls; some of these men were granted estates as a reward for their service.[44] The duties of thegns included taking their share in defence; and some categories of tenants owed bodyguard service. But the basis for calculating obligations remained territorial rather than personal. In both Anglo-Saxon England and Normandy some of the preconditions for military feudalism existed in one form or another, and they were more developed in Normandy; but the much greater systematization of knight service that ultimately took place in England resulted from the circumstances and military needs of the conquest. The first stage of the change came about certainly in the reign of William the Conqueror, most probably early in the reign.

Any arrangements that may have been made with the English earls were transient, since the Godwin family was dispossessed in 1066, Edwin and Morcar in 1069, and Waltheof in 1075, though his wife retained part of his inheritance. But the abbots and bishops of the realm struck their bargains early. William may from the first have required the greater abbeys to take their share in the maintenance of his large army, particularly when they stood in regions vulnerable to attack. The moment for requiring a definite military commitment from an abbot was probably either when he made his submission to the king and fealty was sworn, or when his first successor was appointed. The performance of homage by churchmen, when demanded, was an innovation in England, attributed to King William by Eadmer.[45] It had not necessarily been performed in Normandy when the duke invested an abbot with his temporalities, and it may have been introduced gradually in England. Bishops, who sometimes held substantial personal baronies, were in a different position. But conquest gave King William the opportunity of insisting that all lands were held from him, and possibly spelling out more precisely than before the conditions on which they were held, particularly when a previous landholder was confirmed in his estates. The Norman tradition a century later, not without value even though it cannot be accepted unquestionably as history, was that any member of the conquered race who possessed lands had acquired 'not what he considered due to him by right of succession but only what he had earned by his services or got by some kind of contract'.[46] Contract entered into the tenures of ecclesiastical no

---

[44] For housecarls see the paper by N. Hooper, forthcoming in *Anglo-Norman Studies*, 7 (1985 for 1984).

[45] See below, pp. 60–2, 69.

[46] *Dialogus de Scacccario*, p. 54.

less than lay lords from a very early date. An added consideration was that Norman abbots, some of whom brought with them large contingents of household knights, replaced English abbots in many houses within a few years; but many contracts must have been made before their coming to provide bases for the king's knights already in the country.

The military obligations of the greater abbeys were not based on an assessment of their wealth; and the most likely clue to their uneven incidence is that suggested by David Knowles: that it depended on the actual situation at the moment.[47] But whereas Knowles emphasized the number of armed retainers in the households of the first Norman abbots, only Peterborough among the houses with the heaviest assessments received a Norman abbot as early as 1070. Turold arrived with 160 Frenchmen, all fully armed, as the *Anglo-Saxon Chronicle* records.[48] But Baldwin of Bury St Edmunds, appointed in 1065, lived into the reign of William Rufus; Glastonbury received its first Norman abbot only in 1077 or 1078, and Ely in 1082. The obligations were probably fixed earlier and related to the needs of defence, highlighted by the first rebellions. Glastonbury dominated the marshes of northern Somerset bordering the Bristol Channel. Like Tavistock, which guarded the deep inlet of the river Tamar and was responsible in spite of its small endowment for fifteen knights, it had a part to play in the defence of a vulnerable region far from the centres of power. The marshes surrounding Ely and Peterborough were a potential hiding place for rebels and outlaws. Bury was part of the defence of East Anglia, always open to invasion from Scandinavia. Abingdon, though not quite on a Roman road, was an important crossing point of the Thames, commanding an intersection of important routes. There were strategic reasons for placing garrisons of trained knights in or near most of the abbeys made responsible for a substantial quota. How they were to be maintained was a different matter for the abbeys concerned to decide, though in minor ways the allocation of confiscated estates sometimes helped to determine the outcome.

The lands of thegns who had fought at Hastings were among the first spoils of conquest. The Abingdon chronicler, a monk writing in the reign of Henry I who was very well informed about conditions fifty years previously, stated that Abbot Athelelm gave his stipendiary knights the lands of thegns who had fallen at Hastings. Evidence from Domesday Book shows that many knights on church estates took over the lands once held by Saxon thegns. Some Westminster knights appear to have occupied thegnlands in the more outlying estates. A similar tendency can

[47] Knowles, *Monastic Order*, pp. 608–12.
[48] *ASC* (E) 1070.

0   25   50   75 Miles

Marshes

St. Benet Hulme
3

Peterborough
60

Coventry
10

Ramsey
4

Ely
40

Bury St. Edmunds
40

Pershore
3

Evesham
5

Winchcombe
2

St. Albans
6

Abingdon
30

Westminster
?15

Malmesbury
3

Bath
20

Chertsey
3

St. Augustine's
Canterbury
15

Sherborne

Glastonbury
60

Wilton
5

Winchester
20

Muchelney
1

Shaftesbury
10

Cerne
3

Milton
2

Tavistock
?15

Abbotsbury
1

M.V.

MAP 5   Knight service owed by monasteries
(figures from David Knowles, *The Monastic Order in England*,
2nd edn, Cambridge, 1962)

be seen on the lands of Bury and Ely, Canterbury, Worcester, Shaftesbury
and many other houses. Sometimes this led to confusion, since many
thegns had leased church estates and these temporary tenures could not
easily be distinguished from their family patrimonies by the invading
Normans.[49] When complaints reached the king he preferred whenever

---

[49] *Chron. Abingdon*, ii. 3–4; B. Harvey, *Westminster*, pp. 70–7; Ann Williams, 'The
Knight-service of Shaftesbury Abbey', forthcoming in *Anglo-Norman Studies*, 8.

possible to secure the abbey's title without necessarily evicting the Normans. This process can be traced in the Ely land pleas. When c.1081 King William ordered Archbishop Lanfranc, Robert, count of Mortain, and Geoffrey, bishop of Coutances, to hold an inquest into the lands claimed by Ely and restore all that the abbey had held in King Edward's time, he exempted those which vassals claimed he had given them, and added: 'As for the holders of thegnlands, which certainly ought to be held of the church, let them make the best arrangement they can with the abbot, and if they refuse let the church keep the land.'[50] While some of the intruders who established a claim to church lands in the most troubled years had certainly forced their way in, and sheriffs such as Picot of Cambridge and Urse of Worcester had particularly bad reputations for rapacity, others had been confused about the earlier legal rights to the lands, and these were ordered to make amends. Many men in both categories remained in possession, holding the lands of former thegns as vassals of the church.

If military needs were paramount in the fixing of quotas, they were not the sole determinant. King William had a practical eye to resources; in agreeing to ratify very recent grants of lands, such as Abbot Brand's acquisition of the lands of his family for the church of Peterborough, or the most recent bequests to Tavistock Abbey, he may have seen them as an additional resource that would enable the abbey concerned to support knights. If so the concessions underline the fact that the king's main concern was to keep a substantial army in being without ravaging the lands of his new subjects; subinfeudation came gradually, and the details were, for the most part, left to individual tenants-in-chief. Most of the large manors acquired by Abbot Brand were kept in demesne by Peterborough; his sucessors granted smaller properties to their knights, and planned their subinfeudation with an eye to the potential of their estates.[51]

Sometimes the king intervened directly in special circumstances on behalf of a particular individual. Some of the knights quartered on Abingdon abbey, who had been sent to Normandy on the king's service, were captured by pirates while crossing the Channel, and were robbed and mutilated. One of them, called Hermer, who had not yet received any lands, lost both his hands and could no longer fight. He appealed to the king, who commanded the abbot of Abingdon to provide him with a life tenure of some land.[52] Such intervention, which might be made on

---

[50] *Liber Eliensis*, p. 203.

[51] Finburg, *Tavistock*, pp. 8–9; King, *Peterborough*, pp. 16–18.

[52] *Chron. Abingdon*, ii. 6; see Fowler, *Bedfordshire in 1086*, p. 33, for a grant to a sokeman.

behalf of an English sokeman no less than a Norman knight, seems normally to have been in response to a direct appeal from the individual concerned; but further research may reveal that it was not as unusual as is sometimes assumed.

What was new was the contract; the actual nature of legal tenure and the implications of this were slowly worked out in the course of the next century. Contemporary church chroniclers complained principally of two forms of spoliation: seizure of church lands by powerful lords, which was sometimes due to the confusion of tenures described above, or the granting away of church estates by Norman abbots to their own relatives. The Abingdon chronicler insisted that it would be superfluous to describe in detail exactly how the thegns' estates had been distributed many years before, and hinted that it would be for divine justice to decide if any properties intended for the support of monks and pilgrims had been diverted out of consideration of kinship or secular interest.[53] These were the burdens most clearly visible at the time; as far as the imposition of knight service went, it introduced new concepts as well as new men, but the pressure on church lands of great men whose demands could not be denied was no new phenomenon. When Heming, compiler of the earliest Worcester cartulary, complained of the loss of much land in the eleventh century, he blamed the Danes, the English and Norman nobility and the monks of Evesham.[54] If later writers were louder in their complaints about the burden of knight service than the chroniclers writing in the Conqueror's reign, this cannot be taken to imply that it was imposed later. For ecclesiastical tenants it arose out of the problems and opportunities of the conquest itself; its slightly later and more piecemeal definition for lay tenants-in-chief was a further stage in the settlement of invaders in search of lands and power.[55]

The king's greater vassals brought many of their own vassals with them; providing wages or rewards in lands for these men was their responsibility. But particularly when castles under their control were royal castles, the king had a direct interest in securing castle guard service from his subvassals; and as time went on financial and administrative even more than military needs led him to demand definition whenever it had not taken place. By 1166 the process was still not complete, but it was far advanced. Only in the later stages of subinfeudation, or in the regions where Norman feudalism was a later importation (as in the Scotland of King David), were the precise obligations likely to be defined in writing when a fief was first granted. This was not because the duties

[53] *Chron. Abingdon*, ii. 3–4.
[54] Dyer, *Lords and Peasants*, pp. 17–18.
[55] Holt, *Anglo-Norman Studies*, 6.

of earlier vassals were less; often they were greater if a man wished to keep the favour of his lord and earn further rewards. They were implicit in the act of homage, and they did not exactly correspond with the duties of Saxon thegns or Danish housecarls. There were many similarities in social terms between the distribution of some lands before and after the conquest; but Christopher Dyer, in tracing the history of the lands of the church of Worcester, has rightly stressed the many changes 'within a broad context of continuity'.[56]

By 1070–2 the defence of southern and midland England had been organized; the king could call up troops when and where they were needed right across his domains. There are good reasons for assigning the date 1072 to the writ by which he ordered Aethelwig, abbot of Evesham, to summon all those within his jurisdiction and authority to bring the knights they owed him, and to come himself with the five knights due from Evesham abbey to Clarendon.[57] In that year he was preparing an invasion of Scotland, and needed all the knights he could muster. Aethelwig, one of the few English abbots to win his full trust, may have been one of the first to strike a bargain with him. The chronicler of Evesham records that Aethelwig won and kept the friendship and trust of the king, who gave him judicial authority in Worcestershire, Oxfordshire, Warwickshire, Herefordshire, Staffordshire and Shropshire.[58] If this is to be taken at its face value, it may mean that Athelwig was an important agent in keeping the peace and enforcing order in the period when the death of William fitz Osbern, following closely after the collapse of the native Mercian earldom into rebellion, had left all the marcher provinces vulnerable, until Roger of Montgomery and Hugh of Avranches were established in their earldoms. King William's reforms in Normandy may have gone to the length of discouraging clergy from actually taking part in armed combat themselves; but he never ceased to use them for raising armies and organizing defence. Wulfstan, bishop of Worcester, another trusted English ecclesiastic, helped in the defence of his see against Welsh invaders and rebels of all kinds. From the moment that Remigius moved his see from Dorchester to Lincoln in 1072 it had a vital role to play in the defence of the road to the north, as did Durham. There is every reason to trust the statements of later chroniclers at Abingdon, Ely and Saint-Evroult that King William made provision for the support of a substantial army, and that, as the well-informed Abingdon chronicler relates, he allotted definite quotas of knights to bishoprics and abbeys.[59] If the Evesham writ does not prove that all quotas had

---

[56] Dyer, *Lords and Peasants*, pp. 44–50.
[57] Round, *Feudal England*, p. 304.
[58] *Chron. Evesham*, pp. 88–9.
[59] *Chron. Abingdon*, ii. 3; Orderic, ii. 266–7; *Liber Eliensis*, pp. 216–18.

been fixed by 1072, the weight of the evidence is in favour of a very early date for ecclesiastical quotas, though some houses were able in time to obtain a slight reduction. The obligations of lay lords, particularly in view of the complications of inheritance and the moving frontiers of occupation, remained more flexible for many years.

After 1070 William faced only one more rebellion in England, which was easily suppressed by the men he had left in charge of the kingdom during his absence in Normandy, and one serious threat of invasion from Scandinavia, which compelled him to take temporary measures to support an exceptionally large army in England. There was no reason for him to doubt that any normal needs of the kingdom could be met by drawing on the knights of his household troops established in and around castles, and the feudal dependents of his lay and ecclesiastical vassals. The obligations of fyrd service and ship service that already existed in England could be used to supplement and support the contingents of knights. The exact functions of the so-called 'English knights' who feature in some writs and entries in Domesday Book is a matter for conjecture. Training from an early age was necessary to prepare a hauberked knight to manoeuvre on horseback and charge with couched lance. But on the Welsh frontier the enemy often adopted guerilla type tactics and mailed knights were at a disadvantage in the mountains, as Gerald of Wales acutely observed over a century later; in those regions more lightly armed and mobile riders who knew the country had an important part to play.[60] Auxiliaries were needed everywhere to handle the baggage train and to help in constructing siege weapons. Within a generation sons of thegns might be found training as squires and holding a lord's spare horses in the reserve line, in the hope of mastering in time all the skills of knightly combat. Freeman's dramatic picture of how, when King William's horse was killed under him at the siege of Gerberoi in 1079, Toki, son of Wigod of Wallingford, 'fighting on horseback in the Norman fashion, sprang down and offered his horse to the fallen king', goes far beyond the evidence. The D version of the *Anglo-Saxon Chronicle,* which was Freeman's source for his colourful embroidery, merely records that Toki 'brought him another horse'; presumably the *destrier* that he had been holding in reserve for him.[61] The king used his military resources prudently, wherever he found them, but he did not attempt the impossible; thegns, however loyal, could not have learned Norman tactics overnight. Events proved that he had correctly estimated the military resources needed to hold England. Norman kings augmented their armies when necessary by enlarging their stipendiary household

[60] Giraldus Cambrensis, *Opera,* vi. 220–1.
[61] Freeman, *Norman Conquest,* iv. 648, 731–6; *ASC* (D) 1079.

troops, sometimes by agreement with an independent magnate, like the count of Flanders, or as a last resort by hiring temporary mercenary forces.

The one later rebellion came in 1075, when William fitz Osbern's son Roger, earl of Hereford, conspired with Ralph, the half-English earl of Norfolk, and the last English earl, Waltheof of Huntingdon, was drawn into the plot. Support was promised by Denmark; and the conspirators were said to aim at driving William from the throne. The exact causes of their discontent are not clear; treason was plotted at a wedding feast at Exning to celebrate the marriage of Ralph of Norfolk to Roger's sister, Emma. Although the Worcester chronicler, writing later, alleged that the marriage was against the king's will, the contemporary Anglo-Saxon chroniclers state that he gave his consent.[62] But the rebels may have felt insecure, discontented with their lot, and sympathetic to the disinherited English. Probably the king had never given Roger of Hereford the very extensive authority enjoyed by his trusted father; the prominence of Abbot Aethelwig of Evesham as the king's agent in the region suggests that he was being used in preference to young Roger. Earl Waltheof may have been more deeply implicated than his apologists allowed; the historians of Malmesbury and Saint-Evroult who were loudest in the assertion of his innocence were given the story by the monks of Crowland, where Waltheof's body was buried and miracles were claimed at his tomb.[63] Whatever the causes, the rebellion was suppressed without difficulty by the royal forces under William of Warenne, Geoffrey of Coutances, and Odo of Bayeux, assisted by Richard fitz Gilbert. The Danes retired with heavy losses after an abortive raid on York; one battle and the siege of Norwich ended the rebellion. Earl Ralph withdrew to his Breton lands. Archbishop Lanfranc urged Earl Roger and Waltheof to submit to the king, trusting in his mercy.[64] But Lanfranc had misjudged his own influence; mercy was not forthcoming, and Roger was condemned to life imprisonment, whilst Waltheof, subject to the English law which could punish treachery with death, was executed. For the remainder of his reign William took no risks; when his half-brother and one time loyal supporter, Odo of Bayeux, came under suspicion of treason he too was imprisoned, and his release came only with the king's death.[65]

There was one more serious threat from abroad, in the autumn of 1085. Cnut, king of Denmark, son of King Swein, had never renounced the Danish claim to the crown of England; he had married a daughter of

[62] FW, ii. 10–11; ASC (DE) 1075; Orderic, ii. 310–23.
[63] Kapelle, pp. 134–7.
[64] Letters of Lanfranc, nos 32–34.
[65] Orderic, iv. 38–45, 96–101; Bates, Speculum (1975).

Robert the Frisian, count of Flanders, and relied on help from Flanders for an invasion he was preparing. This time William hurried back to England from Normandy with, according to the *Anglo-Saxon Chronicle*,

> a larger force of mounted men and foot soldiers from France and Brittany than had ever come to this country, so that people wondered how this country could maintain all that army. And the king had all the army dispersed all over the country among his vassals, and they provisioned the army each in proportion to his land.

But Cnut was murdered and the invasion never materialized, so the king 'let some of his army go to their own country, and some he kept in England over the winter'.[66]

The result of the threat was that the king, at his Christmas court at Gloucester, had 'very deep discussion' with those present, and put on foot the great inquest that led to the making of Domesday Book. He had met the threat by rapidly transferring to England a huge force of household knights and mercenaries from campaigns in Normandy; his need, with the frontiers of Normandy no less than those of England to defend, was for trained, mobile troops. Throughout his long reign as duke and king speed was the essence of his success. He did not want a larger, territorialized force of knights; emergencies were met by the ability to mobilize resources and to support a temporarily augmented army for a limited period wherever a crisis required it. To do this he had to have a reliable record of the total resources of his kingdom, the wealth of individuals, the assessed values of the land and the potentialities of the royal demesne administered by the sheriffs. Domesday was the answer: it told much more, but it brought together in a detail remarkable for that age the value of all the land both as a source of traditional taxes and as the wealth of vassals who owed loyal and practical support to the king. Both a geld book and a feodary, it mirrors a society in transition, where the king and feudal lord was feeling his way towards a practical understanding of how best to exploit the various resources of land and men available to him. The task of finding the right balance between what was due to the king and what to the new and old lords of the soil was to occupy his sons to the end of their lives; new outlines emerged clearly only in the reign of his great-grandson.[67]

Domesday Book allows a rough calculation to be made of how the spoils of conquest were divided. The returns were not quite complete; the record omits the cities of London and Winchester, and the four northern counties, and there are difficulties in interpreting its stated 'values'. But a

---

[66] *ASC* (E) 1085; FW, ii. 18.
[67] See below, ch. 4.

rough approximation can be made.[68] Out of a total of about £73,000 for the lands assessed, the king and queen held about 17 per cent (of which Edward the Confessor's widow, Queen Edith, had a life interest in lands worth slightly more than 2 per cent). The church retained or had acquired some 26.5 per cent; and the invaders (including the king's two half-brothers, Odo of Bayeux and Robert of Mortain) held honours amounting to about 48.5 per cent of the total. Pre-conquest tenants-in-chief had a mere 5.5 per cent. The remaining 2.5 per cent went to the king's officials and household servants. The royal demesnes were wealthier and more widely scattered than King Edward's had been, partly because the crown had lost much to the house of Godwin before the conquest. William held lands in every county surveyed except Sussex and the Welsh marcher counties, where he had deliberately set up earldoms and castellanies with exceptional powers.

Of all the pre-conquest landholders to remain in possession, the great monastic houses and the bishoprics were the most conspicuous; and though they lost some properties they were further enriched by new grants. Yet in a sense they too provided some of the spoils of conquest, for within a very few years most of the abbots and bishops were churchmen from Normandy or another of William's continental dominions. Many were drawn from the great Norman abbeys; among the bishops some were royal clerks.[69] William had been a strong supporter of the early movement for church reform, and had won papal approval by calling a series of provincial synods to issue reforming decrees. But the main force of the reform movement had, in its early stages, been directed against the purchase of benefices and clerical marriage. Freedom of election did not then necessarily convey its later meaning; it was interpreted as absence of the pressures of wealth and kinship, and did not exclude the right of a lay patron to propose a nominee for election by the chapter. Provided the candidate was suitable and the office was canonically vacant, no one was likely to object; indeed many reformers regarded intervention by a patron with the interests of the church at heart as the best way of overriding the entrenched family interests of many chapters. Lanfranc of Bec and Canterbury, one of the leaders of reform in Normandy and England, regarded William's nomination of abbots to most of the English houses (usually with Lanfranc's advice) as entirely consistent with the requirements of electoral freedom.[70]

William's zeal for reform was tempered by opportunism. When political expediency made the removal of a prelate desirable, he was careful to appoint a successor of outstanding ability and unimpeachable morals.

[68] The figures are those of W. J. Corbett, *Cambridge Medieval History*, vol. 5 (1926), 505–13. Some details have been corrected, but they give a rough approximation.

[69] Le Patourel, *Norman Empire*, pp. 49–51; Knowles, *Monastic Order*, p. 704.

[70] Knowles, *Monastic Order*, pp.106–19; Chibnall, *World of Orderic*, p. 29n.

After becoming duke of Normandy in 1035 he allowed his worldly uncle, Mauger, to hold the see of Rouen for the first twenty years of his reign; but when Mauger fell under suspicion of treason it was easy enough to find sound canonical reasons for his deposition by an ecclesiastical synod. The man chosen to replace him was Maurilius, monk of Fécamp, an admired spiritual leader. After the conquest of England the fate of Stigand, archbishop of Canterbury from 1052, was much the same. There had been some doubts about the legality of his metropolitan authority from the first, since he had never received a pallium (the vestment symbolizing that authority) from a properly constituted pope; even before the conquest bishops had gone abroad rather than seek consecration at his hands, and Harold, contrary to the stories later spread by the Normans, had carefully avoided being crowned by him.[71] William, equally cautious, received the crown from Archbishop Ealdred of York; but he allowed Stigand to remain at Canterbury until the rebellions of 1069 brought him under suspicion. In 1070 William secured his deposition in a council summoned and attended by two papal legates, and brought in the reformer, Lanfranc, abbot of St Stephen's at Caen, to take his place. Lanfranc, Lombard by birth but Norman by his monastic training and his experience of the Norman church, protested in his early days as archbishop that as an Englishman he was somewhat green. Yet within a few years he could refer quite naturally to 'we English', identifying himself with the interests of his church in a way that was to characterize many of the new abbots and bishops brought from Normandy.[72]

Church reform in Normandy had been one aspect of the restoration of ducal power. The province of Rouen almost coincided with the frontiers of the duchy; the one major discrepancy was the inclusion of the French Vexin in the territory of the archbishopric, and this was an area in which the duke attempted unsuccessfully to keep alive claims to dominion. The work of Geoffrey of Mowbray in restoring the see of Coutances and that of Odo in Bayeux, together with the foundation of the two ducal abbeys at Caen, underpinned the ducal authority in Lower Normandy.[73] It was only natural that after the conquest of England there should be a political side to the reform of the English church initiated by the Normans.

King William lost no time in putting his own men into both archbishoprics. Thomas of Bayeux, a protégé of Bishop Odo, was given York in 1070 within a few months of the death of Ealdred, and was consecrated shortly after Lanfranc's consecration as archbishop of Canterbury. The delay was due to the complex issue of the primacy claimed by

[71] Bates, *Normandy*, pp. 209–10; Brooks, *Church of Canterbury*, pp. 305–10.
[72] *Councils and Synods*, i. 563–76; *Letters of Lanfranc*, nos 2, 49.
[73] J. Le Patourel, 'Geoffrey of Montbray, bishop of Coutances, 1049–1093', *EHR*, 59 (1944), 129–61; Bates, *Speculum* (1975).

Canterbury and disputed by York. This was to cause much bitter rivalry later; but Thomas was prepared to submit personally to Lanfranc during his lifetime, saving the rights of his see, and serious contention over the exact relationship between the two archbishops was postponed. The points at issue were first raised in Rome in 1071, when both men went to receive their pallia from Pope Alexander II, and were deferred pending further investigation. Both archbishops were still in the process of learning the traditional rights of their predecessors, and were anxious to uphold all the lawful privileges of their office.[74]

Lanfranc had the full support of King William in the measures he took to strengthen the English hierarchy and reform the clergy. The king favoured the primacy of Canterbury as a means of unifying the realm.[75] Although Lanfranc failed to win papal recognition for all the claims of his see, he was able to hold a number of reforming councils which the archbishop of York attended, and to determine that the sees of Lichfield, Lincoln and Worcester, claimed by York, belonged to the province of Canterbury. Councils held at Winchester in 1072 and 1076, and at London in 1075, continued the work of reform begun in the legatine council of 1070. They issued decrees of a kind already familiar in Normandy, forbidding simony, attacking clerical marriage, and asserting the right of bishops to admit clerks presented to any benefices with cure of souls.[76] In addition the council of London, citing canons of the fourth-century councils of Laodicea and Sardica, arranged for the movement of three episcopal sees from small townships to urban centres. This was not new; most recently Leo IX had authorized the move from Crediton to Exeter in 1050, but as Martin Brett pointed out, 'the number of sees which were moved in England, and the absence of direct papal assent, were without recent parallel.' Royal assent, on the other hand, was obtained; 'by the beneficence of the king and the authority of the synod' permission was granted to Bishop Hereman to move from Sherborne to Salisbury, Bishop Stigand from Selsey to Chichester, and Bishop Peter from Lichfield to Chester. 'The case of certain others who remained in townships or villages was deferred until the king, who was at that time fighting overseas, could hear it in person.' Dorchester had already been transferred to Lincoln in 1072.[77]

The restructuring of the church, valuable in maintaining discipline, also formed a part of the political reorganization carried out in the years 1070–5. The transfers approved in 1075 had been projected earlier, in

[74] Letters of Lanfranc, nos 3, 4.

[75] Gibson, Lanfranc, pp. 130–1; Councils and Synods, i. 586–91.

[76] Councils and Synods, i. 591–620.

[77] Councils and Synods, i. 609; Letters of Lanfranc, p. 77.

MAP 6   Movements of bishops' sees 1050–1135

consultation with the king. To William, bishops, though forbidden actually to carry arms or to fight in battle, were still responsible leaders capable of organizing defence, like Geoffrey at Coutances or Wulfstan at Worcester. Remigius of Lincoln, a former abbot of Fécamp who had supplied ships and men for the invasion of England, was a prelate who could be trusted with the defence of the route to the north. Chester may have been intended as another outpost of Norman ecclesiastical and military penetration, as Durham was on the frontiers of Northumbria.[78] The characteristic Norman advance by means of castle, town and monastery at the caput of a feudal honour, was parallelled in the upper ranks of the hierarchy and aristocracy by the combination of walled city, earl's seat and cathedral church. William of Malmesbury noted that King William appointed no English bishops; the men he promoted were mostly Normans, though Hereford was given to the Lotharingian, Robert Losinga.[79]

The ecclesiastical aspect was not forgotten, or even seriously diminished, by these political considerations. Most of the new bishops, whether monks or royal clerks, were capable, well-educated men, who set about building their cathedral churches and organizing their cathedral chapters. At Salisbury, Lincoln and York, which were served by secular clergy, energetic prelates established chapters with constitutions similar to those of Normandy, though not exactly modelled on any of them.[80] But it was not surprising that Lanfranc, a monk professed at Bec and experienced as abbot of St Stephen's at Caen, should have looked to Benedictine monks to help in the work of reform. One way of expelling married clerks from prebends they had appropriated as part of the family patrimony was to replace them with monks. He found too that in England, as a result of the tenth-century monastic reform movement, St Oswald's see at Worcester and St Aethelwold's at Winchester, as well as his own archbishopric of Canterbury (reorganized slightly after the time of St Dunstan) already had monastic chapters. These were preserved unchanged, though Winchester was momentarily threatened by the new bishop, Walchelin. Walchelin quickly gave way to advice from Pope Alexander II backed by Lanfranc, and devoted his energies to rebuilding the cathedral church of St Swithun on a scale of unparalleled magnificence.[81] William of St Calais expelled the married secular clerks from Durham and established monks from the newly refounded houses of Jarrow and Wearmouth in 1082; Rochester became monastic in 1083. Some bishops attempted to annex wealthy and ancient monasteries as their seats, but Malmesbury successfully repelled Hereman of Sherborne, and Bury resisted William's former chancellor, Bishop Herfast of Elmham.

In later reigns monastic chapters were established in Norwich, where the East Anglian see was finally settled, in Bath, where John de Villula

[78] On the position of Lincoln see Hill, *Lincoln*, pp. 64–7.
[79] Malmesbury, *GR*, ii. 312–13.
[80] Edwards, *Secular Cathedrals*, ch. 1.
[81] Knowles, *Monastic Order*, pp. 129–34; and see below, ch. 9.

moved his see from Wells in 1090, and in the new bishopric of Ely, carved out of the huge diocese of Lincoln in 1109. When Robert de Limesey moved his main seat south from its temporary location at Chester in 1102, he placed it in the priory of Coventry. So the establishment of monastic chapters in line with English traditions went side by side with the reorganization of secular chapters on continental patterns. Half the cathedrals of England continued to be served by monks until the Reformation, although elsewhere, in almost the whole of continental Europe, monastic chapters either never took root or withered away. It was typical of the kind of synthesis and change that followed the Norman conquest.

2

The Moving Frontiers

Wales

In claiming the crown of England by hereditary right William set out to secure all the royal authority exercised by Edward the Confessor. This meant not only that he would attempt to push his frontiers to their previous limits, but that he would also aim at establishing lordship over any regions beyond the frontiers whose rulers had submitted to his predecessor. Relations with the Welsh princes and Scottish kings were far from stable in the years before the conquest; William's intention seems to have been to insist on all possible claims, and to renounce no conceivable rights. The frontiers of his new kingdom, like those of his Norman duchy, were in places ill-defined zones in which conflicting claims and rights were intermingled; the neighbouring princes were prepared to renew oaths of loyalty or allegiance made to King Edward only if William's power showed that it was in their interest to do so. He won some initial success, particularly in Wales, and at least staked out claims that his descendants were to pursue.

The frontier between the English kingdom and the lands of the Welsh princes was still in process of definition. There was an area of disputed settlement, particularly between the Wye and Offa's dyke, subject to raids from either side. In the tenth and eleventh centuries the strongest pressure had come from England, but the region suffered some violent Welsh incursions in Edward the Confessor's reign.[1] Wales was then politically fragmented among a number of princes, even if the victories of Gruffydd ap Llewelyn, prince of Gwynedd, gave an illusion of unity. When he defeated and slew the greatest of the southern princes, Gruffydd ap Rhydderch of Deheubarth, in 1055, he established a short-lived

---

[1] Stenton, *Anglo-Saxon England*, pp. 574, 615–17; Wendy Davies, *Wales in the Early Middle Ages* (Leicester, 1982), pp. 113–16; for a general account Lloyd, *Wales*, ii. 357–486.

domination over much of the south. Added to the threat of his rising power, his alliance with disaffected English leaders – Sweyn of Hereford in 1046 and Aelfgar of Mercia in 1055 – helped to provoke a strong English reaction. Edward the Confessor certainly believed that he had a right to some kind of dominion in Wales, going back perhaps to the tenth century, when a few Welsh princes had submitted to the rulers of Wessex and had witnessed charters at the English court as *subreguli*. Claims, long dormant, were revived in the face of an apparent threat from Wales. In 1056, according to the *Anglo-Saxon Chronicle*, Gruffydd was forced to swear that he would be a loyal and faithful underking to Edward. When peace broke down again in 1063, an army led by Harold found support among the disaffected Welsh princes, and Gruffydd was killed by some of his own men. Harold took oaths of vassalage from Gruffydd's two half-brothers in the north, and the separate southern principalities re-emerged. English pressure along the frontier was renewed.[2] This was the situation inherited by King William, who firmly believed in his right of dominion over Wales. After some of the dispossessed English rebels had sought refuge and support among the Welsh princes, his determination to assert effective authority hardened into a resolve to replace disloyal Welsh leaders by Norman lords wherever possible.

The lordships established along the Welsh frontiers in the early years of his reign were military authorities, effectively defensive, and poised for further conquest. The king himself took little direct part in the campaigns; he seems to have given licence to conquer in the lands of any Welsh prince who proved disloyal. With this licence went the necessary resources in English estates, exceptional rights of government, and authority to build castles freely in a way he permitted only in disturbed frontier regions. In the north the initiative was left, after the departure of Gherbod, to Hugh of Avranches, earl of Chester, and his ruthless and aggressive nephew, Robert of Rhuddlan. They struck into North Wales across the Dee, and penetrated as far as Conway. According to an entry in Domesday Book, by 1086 Robert of Rhuddlan had obtained from the king a grant of the whole of 'North Wales' (whose exact extent is uncertain) for an annual payment of £40. So he preserved the tradition of tribute allegedly owed, though perhaps never paid, by earlier Welsh princes who had made submission.[3] The advance continued into the next reign; Robert established castles at Rhuddlan and Deganwy on the river Conway. Hugh probably built those at Bangor, Carnarvon and Anglesey before the violence and brutality of the Normans provoked a rising.

[2] Barlow, *Edward the Confessor*, pp. 91, 99, 203–13; *ASC* (CD) 1056.
[3] D. Walker, 'The Norman settlement in Wales', *Anglo-Norman Studies*, 1 (1979 for 1978), 131–43; DB, i. 269a; Malmesbury, *GR*, i. 237, ii. 316.

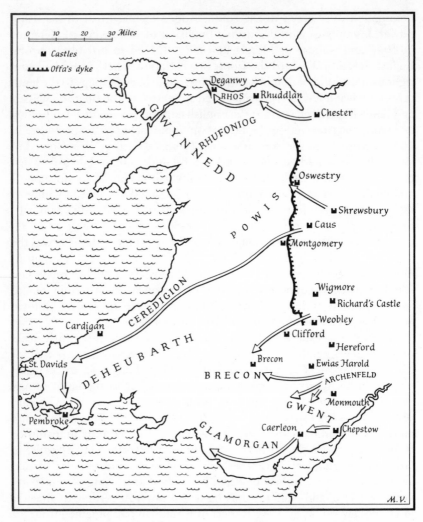

MAP 7   The Norman advance into Wales 1066–1100
(based on William Rees, *A Historical Atlas of Wales*, London, 1972, plates 29 and 30)

Robert was killed by a raiding party, probably in 1093, and the advance was halted.[4]

In mid-Wales the conquest was spearheaded by Earl Roger of Montgomery. From his base in Shrewsbury he advanced into the region to which he gave his name, and built a new castle at Montgomery. Thence he struck into the heart of Cardigan, building castles all the way; before

[4] Orderic, iv. pp. xxxiv–xxxviii, 138–43.

his death in 1094 his men had pushed south along the coast towards Dyfed. His son Arnulf built a castle at Pembroke on a site of great natural strength; alone of all the fortresses it remained unconquered in the wars of the next century. Here his men linked with the Norman advance along the northern shores of the Bristol Channel, where the most lasting settlements were made.

The southern march should have been the sphere of William fitz Osbern, first of the marcher lords to be established. But he had barely pushed his frontier to the Wye and built the great keep at Chepstow before his death in 1071. The treason of his son in 1075 put an end to the family's power, and brought the king more directly into the region. William the Conqueror established no new earldom; he left the military strategy to powerful vassals, such as the lords of Lacy, Mortimer, and Neufmarché. But he himself visited the region in 1081 when, according to the *Anglo-Saxon Chronicle*, he 'led an army into Wales and there liberated many hundreds of men'. Although the Welsh *Chronicle of the Princes* stated that his purpose was pilgrimage to offer prayers at the shrine of St David, politics were certainly mixed with prayers.[5] It was probably in that year that he came to terms with some of the princes of South Wales. Sulien, one of the most learned of the Welsh clergy, was then bishop of St Davids, and he may have acted in his traditional role of mediator between William and Rhys ap Tewdwr, ruler of Deheubarth. In 1086 the Domesday entry for Herefordshire recorded that 'Riset of Wales' (who must by Rhys ap Tewdwr) paid a render of £40 to the king: the sum that Robert of Rhuddlan paid as tribute for North Wales.[6] William was keeping alive the claims of his predecessor, Edward, in Wales.

It may have been on this visit that he cast an eye further afield: the coast of Ireland is clearly visible from the hills above St Davids, and Harold's sons had taken refuge there and attempted to invade England. Settlers in Pembroke were soon drawn into Irish politics; Arnulf of Montgomery, once established there, formed a marriage alliance with Muirchertach, king of Munster.[7] There must have been some reason for the statement of the *Anglo-Saxon Chronicle* that King William 'would have conquered Ireland by his prudence and without any weapons, if he could have lived two years more'. The church of Canterbury had some ill-defined claims to authority in Ireland, which Lanfranc voiced in several of his letters; and William made what use he could of the authority of the church in all his conquests.[8] But neither he nor his son

[5] ASC (E) 1081; *Brut-y-Tywysogyon*, p. 31.
[6] DB, i. 179a.
[7] Orderic, vi. 30–1; *Brut-y-Tywysogynon*, p. 43.
[8] ASC (E) 1087; *Letters of Lanfranc*, nos 4, 9–10, 49.

William Rufus, who also cast covetous glances across the Irish Sea, took any practical steps to secure dominion in Ireland. That particular enterprise was left for Henry II, in the later part of his reign. The immediate concern of William and his sons was to guard their own shores against invasion from Ireland, and this was one motive that led to their determined move to establish settlements along the northern shores of the Bristol Channel. An additional incentive was that this was one of the areas of natural expansion for the families settled in Somerset and Devon, among whom Braose, Chandos, and fitz Gilbert were conspicuous.[9] It was too a land of opportunity for enterprising household knights in search of a patrimony. Gerald of Windsor, a younger son of William I's constable at Windsor, was outstandingly successful. From being a steward to Arnulf of Montgomery he became royal constable at Pembroke, and married a Welsh princess, Nest, the daughter of Rhys ap Tewdwr; his descendants, the Fitzgeralds, prospered both in Pembroke and later in Ireland, and his daughter married William de Barry.[10]

Both William the Conqueror's sons continued their father's interest in this region. Henry was responsible for an unusual enterprise: the successful settlement of Flemings in Pembrokeshire. Some of these were brought c.1111 from an earlier settlement in Northumbria, but some may have come direct from Flanders to escape the disastrous floods there. In the early twelfth century Flemish entrepreneurs known as locators sometimes organized the settlement of whole colonies in lands needing to be brought under cultivation; the services of one of these men may have been used, though Henry gave one district to a Flemish leader, Wizo, possibly a military captain from the auxiliary forces he employed by treaty with the count of Flanders. The Flemings soon formed a thriving community of farmers, traders and craftsmen, which survived the Welsh risings later in the century.[11] Henry was in several ways responsible for more direct intervention in Wales; he established a royal castellan and sheriff in Pembroke, and led two expeditions in person against Welsh risings, as well as helping to strengthen the authority of Canterbury over the Welsh sees.

The North

King William gave his close personal attention to the north. This provided an extensive border area of potential settlement and exploitation, with the earldoms only partly assimilated by the English kings who claimed lordship over them. The eastern seaboard lay temptingly open to

---

[9] Rowlands, *Anglo-Norman Studies*, 3, pp. 142–7.
[10] Lloyd, *Wales*, ii. 401, 407–8, 416; Richter, *Giraldus Cambrensis*, p. 4.
[11] Lloyd, *Wales*, ii. 424, and below, ch. 5.

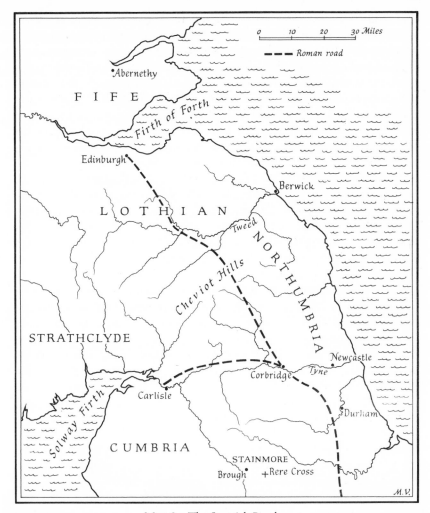

MAP 8   The Scottish Borders

invasion from Scandinavia, or from across the still contested border with Scotland. And north of the border was a monarchy of growing power, expanding from its heartland between the Moray Firth and the Firth of Forth into Lothian. Its king, Malcolm Canmore, gave refuge to English exiles, and married the English princess Margaret, sister of the pretender Edgar Atheling. To secure his formal subjection was of prime importance to William. Whatever claims to authority, secular or ecclesiastical, might be put forward, they could be enforced only by an impressive show of military power.

How far earlier kings of England had succeeded in incorporating the northern provinces in their realm was a matter on which opinions differed. The local nobility was always ready to assert loyalty to their native earls, the Scottish kings to insist on their rights to lordship as far south as the Rere Cross on Stainmore. Their claims were most tenacious in the west where, after the collapse of the ancient kingdom of Strathclyde, they had exercised intermittent lordship; ecclesiastically much of Cumberland and Westmorland lay in the diocese of Glasgow until 1133.[12] The local aristocracy included immigrants from Scotland and members of the Northumbrian house of Bamburgh. Nevertheless the tenth-century kings of Wessex had occasionally asserted lordship in the region; in 945, after ravaging all Cumbria, King Edward granted it to Malcolm, king of Scots, 'on condition that he be his helper, both on sea and on land'. His successors maintained claims to lordship; in 973 the eight underkings who, according to Florence of Worcester, came to Edgar at Chester included 'Malcolm, king of the Cumbrians' as well as Kenneth, king of Scots. These traditions were remembered in England, and in time both Cnut and Edward the Confessor obtained some form of submission from Scottish kings.[13]

William the Conqueror's immediate concern was to come to terms in person with Malcolm Canmore. His northern expeditions took the east coast route and were in part shows of strength against the turbulent Northumbrians rather than against Cumbria, which he left to his barons. In Northumbria he inherited particularly difficult conditions from his predecessors.[14] Up to 1055 the Northumbrian earls were taken from local families, particularly the house of Bamburgh; but in that year Waltheof, the young son of Earl Siward, was passed over in favour of Earl Godwin's third son, Tostig. Tostig's authority was never secure; his uneasy tenure of the earldom made incursions by Malcolm, king of Scots, possible, and finally provoked a revolt in 1065 which forced him to flee for his life. The Northumbrians invited Morcar to be their earl; his troubled rule was ended by the Norman conquest, and the conquest did not at first subdue the disaffected earldom.

William's first expedients of government were based on inadequate knowledge of a sturdily independent region. The Northumbrians would accept neither his men (even when, like Cospatric, they were chosen from the local aristocracy) nor their methods of exacting tribute. William's savage expedition to the north in 1069 established his rule in Yorkshire and fought off Scandinavian invaders, but left Northumbria and Cumbria still open to invasion from Scotland. Cumbria in particular suffered from the harrying raids of King Malcolm. Not until 1072 was William

[12] Barrow, *Kingdom of the Scots*, pp. 142–61.
[13] *ASC* 945, 973 (DE); Anderson, *Scottish Annals*, pp. 74–6, 84–7.
[14] Kapelle, ch. 4.

free to take action against him, but his expedition in that year established a relationship which, however fragile in apperance, was never forgotten by the Normans. In the terse words of the *Anglo-Saxon Chronicle,* William 'led a ship force and a land force to Scotland, and blockaded that country from the sea with ships. And he led his land force in over the Forth . . . And King Malcolm came and made peace with King William, and gave hostages and was his man.' The meeting, according to Florence of Worcester, took place at Abernethy; the nature of the homage is not defined in the sources, and its implications were to be a recurrent cause of friction.[15] After Malcolm had once again invaded and plundered Northumbria in 1079, William sent his son Robert northwards; again the armies met without a battle, and Malcolm renewed his earlier promises and gave hostages. To the Scottish king the oath was a personal promise of allegiance; it seems to have been a form of homage in the marches, of the type sworn to the king of France by the powerful counts whose lordships encircled the royal demesne lands. Malcolm appears to have thought of it in this way, for after the accession of William Rufus (to whom he had taken no oath) he was unwilling to promise allegiance until Robert Curthose accompanied his brother to support his demands. And it was with extreme reluctance that Malcolm agreed to attend the court of William Rufus at Gloucester. He alleged, according to Florence of Worcester, that he would not agree to justice being done 'unless upon the borders of their realms, where the kings of the Scots were accustomed to do right by the kings of the English, and according to the judgement of the chief men of both kingdoms'.[16]

Nevertheless William I established a precedent of exacting allegiance, and pending some less fragile agreement between the two rulers, he concentrated his energies on securing firm bases in the north for further advance and more effective defence. Here, as in the Midlands and the Welsh marches, authority was first established by means of strategically placed castles. Settlements, firmly based administration, and ecclesiastical authority followed by rapid stages. William was chary of giving the almost viceregal powers that had been necessary in the first stage of conquest for William fitz Osbern, Hugh of Avranches, Roger of Montgomery and Odo of Bayeux. He planted in his castleries men more of the type of Henry of Ferrers, and granted them powers that were analogous or only slightly greater. Roger of Bully at Tickhill, Ilbert of Lacy at Pontefract, Count Alan Rufus at Richmond, Drogo of La Beuvrière in Holderness, and Roger of Montgomery's son Roger the Poitevin in the

[15] *ASC* (D) 1073, (E) 1072; FW, ii. 9.
[16] FW, ii. 31; Barlow, *William Rufus,* pp. 288–95. For homage in the marches see Lemarignier, *L'hommage en marche.*

lands between Mersey and Ribble, were given compact fees around their principal castles, and extensive estates in the more peaceful and productive English shires to support their military establishments. But the king kept control of the royal demesnes in Yorkshire, and took over some confiscated estates, so that there was a sound financial basis for the sheriff's administration.[17] The lords of Holderness, where Odo count of Champagne had succeeded Drogo before the end of the reign, in time acquired sheriffs of their own; the promontory they controlled was almost cut off from the mainland by rivers and marshes, and formed a compact unit where strong control was vital to keep invaders at bay.[18] Durham, in time to become the seat of a princely bishop, was *sui generis*. Elsewhere, as settlement advanced, direct royal government advanced with it.

Recent changes in tenure recorded in Domesday Book suggest that the grants of some of these northern lordships came relatively late in the reign. Roger the Poitevin, indeed, can scarcely have been old enough to carry conquest into a disturbed region before about 1080. Domesday shows the advance northwards in progress, with new concentrations of power in the north, and a reallocation of supporting estates in safer regions such as Lincolnshire and Norfolk. The new lords brought with them vassals from their own patrimonies across the Channel; but the supply of knights for settlement may have been inadequate, and in both Yorkshire and Lancashire, particularly in the more inhospitable mountain regions, the number of native landholders was exceptionally large.[19] Shortage of Norman or Breton knights may not, however, have been the sole reason, in this age of land-hungry third and fourth sons; the English had experience of the guerilla type raids characteristic of the region, and their knowledge of local conditions made them a particularly valuable element even in a Norman army. In spite of their hostility to the invading Normans, their traditional allegiance was to their native earldoms; when both Bernicia and Cumbria were cut in half by advancing Scottish kings the effect, as Geoffrey Barrow has suggested, was 'to strengthen the Englishness of Northumberland and Cumberland, whose communities, however independent they might feel . . . showed no tendency to become Scottish'. A territorial stake in the country was the best guarantee of their loyalty in the face of an invading army of Scots.[20]

Key royal fortresses were established by William's son, Robert Curthose,

---

[17] DB, i. 299–301b; Kapelle, p. 120.
[18] English, *Holderness*, pp. 70–2; C. H. Hunter-Blair, 'The sheriffs of Northumberland', *Archaeologia Aeliana*, 4th ser., 20 (1942), 24–6.
[19] Kapelle, ch. 6; Greenway, *Mowbray Charters*, pp. xxxix–xl.
[20] Barrow, *Kingdom of the Scots*, pp. 160–1.

at Newcastle-on-Tyne in 1080, and by William Rufus in 1092 at Carlisle. The advance of Rufus into Cumbria was his most successful attempt to build on the foundations laid by his father. The castleries established under the Conqueror protected routes across the Pennines, and made possible a consolidation of settlement west of the mountains. In 1092 Rufus led a great army northwards, rebuilt the borough of Carlisle, erected a castle there, and garrisoned it with his men. He appointed a sheriff, and gave the lordship of Carlisle to Ralph le Mesquin of Briquessart. Most remarkably, he brought peasants with their families and livestock from the south to people the devastated region; an attempt at settlement in depth that was to be repeated by his brother Henry, when he planted Flemings in Pembrokeshire.[21] Henry rounded out the northern conquest in 1133 ecclesiastically, by establishing a bishopric at Carlisle, subject to the archbishop of York.[22] Relations with Scotland were easier in his reign, because both King Alexander and King David were brothers of the English queen, Matilda; David, indeed, had been brought up at the English court.

---

[21] Barlow, *William Rufus*, pp. 297–8; *Regesta*, i. 463, 478; ii. 407; *ASC* (E) 1092.
[22] Le Neve, ii. 19; John of Hexham, in Simeon of Durham, ii. 285.

3

Settlement and Succession

William the Conqueror and his Sons

In the mid-tenth century succession to the English crown became firmly settled in the line of the West Saxon kings. The next hundred years produced a series of disputed successions and military conquests, complicated by the rival claims of Scandinavian kings and Norman dukes. If the crown seemed at times to belong to the man who could successfully seize and hold it, this was never the whole truth. Success even in the short run depended on carrying the support of leading churchmen and magnates. And to establish a secure royal line was possible only by showing respect, at least externally, for accepted customs of king-making. A ruler had to convince his powerful subjects of his right to rule.

His position was strongest if, in addition to being eligible by birth, he had been designated by the late king, recognized by the chief magnates, and consecrated by the church.[1] William the Conqueror took great pains to convince his subjects of his eligibility on all counts, even if this involved twisting the facts. As far as birth went, only one other contender had an obviously stronger claim: Edgar Atheling, the great-grandson of King Aethelred and his first wife, Aelfgifu. Had Edgar's father, Edward the Exile, not died prematurely in 1057 the opposition from the line of Cerdic might have been much more formidable; but the young and inexperienced Edgar was not considered for the succession when King Edward died; his claim was not voiced until after Harold's defeat at Hastings, and it was quickly dropped. Harold himself had no more than the shadow of a right through kinship; he was the brother of Queen Edith, and was distantly allied with the Danish royal house through his mother Gytha. Swein, king of Denmark, a nephew of Cnut, took no steps

---

[1] See below, Appendix 1; Barlow, *Edward the Confessor*, p. 54; J. S. Beckerman, 'The role of testamentary custom', *Speculum*, 47 (1972), 258–60; Ann Williams, 'Some notes . . . on the royal succession, 860–1066', *Anglo-Norman Studies*, 1 (1979 for 1978), 144–67.

to lay claim to England; and Harold Hardrada, king of Norway, who had aspirations to extend his rule, had no real hereditary right. William, on the other hand, was the great-nephew of Queen Emma, sister of Duke Richard II of Normandy, who had married successively King Aethelred and King Cnut. It was a slender right, based on collateral descent, but in default of direct descendants of either Edward the Confessor or Cnut it sufficed to give a show of legitimacy to William's claim.

As for designation, the conflicting evidence suggests that King Edward looked with favour on the possible succession of his Norman cousin for a time, once his own childlessness made it necessary for him to think of naming an heir. He had been brought up in exile in the court of Normandy, and began his reign with a deep suspicion of the house of Godwin, which he learned to temper only when it became quite clear that he could not rule without them. The Norman chroniclers, who stated the case for William too neatly and emphatically to be wholly convincing, insisted that Edward had sent for his cousin in 1051, and named him as his heir. Since some corroboration comes from a Canterbury tradition, recorded by Eadmer, of a promise made to William by young Edward during his exile in Normandy, it is likely that at some date William was given encouragement. Edward, however, designated different heirs at different times, and he gave his voice to Harold on his death-bed. The Norman sources knew of this, and William of Poitiers explicitly rejected it, claiming that Edward's earlier designation of William as the man most likely to succeed him remained valid.[2] In this interpretation the recourse to battle was an appeal to the judgement of God.

Thereafter William's claims were more solidly based. On the field of Hastings Harold was removed by the only acceptable method of eliminating a rival king: death in battle. Even then William took care to keep the favour of the church by penance and reparation for the bloodshed; his foundation of Battle Abbey a few years later was his own most dramatic and visible act of reparation.[3] His acceptance as king by the leading men of the realm, and his coronation by Archbishop Ealdred of York in preference to the schismatic Stigand of Canterbury were public ceremonials that none could deny. But his acceptance as king of England as well as duke of Normandy left open the problem of succession. Would he pass on all his territories as an undivided inheritance to one of his sons; and if so, to which one?

---

[2] William of Poitiers, pp. 172–9, gives an eloquent statement of the Norman case. See also *ASC* (D) 1052 for 1051, 1057; William of Jumièges, vii. 13–14, pp. 132–4; Eadmer, *HN*, p. 7.

[3] *Battle Chronicle*, pp. 16–23; for the penitential ordinances see *Councils and Synods*, i. 581–4.

William had three surviving sons; one son, Richard, had been killed in
a hunting accident before receiving the belt of knighthood. Although the
descent of a kingdom to the eldest son was not an invariable rule there
was a strong presumption in favour of the first born unless he was
manifestly incapable of governing. Kingdoms and counties were already
regarded as impartible; younger sons might be provided with apanages,
for which they swore fealty to their brother. Serious problems began if a
ruler died without male descendants, or if he had brought together by
conquest or marriage a number of separate principalities. William I
committed his fortunes to his eldest son, Robert Curthose, some years
before 1066. By arranging the betrothal of Robert to Margaret, heiress of
Maine, he established a claim to a long-coveted territory. Both the
betrothed were children at the time, and Margaret died before the
marriage could be consummated; nevertheless William based his claim
on the betrothal when he invaded Maine, and his legal right depended on
Robert. In addition, before he embarked on the hazardous invasion of
England, he made his barons do homage to Robert, to secure the
succession to the duchy in his line. This homage was repeated later.[4]
Unfortunately Robert proved an unruly son, champing for more effective
power and patronage during his father's lifetime; two bitter quarrels with
his father forced him into exile in France, where he went to the length of
taking up arms against the Normans. He was still absent and unreconciled when William died. Normandy could not be taken from him; and
William was determined that he should not have England. There was no
alternative to a temporary division of the inheritance, inconvenient
though that was to lords with great estates on both sides of the Channel.

No share in the royal inheritance had been provided for the two
younger sons, and in 1086 they were virtually without landed estates.
Both had received the normal aristocratic training in the arts of war, and
had been knighted; they attended their father and fought in his household troops, living the life of young knights bachelor. Both had received
some teaching from Archbishop Lanfranc, and William Rufus may have
been groomed for kingship. Neither had been provided with a wife; and
Robert too remained unmarried after the death of his first betrothed.
William deferred taking a decision; he was not quite sixty when he died
at Rouen after a short illness, with only enough time to leave verbal
instructions for his heirs.[5] Robert retained his right to Normandy, and
also to Maine if he could succeed in holding it against a claimant from

---

[4] For Robert's position see R. H. C. Davis, 'William of Jumièges, Robert Curthose and
the Norman Succession', *EHR*, 95 (1980), 597–606; J. Le Patourel, 'The Norman succession 996–1135', *EHR*, 86 (1971), 225–50.

[5] Orderic, iv. 78–101; Chibnall, *World of Orderic*, pp. 182–7.

the older comital line. William Rufus was sent to England with a letter instructing Lanfranc to crown him king. Henry's legacy consisted only of money, or possibly a right to his mother's lands. Robert lived until 1134; and his existence never ceased to be a potential threat, though he was only twice at the centre of a major plot to win the English crown, and after Henry defeated and imprisoned him in 1106 his claims to Normandy remained dormant. When Henry died, less than two years after Robert, he left no surviving legitimate son. So for a hundred years after the Norman conquest it was doubly important for the reigning king to uphold the legitimacy of his rule by keeping the support of the baronage and the approval of the church. Coronation and unction, long important to set the seal on succession to the throne, might seem in such circumstances actually to make a king.[6] The Norman kings dated their acts from the time of their coronation, though William's first three successors allowed only the smallest interval to elapse between the death of their predecessor and their own crowning. Every reign began with a swift seizure of the royal treasure, and coronation by the best-qualified prelate who was within call. Since the prelates controlled substantial landed wealth and could raise a force of some 700 knights, church support was more than merely moral.[7]

Whatever William the Conqueror's intentions, his sons seem to have resolved that the divided inheritance should ultimately be reunited. In an agreement made in 1091 William Rufus and Robert each recognized the other as the heir to all his lands if he should die without a son; and a similar arrangement was made by Robert and Henry in 1101.[8] Apart from the agreement with Robert, William Rufus made no attempt to provide for the succession; he never married. The matrimonial alliances of medieval kings can never be explained solely in personal, psychological, terms; it was the acknowledged duty of any ruler to endeavour to provide an heir. Whatever his personal inclinations, one possible political reason for William's prolonged bachelorhood may have been his failure to find a suitable heiress; a later rumour suggested that he cast covetous eyes on Matilda, the daughter of Queen Margaret of Scotland and niece of Edgar Atheling, and withdrew only because she was alleged to be a nun.[9] Thirteen years of celibate rule was exceptional, but he was still

[6] P. E. Schramm, *A History of the English Coronation*, trans. L. G. W. Legg (Oxford, 1937), gives a general survey in some need of revision; a study of the Norman coronations is being prepared by George Garnett.

[7] Jacques Beauroy, 'La conquête cléricale de l'Angleterre', *Cahiers de civilisation médiévale*, 27 (1984), 35–48.

[8] Barlow, *William Rufus*, pp. 281–3; David, *Robert Curthose*, pp. 134–5.

[9] Southern, *St Anselm*, pp. 184–5.

young when he met his death while hunting in the New Forest, and his territorial ambitions were only partly satisfied.

Both William Rufus and Henry showed something of their father's 'creative power in both fighting and ruling'; with Rufus the emphasis was on the fighting, with Henry on the ruling. Robert Curthose lacked the gift, though he was a brave fighter and a popular ruler with the clientele who profited from his generosity. His ambitious younger brothers recognized that he was not capable of maintaining intact the ducal rights which his father had fought to secure. He gave away castles in fee, and surrendered lands and rights of jurisdiction, so that his resources were not enough to pay his knights. William Rufus and Henry used his weakness to keep him out of England, as their father had intended, and to take over as much as possible of his authority in Normandy. If they alleged filial duty as a cloak for private ambition the ambition was as much dynastic as personal; they wished to reunite the inheritance and to develop its potential as their father might have done. Both, as feudal and administrative changes in England showed, possessed some creativity in the art of government.

On the English side of the Channel, Rufus concentrated on military success in Cumbria and the southern marches of Wales. But he kept his father's ablest administrators, notably Ranulf Flambard, and encouraged them to exploit all the potential resources of the crown to raise the money that built castles and kept his household troops contented and loyal. To retain the support of his barons and prevent them from rejoining Robert in a bid for the crown he had to go a little further than he might have wished in creating new titles. Mostly, however, his earldoms were titular awards to powerful vassals of proven loyalty, like William of Warenne or Henry of Beaumont, who became earls of Surrey and Warwick respectively.[10] But he also manipulated patronage in a way that favoured some new men, chosen from his younger knights and vassals. Simon of Senlis, a gallant knight of obscure origins, was given the hand of Earl Waltheof's daughter Matilda and the title of earl of Huntingdon and Northampton. The second and third husbands of the Lincolnshire heiress, Lucy, were both household knights of good family; Roger fitz Gerold of Roumare, the castellan of Neufmarché, and Ralph of Bricquessart, vicomte of Bayeux. Both established powerful families in England who were to play a major part in the politics of Stephen's reign.[11] Robert fitz Haimo, son of the sheriff of Kent, was married to Roger of Montgomery's daughter Sibyl. These able and powerful military commanders, with patrimonial interests in Normandy and new

---

[10] Southern, *St Anselm*, p. 4; Barlow, *William Rufus*, pp. 167–9.
[11] *Complete Peerage*, vi. 639n; vii. App. J; Barlow, *William Rufus*, pp. 172–3.

English honours *iure uxoris,* could be relied upon to lead the king's knights as they campaigned in Normandy, Maine and the French Vexin, and to further the ultimate reunion of Normandy with England. Other rising families were established in Yorkshire and south Wales, to secure the Norman advance in these regions.

William Rufus did not accept Robert's position in Normandy without demur. Robert had invited retaliation by giving support in 1088 to a rebellion in which his uncles Odo of Bayeux and Robert of Mortain played a part, and the dissidents included William of Saint-Calais, bishop of Durham. But the rebels were defeated and punished; Odo was deprived of his English estates and banished from the country; the earldom of Kent was not revived. For some years William intervened in the disturbed politics of Normandy, frequently against Robert; his opportunity came when Robert answered the call made by Urban II at Clermont in 1095, and left the following year on the first crusade. In return for a substantial loan to finance his expedition, he entrusted Normandy to his brother. So for the last four years of his life William ruled Normandy as king of England, and carried his campaigns into Maine and the Vexin.[12] He had already come to terms with his younger brother Henry, who appears, biding his time, in William's household. Rufus was thought to be planning an expedition still further afield into Poitou in the summer of 1100;[13] and although Robert was then on his way home from Jerusalem, having married the Norman, Sibyl of Conversano, in Apulia, and acquired with her a dowry sufficient to repay his debt to his brother, it is doubtful whether William would have been willing to relinquish Normandy after four years of successful rule. At the moment of his sudden death Normandy and England were both firmly in his grip, however different the nature of his title in the two, and Henry's six-year struggle to drive Robert out of Normandy was a continuation of his brother's general policy. But the means he was able to use were conditioned both by the circumstances of his own accession, and the need to conciliate those important barons and prelates who had been dissatisfied with William's methods of government.

William Rufus's great failure was with the church. The extent of that failure is shown in the hostility of all the leading ecclesiastical chroniclers, who were ready to blame him for the actions of his father and his brother Henry as well as his own. Moreover, to the general problem of adjusting a still developing feudal custom to the pre-existing financial and ecclesiastical structure of the Anglo-Norman realm was added the

---

[12] J. Le Patourel, 'Norman kings or Norman "king-dukes"?', *Droit privé et institutions régionales: Études historiques offertes à Jean Yver* (Rouen, 1976), pp. 469–79.

[13] Malmesbury, *GR,* ii. 379.

difficulty caused by a more rigorous definition and papal enforcement of church law. William the Conqueror made some effort to adjust the rights he took for granted in Normandy to the traditional rights of the churches in his new realm. But the circumstances of the conquest created a new situation; and the contemporary sources have unfortunately left very little record of how he exercised his rights and fulfilled his obligations during church vacancies, or exactly how new prelates who were also great territorial magnates were invested with their office. Most of the chronicles were written a little later, emphasized the issues that were contentious at the time of writing, and generalized from a handful of precedents that seemed to prove their point. So the Battle and Ely chroniclers looked for signs of monastic exemption from the diocesan bishop, and Eadmer was obsessed with the questions of homage and investiture.

The persuasive generalizations of Eadmer, monk of Canterbury and biographer of Anselm, have been accepted without question by many historians up to the present day. He stated his intention unequivocally in the preface to his *Historia novorum in Anglia*:

> The chief purpose of this work is, after describing how Anselm, abbot of Bec, was made archbishop of Canterbury, to show why, when disagreement arose between him and the kings of England, he was exiled from the kingdom so often and so long, and how the cause of dispute was resolved. The root cause was a novelty in this age, unheard of in England before the Normans began to reign there. From the time that William, count of the Normans, conquered the land no one before Anselm was made bishop or abbot unless he had previously done homage to the king, and received investiture of his bishopric or abbacy by the handing over of a pastoral staff.

The only exceptions, he added, were the two bishops of Rochester, who had been invested by Lanfranc in the chapter of Christ Church, Canterbury. There were other reasons for Anselm's exile, but they were subsidiary to this. Some of these other 'novelties' are listed later: the Conqueror's insistence on seeing letters to and from Rome, on approving any constitutions issued in an archiepiscopal council, and on giving permission for the excommunication of any one of his barons or officials, even for such a crime as incest or adultery.[14] All this is clear enough. But was it true?

Little as we know of procedure in Normandy before 1066, it is certain that in some well-attested appointments to abbeys homage was not done. An isolated example of the abbot of St Julian at Tours kissing the duke's

---

[14] Eadmer, *HN*, pp. 1–2, 10.

knee when he was invested with land in Normandy is as much an imperial relic of submission as feudal homage. William regularly invested new abbots of Saint-Evroult with their temporalities by handing over the pastoral staff of one of the bishops present in his court. The new abbot then went away to be blessed and invested with his spiritual authority by a bishop. It is not clear whether this was the normal procedure for investing all Norman abbots; but as long as investiture by the duke was recognized as involving only the temporalities it was perfectly acceptable. Even the canonist Ivo of Chartres found it appropriate as late as 1097.[15] The position of Norman bishops, who were great vassals often holding family estates, is more doubtful; often they must have done homage before becoming bishops. But it cannot be assumed from the Norman evidence that the king would have required homage as a matter of course from English prelates, as long as he was not denied the right of investiture. And, Eadmer apart, the monastic historians writing during and shortly after the Conqueror's reign are almost uniformly silent on this question. The conditions of the conquest may have brought about, or hastened, a change.

English abbots or bishops who did not choose the course of rebellion came at some time to the king's court and made their peace with him; this may have involved homage as well as fealty. As military obligations became imposed and clarified, the prelates who received homage from their own vassals may have been required to perform homage to their own lord, the king. Norman bishops who were granted personal honours in England, notably Odo of Bayeux with his earldom of Kent and Geoffrey of Coutances with over 280 manors, must have taken homage in their stride. There is no reason to doubt Eadmer's explicit statement that Lanfranc had done homage, even if he was overhasty in generalizing from a few known examples.[16] Since during the great invasion scare of 1085 William summoned his vassals and their men to Salisbury, and insisted that the knights of his barons should 'bow down to him and become his men', it is unlikely that he required any less from those churchmen who had military obligations. But the chroniclers were usually content to describe a new appointment with some such formula as 'the king sent him', or 'he was made abbot'. Whatever ceremonies may have been performed were not so shocking to monks and cathedral clergy that they recorded any protests. We cannot assume that the change was as sudden and sweeping as Eadmer makes it, or even

[15] Fauroux, no. 142; W. Ullmann, *The Growth of Papal Government in the Middle Ages* (London, 1955), pp. 315–16; J. Yver, *BSAN*, 57 (1965 for 1963–4), 189–283; O. Guillot, *Le comte d'Anjou et son entourage au xie siècle* (Paris, 1972), i. 185–8.

[16] Eadmer, *HN*, p. 41.

that priors and abbots without military obligations were required to do homage at all.

There were certainly difficulties and delays in some sees. As far as the evidence goes, the reasons were ecclesiastical. Sometimes it was uncertain whether an abbey was canonically vacant when the incumbent had been suspended for rebellion. Abbot Aethelwig of Evesham, for example, administered Winchcombe for some years together with his own abbey. But William lost no time in securing the consent of papal legates to the deposition of prelates who, for any reason, could be charged with misconduct; and after 1070 delays in consecration were mostly for other reasons.[17] In 1075, after the death of Theodwin, abbot of Ely, Godfrey, a monk who had been chosen as administrator by Theodwin himself and approved by the king, administered the affairs of the abbey in every way as though he had been abbot. The reason for his failure to be blessed as abbot may have been friction with the diocesan; the Ely chronicler, writing in the next century, criticized the next abbot, Simeon, for consenting to be blessed by his diocesan, Remigius of Lincoln, whose authority was questioned by the abbey.[18] King William ordered that the claims of the abbey to its spiritual immunities and temporal possessions should be investigated, and several pleas were heard during the later years of his reign. The monks failed to prove exemption from their diocesan, but the case shows the king's anxiety to find out the truth about existing customs. There is no hint of any objection at that time to his method of investing an abbot with the temporalities, whatever form it may have taken.

Nor does it appear that abbeys and bishoprics were deliberately kept vacant, even if during William's reign they normally came under the care of the king rather than the diocesan bishop during vacancies.[19] The *Anglo-Saxon Chronicle* complained that in 1070 'the king had all the monasteries that were in England plundered.' But the Worcester chronicle was more exact: 'on the advice of William, earl of Hereford, and certain others, King William had all the monasteries of England searched, and ordered that the money, which the wealthiest of the English had deposited in them, on account of his plundering of the land, should be removed and placed in his treasury.' Much of the confiscated wealth was not monastic property; and sometimes on later occasions when he insisted on inventories being made and church treasures removed this was ostensibly for safe keeping only. When Theodwin was appointed abbot of Ely he refused to enter the abbey until all the gold and silver and

[17] *Chron. Evesham*, p. 90; Gibson, *Lanfranc*, pp. 113–15.
[18] *Liber Eliensis*, p. 197.
[19] Howell, *Regalian Right*, pp. 5–11.

precious stones that had been carried off were restored, and this was done.[20] Some exploitation of estates by royal custodians certainly took place; St Albans remembered that in 1077 trees had been cut down and men impoverished on the abbey's estates until Lanfranc intervened to restrain the king.[21] And in general the regalian rights already well established in France were slowly replacing the earlier practice of guardianship by churchmen. But there was no systematic exploitation of rights, and most chroniclers praised William I for protecting church rights more than they condemned any infringement of liberties. Complaints built up during the reign of his son, William Rufus. They came from two sides; from reformers like Anselm and his faithful biographer Eadmer, who insisted on a stricter application of the most recent church legislation, and from the general run of prelates, monks and their tenants, who resisted the attempt of the king to systematize his financial rights in his interest rather than their own.

The resentment aroused by Rufus was not due to any abuse of accepted feudal rights, though it has sometimes been interpreted in this way. These rights still varied according to the terms of individual enfeoffments; much was unsystematic, and changing feudal customs had to be adjusted to old-established rights of the English crown. The more precisely defined military obligations of the greater spiritual lords created new problems. And the important role of the church at the time of each new accession and coronation was exploited to the full. William Rufus's designation by his father and his coronation by Lanfranc gave him a firm hold on the kingdom; he was not obliged to make concessions. Eadmer, wishing to argue that he had struck a bargain to secure the crown, gave his own version of events:

> When he set out to snatch the government of the kingdom from his brother Robert, he found that Lanfranc, without whose assent he could not hope to win the kingdom, was not wholly willing to fall in with his plans. Fearing that to delay his consecration would lead to the loss of the dignity he sought, he began both in person and through others to promise on oath to Lanfranc that if he became king he would observe justice, mercy and fair-dealing throughout the whole kingdom, preserve the peace, liberty and security of the church against all others, and obey Lanfranc's precepts in everything.

This may be no more than a dramatization of the coronation oath. Lanfranc, by whatever means he was persuaded, gave Rufus loyal support until he died in 1089, and used his legal skill to judge the rebels

[20] ASC (DE) 1070; FW, ii. 4–5; Liber Eliensis, p. 196.
[21] Gesta abbatum (RS), i. 51.

of 1088, arguing that the bishop of Durham, having acted treasonably as a vassal, could not claim immunity as a bishop. William of Malmesbury saw Lanfranc's influence in terms of personal example rather than contract when he wrote that Rufus acted with restraint and judgement as long as the archbishop lived, but gradually fell away into bad habits after his death.[22]

Much that Rufus did was a logical development of his father's lines of action. There was nothing new in giving bishoprics to clerks who had done good service in the royal court, and not all were unsuited to their new office. Orderic Vitalis, though complaining that Rufus gave away ecclesiastical honours like hirelings' wages to clerks and monks of the court, added that some made good and conscientious prelates.[23] But the progressive definition of the feudal obligations of all vassals revealed how incompatible some of these were with the demands of church reformers and the precepts of developing canon law. Feudal reliefs, if demanded from newly-elected bishops or abbots, might easily be confused with simony. Even as duke of Normandy, William the Conqueror had supported the condemnation of simony by church councils; he avoided the open sale of English bishoprics. His son Rufus, less scrupulous, made some effort to follow this example, provided he could take some profit from the feudal honours of his ecclesiastical tenants-in-chief. When, in 1091, Anselm of Bec reluctantly accepted the archbishopric of Canterbury, he refused to make any grant to the king that might be interpreted as payment for office. Bishop Herbert Losinga, who paid for promotion to the East Anglian bishopric, repented and went to Rome to obtain absolution, probably in 1094.[24] It seems that these rebuffs made the king walk more warily for a time. A writ, issued during a vacancy in the see of Worcester to the bishop's tenants, shows one alternative that he attempted.

Addressed to all the men, French and English, holding free lands of the bishop of Worcester, the writ specified the exact amount that twenty-nine named tenants were to pay the king as a relief; the total sum demanded was £250. Often regarded as a breach of 'accepted feudal custom', since subtenants did not normally pay reliefs directly to an overlord, it is much more likely to be an expedient to secure a relief without appearance of simony.[25] The writ was issued in 1095, after the death of Wulfstan, the last surviving English bishop. Wulfstan had made his peace with William I very shortly after the conquest of England, and for the rest of his long life had consistently shown both loyalty to the king

---

[22] Eadmer, *HN*, p. 25; Gibson, *Lanfranc*, pp. 159–61; Malmesbury, *GR*, ii. 367.
[23] Orderic, v. 202–4.
[24] *Councils and Synods*, i. 642–3.
[25] Round, *Feudal England*, p. 309.

and respect for the customs of his diocese and the law of the church. With a see on the Welsh border he had no difficulty in viewing the maintenance of peace and order as part of his duty; he was ready to help in mustering forces to resist either Welsh raiders or local rebels, as he did in 1088. His biographer noted that his custom was to dine either with his monks or with his knights, thereby acknowledging the dual role he accepted and discharged with honour.[26]

After his death the king did not prolong the vacancy unduly; Samson of Bayeux was appointed a year later. One of the ablest of the king's clerks, who played an important part in the Domesday inquest, Samson was 'a man of wordly tastes and habits'; yet he had virtues that won and kept the friendship of Marbod of Rennes and the canonist Ivo of Chartres. If, as Orderic Vitalis suggests, he had already refused the bishopric of Le Mans because he knew that a reformer of more ascetic tastes than he was needed to secure papal approval, he was just the man to recognize that in accepting Worcester he must avoid all shadow of suspicion of simony and, at the same time, to suggest an expedient for meeting the king's financial needs.[27]

Whatever lay behind the Worcester writ, the measure was disliked and rejected later; it may not have been tried elsewhere. William Rufus throughout his reign, as Margaret Howell has shown, was experimenting in the application of his rights of regale; and it is equally clear that he was also experimenting in his demands for feudal dues.[28] His government was not consistently extortionate. But some expedients were resented; and rights of regale were overstrained when vacancies were prolonged and most of the revenues taken for the royal coffers. When William died two bishoprics and eleven abbeys were in the king's hand. Archbishop Anselm had gone into exile because, as Eadmer wrote, 'little was done lawfully or as directed', and he wished to consult the Pope about his troubles.[29] There were many causes of friction, though it was only after Anselm's sojourn at Bari with Urban II that he grasped the full force of the papal attack on lay investiture and the performance of homage by churchmen. It is possible now to see, with hindsight, that these abuses lay at the root of the apparently petty disagreements between 'the most secular of all medieval kings' and his conscientious archbishop. But it was not until Anselm returned to England after the death of Rufus with a clearer grasp of what he had previously only dimly perceived that he attacked them relentlessly. Nevertheless clerical resentment against

[26] *Vita Wulfstani*, pp. 24–6, 46.
[27] Galbraith, *EHR* (1967), 86–101; Orderic, ii. 300–2.
[28] Howell, *Regalian Right*, pp. 12–19.
[29] Southern, *St Anselm*, pp. 142–60, gives the best account of Anselm's difficulties.

Rufus was strong enough for his brother Henry to feel obliged to bolster up a dubious right of succession with promises that went beyond the general expressions of just government included in the coronation oath.

Henry, the ablest of the Conqueror's sons, had a weaker title to the throne than his brother William. He could not claim designation. In spite of his father's avowed intention not to allow Robert Curthose to have the English crown, William Rufus had agreed at Rouen in 1091 to make Robert his heir if he himself died childless. This agreement seems to have been abrogated two years later, but William left the succession an open question. By 1100 Robert had been absent on crusade for over four years, and Henry, after a period of vacillating between both brothers, and even at one stage uniting both against himself, had made his peace with William in 1095. He appeared at times in William's company, witnessing at least one charter, and leading a contingent of knights in the Vexin wars.[30] He was hunting with his brother in the New Forest on 2 August 1100. Whatever William's intentions for the succession, Henry was ready to seize his opportunity whenever it came. By fighting and bargaining with his brothers he had secured a territorial base in the fortress town of Domfront, and in the Cotentin, where he had the status of count. He had the nucleus of a household, and loyal contingents of knights drawn mainly from lower Normandy and the Breton frontiers.[31] He understood the Anglo-Norman magnates, and knew the importance of support by the church. His swift and unerring actions when William was struck down without warning by an arrow on his fatal hunting expedition were made possible by his constant readiness and instant response to any crisis. Although some historians have argued that William was murdered, the balance of the evidence indicates that his death was accidental.[32] Hunting accidents were common; his younger brother Richard and one of Robert Curthose's illegitimate sons had both met with similar accidents. The aristocracy lived dangerously; Louis VI's son and heir, Philip, was fatally injured by a fall from his horse; Miles of Gloucester was killed while hunting in 1143. At the time of William's death there was no suggestion of foul play; and in any case murder was not in Henry's character, relentless though he was. He would never have risked his reputation in the hands of an assassin.

However, from the moment of William's death on 2 August he knew what he had to do to seize and reunite his father's inheritance. Within a day he had persuaded the keepers of the king's castle at Winchester to

---

[30] Barlow, *William Rufus*, ch. 6 and pp. 363–4; *Regesta*, i. 398; Orderic, v. 214–15.

[31] Le Patourel, *Norman Empire*, pp. 342–8.

[32] C. Warren Hollister, 'The strange death of William Rufus', *Speculum*, 48 (1973), 637–53; Barlow, *William Rufus*, p. 425.

surrender the castle and treasure to him. On 5 August he was crowned and anointed at Westminster by Maurice, bishop of London, and made the promises incorporated in his coronation charter. He immediately sent for the exiled Anselm. On 11 November he married Matilda, daughter of Malcolm Canmore and Margaret, 'of the true royal family of England'.[33] Within three years she had given him two children, a boy and a girl, who survived infancy. The crown of England, and the succession to the crown, were for the time being as secure as he could make them. By 1106 he had Normandy also.

Each step in his advance was important. He justified his haste by the need to establish firm government immediately in the interests of peace. Whatever Robert's claim, he was not yet back in his duchy of Normandy after a long absence, and was out of touch with conditions both there and in England. Henry, though a younger son, was of Norman royal birth, and a special claim could be advanced on his behalf because he had been born in England after the coronation of both his parents; he was in a sense born in the purple. He could not claim designation; but he secured consent to his accession from all the magnates who were present, first at Winchester and then at Westminster. A few had scruples, because Henry as count of the Cotentin had done homage to his brother Robert. But dissidents, including William of Breteuil, were won over; and he had the backing of the powerful family of Beaumont. Both Robert, count of Meulan, and his younger brother Henry, earl of Warwick, are named among his supporters. Orderic Vitalis, with his finger firmly on the pulse of Norman baronial feeling, attributed to Count Robert in a later crisis advice that seems to have guided Henry's actions from the first.[34] The king's chief care should be to secure peace and justice for his people; rebels who tried to snatch their own profit in a time of disorder were to be placated until the danger was over, and then dealt with as they deserved. Even if they asked for London or York, 'it is better to give a small part of the kingdom than to sacrifice victory and life itself to a host of enemies'; alienated demesnes could be recovered later, by due process of law. Some such thinking was behind Henry's grant of a coronation charter; promises had to be given to secure the crown, but the implementation of the promises would depend on keeping a balance between the reasonable demands of the great vassals and churchmen, and the king's customary rights. Prudence, not cynicism, was his guiding principle. His later practice shows that he was prepared to renounce any demands made by his brother that had been found unacceptable.

He was not, however, prepared to concede all that might be read into

[33] *ASC* (E) 1100.
[34] Orderic, v. 290–2, 314–17; Malmesbury, *GR*, ii. 470.

the wording of the charter; it is worth noting that the charter itself, though included in the contemporary compilation known as the *Leges Henrici primi,* had a negligible place in the political thinking of his reign. A revised version may have been issued in 1101, but most of the manuscripts date from the thirteenth century, when charters of liberties achieved a significance they never had in the Norman period.[35] The clauses cited by Florence of Worcester show what seemed important to a contemporary monastic chronicler. The king

> on the day of his consecration made free the Church of God, which in his brother's time had been sold and let out at farm, abolished all evil customs and unjust exactions by which the realm of England was wrongfully oppressed; established firm peace throughout the kingdom, and restored to all the laws of King Edward with such emendations as his father had made, but retained in his own hand the forests that his father had established.[36]

For the pragmatic Norman kings what most mattered was the visible ceremony of coronation.

Henry knew that he could never afford to quarrel irreconcilably with the church, though he was prepared to press his rights to the furthest limit. This went a good deal beyond the limits that reformers in Rome wished to impose even in 1100, much more in 1135. He never failed to recognize just when, and how far, he must give way. Maurice, bishop of London, crowned Henry; he was on the spot, and delay might have meant civil war. But Henry immediately sent for Anselm of Canterbury, and set about filling vacant sees and authorizing the holding of a church council. Anselm was as anxious as Henry to avoid conflict; his support was crucial in the first perilous year of the reign. Henry's chosen bride had been educated in a nunnery, and some believed that she had taken the veil. Although Anselm's letters show his deep repugnance for any attempt to evade genuine religious vows, he was prepared to allow a case to be made before a court of bishops, based on an earlier ruling by Lanfranc that women who wore the veil to protect themselves in lawless times might be free to leave the cloister. Whatever regrets Anselm may have felt at Matilda's decision, he allowed the marriage to take place and performed the ceremony himself.[37] That he did so was later to be the strongest argument of the Angevin party against allegations that Matilda's daughter was illegitimate and so could not inherit the crown because her mother had been a nun. Anselm also ensured the support of the church

[35] Stubbs, *Charters*, pp. 116–19; *EHD*, ii. 400–2; see also *Councils and Synods*, i. 652–5; *Regesta*, ii. 488.
[36] FW, ii. 46–7.
[37] Southern, *St Anselm*, 188–90.

for Henry when, in 1101, he faced the one serious attempt made by Robert Curthose to invade the kingdom and take the crown.[38] Unfortunately for Henry, Anselm returned to England with full knowledge of the papal prohibition of homage and investiture, and nothing would induce him to give way. Consequently William Giffard, newly appointed to the see of Winchester, and a number of other prelates remained uninvested and unconsecrated for six years or more.

The root cause of the trouble was the dual role of bishops and great abbots who were both prelates with spiritual duties and the lords of temporal baronies. To King Henry two things were important: first, to secure visible recognition from them that they held their baronies from him and would render loyal service in return; second, to keep a controlling voice in appointments, which were a valuable source of patronage. If he were forced to abandon investiture in the face of a claim that it conferred spiritual powers (especially when the symbol handed over was a bishop's pastoral staff), homage was more important than ever as the ceremony which bound any vassal to serve his lord. However, homage and its implications were becoming unacceptable to strict churchmen, who found it repugnant that hands consecrated to celebrate the Mass and bestow blessings should be placed (as they were when homage was done) between the hands of a layman which might have shed blood or committed hideous crimes. Only the bond of fealty, which involved no more than an oath, was acceptable to reformers.

The conflict of spiritual and lay authorities in western Europe at this time has become familiar to historians as the investiture contest, but the real issues were much wider and involved the independence of the ecclesiastical hierarchy and the acceptance of a clear sphere of operation for the law of the church. Genuine freedom of election became as much an issue as investiture. Pope Paschal II, a zealous reformer, demanded an end not only to lay investiture and the homage of prelates, but also to all lay intervention in elections. Henry I indignantly stood on all his traditional rights. Homage had become normal for almost all English bishops; no one had objected to the investiture of Norman abbots by his father when it was intended to imply no more than the grant of temporalities. As for elections, he expected to have a voice in all major church elections as his father had done; free election had come to mean no more than the formal acceptance by the chapter of cathedral or monastery, frequently in the king's court, of a candidate nominated or at least approved by the king.

The dispute dragged on from 1101 to 1107, while embassies to Rome

---

[38] Orderic, v. 310–11; Malmesbury, *GR*, ii. 471–2; Eadmer, *HN*, p. 127; C. Warren Hollister, 'The Anglo-Norman civil war: 1101', *EHR*, 88 (1973), 315–34.

attempted to find a solution acceptable to both sides. Long-distance negotiations on such delicate matters led to misunderstanding and deadlock. Anselm went into exile again in 1103. Henry gave enough ground to allow an acceptable compromise only when he was threatened with excommunication in 1105 on the eve of the final campaign he undertook in Normandy to wrest the duchy from Robert Curthose. He knew he must have the backing of the church to justify his claim that he acted in the interests of the Norman church and people. In fact Paschal gave most ground, for from 1102 he ceased to forbid homage and intervention in elections, and concentrated on investiture.[39] The compromise finally reached in 1107 was, according to Eadmer, an agreement that no king or other layman should invest a prelate with a bishopric or abbacy, and that the archbishop would not refuse investiture to any prelate on the grounds that he had previously done homage to the king. Nothing was said about elections; though Anselm's refusal in 1108 to consent to consecrate the abbot-elect of St Augustine's, Canterbury, in the royal chapel may have been designed to avert any attempt the king might make to turn election in his presence, which opened the way to coercion and was already on the way to becoming a tolerated anomaly, into a customary right.[40]

The king complained that his customary rights had been diminished; but he lost nothing of substance. The fragile compromise lasted; the silences were interpreted in Henry's favour, at least during his lifetime. This was all the more remarkable because the customs he claimed cut across the principles held by many reformers and the decrees of church synods. The election of William of Corbeil as archbishop of Canterbury in 1123 nearly foundered, because when the archbishop-elect went to seek his pallium at Rome the election was contested on several grounds. One objection was that it had taken place in the king's court, which was not a suitable place for the creation of prelates. The scales were tipped in Henry's favour by the support of his son-in-law, the Emperor Henry V.[41] By this time the most critical stage of the investiture contest in Germany was over. Calixtus II had agreed, in return for the Emperor's renunciation of investitures, that elections might take place in his presence. In such circumstances the English king's demand seemed acceptable, and Calixtus could not afford to risk conflict with the Emperor at that moment. William of Corbeil received his pallium in May, 1123. This was fortunate for the English king, who faced one of the greatest crises of his reign; he needed papal help to annul a marriage that threatened his hold

[39] *Councils and Synods*, i. 655–61, 690–1; Southern, *St Anselm*, p. 171.

[40] Eadmer, *HN*, pp. 186, 188–90.

[41] K. Leyser, 'England and the Empire in the early twelfth century', *TRHS*, 5th ser., 10 (1960), 72–83.

on Normandy and even the right of his own descendants to inherit the crown.

Throughout his reign Henry exercised the regalian right, customary in western Europe, of administering the estates of vacant abbeys and bishoprics, and appropriating the profits. Probably the vague wording of the coronation charter never implied a renunciation of that right. The one concession the Worcester chronicler thought worthy of mention was the promise not to sell or put at farm the church of God, which probably combined a rejection of simony with an undertaking not to farm out vacant bishoprics to the highest bidder as his brother had sometimes done. The 1130 Pipe Roll shows that in two years he drew over £800 from the vacant bishopric of Durham, and no one is known to have challenged his right to do so. Avoidance of simony did not prevent him from taking a free gift from the kinsmen of a new bishop.[42] As has been seen, he won the battle of elections; free election continued to involve obtaining the king's approval at some stage, and as often as not electing his candidate. The number of royal clerks elected to bishoprics rose steadily until 1125.[43] Most were able, well-educated men; the schools of Laon were particularly favoured as a training ground for the royal chapel. The service of many bishops continued after their election; Roger of Salisbury was supreme in the financial organization and acted as the king's viceroy when he was in Normandy. Most carried out their episcopal duties conscientiously; even some of the most worldly were respected in their own dioceses. Ranulf Flambard, bishop of Durham, who was generally condemned by chroniclers for his personal morals, won the support of his own chapter by his defence of his church's rights and his rebuilding of the great cathedral.

Other promotions went to kinsmen. The king's nephew, Henry of Blois, who was elected abbot of Glastonbury in 1125, was allowed to hold the abbey after he became bishop of Winchester in 1130. His monks, far from resenting such pluralism, regarded him as a model abbot, who restored the prosperity of his house. Peterborough, however, was able to rid itself of an unsatisfactory abbot. Henry of Poitou, a kinsman of the king, continued to hold the abbey of St Jean d'Angély after his appointment to Peterborough in 1127; after unwillingly enduring his oppressions for four years the monks succeeded in obtaining the royal consent to his removal.[44] If in many ways Henry's treatment of the

---

[42] Howell, *Regalian Right*, pp. 20–9; *PR 31 H.I*, pp. 31, 34, 128, 130; Simeon of Durham, ii. 283.

[43] See the graph in Barlow, *English Church 1066–1154*, p. 318.

[44] See for Durham, Southern, *Medieval Humanism*, pp. 199–205; for Glastonbury, Adam of Domerham, pp. 305–15; for Peterborough, C. Clark, *EHR*, 84 (1969), 548–60.

church carried on the traditions of his father and brother, he was a better judge than Rufus had been of what was acceptable to his countrymen, and just how far he would have to go to meet new reforms at Rome without losing their allegiance.

A number of clauses in the coronation charter show the measures he took to win the consent of the secular magnates to his accession. Most relate to the definition of feudal custom; the Worcester chronicle did not trouble to record them. Neither the financial obligations that might be implied in vassalage nor the implications of hereditary feudal tenure had yet been spelled out in detail; and Rufus had attempted to go too fast and too far in the king's interest. By the end of Henry's reign it had become far more possible to translate feudal custom into legal and financial terms. This was achieved by working with the baronage and occasionally by pushing the law to the utmost limits of severity against recalcitrants, not by invoking the coronation charter. It was not that the king cynically disregarded it, or gave thought to wringing a legal justification out of the obscure wording of the hastily drafted clauses. The charter had simply, for the time being, ceased to be relevant to the needs of government and to keeping the peace and dispensing justice.

Some modern historians have seen Henry as a cruel, hard ruler, and have overemphasized the occasional complaints of the chroniclers. Yet, as Hollister has shown, he was not cruel by contemporary standards; he used harsh punishments prescribed by custom to restrain men who were far more brutal to those in their power. William of Malmesbury and Orderic Vitalis regarded him with admiration, as did Suger of Saint-Denis, the biographer of his great French opponent, Louis VI. It should be noted that the Anglo-Saxon chronicler complained of heavy gelds in proportionately less years of his reign than in the reign of William Rufus, and that the same chronicler, in describing the mutilation of the money-ers in the year 1125, wrote, 'It was done very justly because they had ruined all the country with their great false-dealing, which they all paid for.'[45] Henry, on the whole, earned his title of 'lion of justice'; lions are not lambs.

To those of us, however, who try to read between the lines of the charter, it is important as an expression of what seemed acceptable custom in 1100. Many terms were still undefined. The heir entitled to offer a relief for his predecessor's land cannot be assumed to be the eldest son; parage customs, which allowed a choice of heir, were only slowly giving way to rules of primogeniture, and the rights of collaterals were far from clear. The king had a right to withhold consent to the marriages

---

[45] C. Warren Hollister, 'Royal acts of mutilation: the case against Henry I', *Albion*, 10 (1978), 330–40; Chibnall, *World of Orderic*, p. 196; *ASC* (E), 1125.

of his vassals if the suitor was considered to be one of his enemies. The kindred still had some rights to the wardship of minors, but the king as overlord was encroaching on them, and he could exercise control over the marriages of heiresses, provided he consulted his barons. At this date consultation and agreement between king, magnates and kindred were more important than defining complicated legal rules. In practice, as long as the king avoided totally disinheriting a whole family, there was scope for him to manipulate marriages and doubtful inheritances in the interests of royal authority. Only very occasionally, and then in Normandy rather than England, was he forced to give way to claims that he considered dangerous to the realm. There was room within acceptable custom both to punish dangerous enemies and to reward loyal supporters without seriously depleting the royal resources.

The most dangerous of the rebels who supported Robert Curthose when he invaded the kingdom in 1101 was Robert of Bellême. The eldest son of Roger of Montgomery and Mabel of Bellême, he had inherited their Norman and French lands, to which he added the earldom of Shrewsbury after the death of his younger brother Hugh in 1098. He had also acquired the inheritance of Roger of Bully, which included the strategically important castle of Tickhill, though by what title he secured it is not entirely clear. A cruel, ruthless, able and very wealthy vassal, he preferred Robert Curthose whom he could manipulate to the masterful Henry. Although he accepted the uneasy peace agreed between the brothers at Alton in 1101, when Robert withdrew his army without striking a blow, he remained unreconciled. Within a year Henry was able to accumulate sufficient evidence against him to summon him to his court on a number of charges, including building a castle at Bridgnorth in defiance of the king's prohibition. Robert treated the summons as a challenge, rebelled openly, and fortified his castles. The outcome was complete victory for the king and the confiscation of all Robert's English estates. Robert went into exile, and two of the brothers who had supported him also lost their English lands. Roger the Poitevin forfeited his lands between Ribble and Mersey, and Arnulf lost Pembroke.[46]

The family survived in England only through the female line. Roger of Montgomery's daughter, Sibyl, was married to Robert fitz Haimo, a loyal supporter of Henry I; and their daughter was later given in marriage to Henry's favourite bastard, Robert of Gloucester. This was one of Henry's few acts of almost complete disinheritance; nothing that the Bellême had held in England went to any of their kindred, though for the time being they retained what they had across the Channel. Henry had decided that they must go if he was ever to be master in his own

---

[46] Orderic, vi. 20–33; Mason, *TRHS* (1963), 13–28.

realm; their dispossession is parallelled by that of the rebel Odo of Bayeux in his brother's reign. Their position in Normandy, where they had powerful support from the counts of Anjou and the king of France, was more secure. Even when Robert later challenged Henry's authority in Normandy and was punished with life imprisonment, Henry could do not more than hold the Norman lands until Robert's son came of age to inherit them. In England, however, no comparable power was allowed to rise; no new earl of Shrewsbury was appointed. A royal clerk, Richard of Belmeis, later bishop of London, acted for a time as administrator in Shropshire.[47] Other recipients of Bellême lands included the Clare family and Stephen of Blois. The king kept the principal castles, including Pembroke, in his own hand.

One other great magnate suffered total confiscation: William, count of Mortain and earl of Cornwall, the son of the Conqueror's half-brother Robert. He too was spared in 1101, and even trusted for a while. But in 1104, frustrated, if William of Malmesbury can be believed, by his failure to secure his uncle Odo's county of Kent, he threw in his lot with Robert Curthose and became one of Henry's most implacable enemies.[48] The decisive battle of Tinchebray was fought in 1106 beside his own castle; he himself was captured and imprisoned for life, forfeiting all his lands. As he had no children and his patrimony of Mortain was given in 1112 to his cousin, Stephen of Blois, there appear to have been no complaints about disinheritance. His English lands were held for a time by King Henry, who used them to reward his adherents as need arose. In time Pevensey was granted to Gilbert of Laigle, Helmsley to Walter Espec, and Berkhamsted to the chancellor, Ranulf. The earldom of Cornwall was not revived until the next reign.

Among the families whose fortunes were diminished at this time must be counted the Grandmesnils and the Mandevilles. Hugh of Grandmesnil's great English honour of Leicester passed on his death in 1098 to his son Ivo, a man of unstable temperament who had ruined his reputation in the first crusade by joining the group who ran away from the siege of Antioch. After incurring the king's displeasure by waging private war in England, he pledged all his lands to Robert, count of Meulan, in return for a loan to enable him to return to Jerusalem and expiate his previous cowardice. He and his wife died on the pilgrimage, and the inheritance passed, not to his young son Ivo, but to Robert of Meulan.[49] The exact nature of the transaction is not clear; there was talk of a marriage which never took place between young Ivo and a niece of the count of Meulan;

---

[47] The *Brut-y-Tywysogyon*, pp. 57, 63, 75, calls him 'the king's steward' and 'the man holding the king's place at Shrewsbury.'

[48] Malmesbury, *GR*, ii. 473–4.

[49] Orderic, vi. 18–21.

but if any claims of kinship were adduced they were even sketchier than Robert Curthose's claim to Maine. Robert of Meulan may have pleaded a right to foreclose on mortgaged property; in any case he stood so high in the king's favour that he could confidently anticipate a substantial reward. There was no question of confiscating the great Norman estates of the Grandmesnil family, held by Ivo's elder brother.

The history of the Mandevilles vividly illustrates Henry's management of a doubtful inheritance.[50] The Conqueror's vassal, Geoffrey, had earned substantial estates valued at £782 in 1086, besides being sheriff of London and two or three other counties, and custodian of the Tower of London. His son William, who succeeded him as custodian, incautiously allowed Ranulf Flambard to escape from imprisonment in 1100, and was so heavily fined that he had to surrender some of his richest manors. Some time after his death they were granted, with the custodianship of the Tower, to Othver fitz Earl, the second husband of William of Mandeville's widow. Othver, an illegitimate son of Hugh, earl of Chester was drowned in the *White Ship* in 1120, and this opened the way for William's son, Geoffrey of Mandeville, to make a bid for his patrimony. He had won back something by 1130, when he was still paying off a huge fine of 1,300 marks; but at the time of King Henry's death he was still one of the group of household knights characterized by Anselm as serving in the hope of recovering a lost inheritance, and he nursed his unfilfilled hopes and ambitions into the next reign.

Other forfeitures, such as those of Robert of Lacy and Robert of Stuteville, involved only one branch of a family; the Lacy family continued to flourish in Herefordshire and Pontefract, and the Stutevilles in Yorkshire.[51] The break-up of the Mowbray honour was a complicated business arising from a confiscation in the previous reign. After Robert of Mowbray rebelled in 1095 and was imprisoned for life, his wife Matilda of Laigle obtained an annulment of the marriage from the pope. To keep the friendship of the family of Laigle, enfeoffed on the southern Norman frontier and related to the powerful counts of Perche, was important to Henry in his struggle with the king of France. He arranged for Matilda's remarriage to Nigel of Aubigny, a landless younger son who was one of his favoured household knights. With her hand went the Norman fee of Mowbray, but not Robert's English lands; the bulk of the English fee gradually built up for Nigel came from the confiscated Stuteville lands. Even when Nigel repudiated his childless wife and married Gundreda de Gournay with the king's consent in 1118, he kept the Mowbray lands in Normandy.[52]

[50] Hollister, *History*, 58 (1973), 18–28.
[51] Wightman, *Lacy Family*, p. 66; Clay, *Yorkshire Families*, pp. 85–6 *et passim*.
[52] Greenway, *Mowbray Charters*, pp. xviii–xx.

By judicious control of marriages or the transfer of forfeited lands to collaterals, Henry was often able to establish his loyal vassals in great honours without undermining the patrimonial claims cherished by all his vassals. If one branch of a family retreated to Normandy, disgruntled and shorn of its acquisitions in England, another branch remained to create a new patrimony of its own and resist any attempts to take it back. As far as possible, Henry avoided permanently alienating any of his vassals once Robert of Bellême, William of Mortain, and his own brother Robert Curthose had been securely locked away for life. He succeeded so well that after 1102 he never had to face rebellion in England; one conspiracy involving a royal chamberlain was mercilessly suppressed in 1119.[53] But there were moments of great danger in Normandy, where malcontents rallied in support of the claims of Robert Curthose's son, William Clito, and received help from the king of France. The worst crises came in 1112–13, and in the period between 1118 and 1125; but the danger was not over until William Clito was killed in battle in Flanders in 1128. In all that he did to consolidate his power in England, Henry never ceased to regard Normandy as an integral part of his realm, and to work to strengthen its ties with England. The building up of the new Mowbray inheritance for Nigel of Aubigny is merely one example of the way in which he consolidated cross-Channel lordships, and won the loyalty of his vassals either through gratitude or through fear.

Contemporaries noted the rise of new men, like the landless Nigel, and many of the royal household officials. But the great old families, if trustworthy, were equally favoured.[54] Conspicuous among these was the house of Beaumont, whose loyalty was almost proverbial, and who showed a remarkable talent for loyalty to the winning side. Robert, count of Meulan, was one of Henry's closest advisers from the moment of his accession, and showed such devotion to him even during the quarrel with Anselm, when Pope Paschal was threatening excommunication, that Ivo of Chartres accused him of being more ready to serve the king of the English than the King of the angels. He was given the Grandmesnil honour of Leicester, and was one of the two men to be made earls by Henry; the other was Henry's bastard son Robert, who became earl of Gloucester. Three years after the birth in 1104 of Robert of Meulan's twin sons, Robert and Waleran, a plan was made to divide the Beaumont inheritance.[55] Waleran, the elder twin, was to have the Norman patrimony centred in the valley of the Risle, with the county of Meulan, and in England Sturminster in Dorset; the grant of one or two English manors

---

[53] Malmesbury, *GR*, ii. 488.

[54] C. Warren Hollister, 'Henry I and the Anglo-Norman magnates', *Anglo-Norman Studies*, 2 (1980 for 1979), 93–107; Hollister, *Viator*, 8 (1977), 63–82.

[55] Migne, *PL*, clxii. 157–8; *Regesta*, ii. 843.

to vassals with predominantly Norman honours both strengthened cross-Channel ties and provided them with a convenient base outside the court when the king and his household were in England. Robert was to have the earldom of Leicester and the bulk of the English lands.

The twins inherited when their father died in 1118, and Robert was not left long without a Norman interest. In 1119 Eustace of Breteuil rebelled and forfeited the greater part of his honour of Breteuil, which went at first to a Breton kinsman, Ralph of Gael. But the Normans of Breteuil hated and resisted the Breton; and the honour was finally given to Robert of Leicester with the hand of Ralph's daughter, Amice.[56] With wealth and vassals in both England and Normandy, Robert never wavered in his loyalty, even when his more volatile brother Waleran joined Amaury of Montfort in an unsuccessful rebellion in 1124. It was probably Robert's standing with the king that saved Waleran from forfeiture after his capture at Bourgthéroulde, though it could not save him from five years' imprisonment. Waleran was released and restored to his estates in 1129, to remain loyal thereafter. His temporary defection may have tempted his cousin, Roger, who had succeeded to the earldom of Warwick in 1119 and was far less trustworthy than his father, Earl Henry. Perhaps because Roger was judged unreliable, King Henry set up another of his new men, Geoffrey of Clinton, as a counterpoise to his power in Warwickshire.[57]

Among the great, established families to maintain or improve their position were those of Giffard, Warenne, and Clare, The chronicler of Ely, where a son of Richard fitz Gilbert of Clare was appointed abbot in 1100, described the families of Clare and Giffard as illustrious through their valour and high birth, and capable with their numerous dependents of overawing assemblies of nobles; he added that even the royal majesty was sometimes shaken by the terror they inspired, though he made it clear that Henry I was not shaken.[58] The Clares, like the Beaumonts, received favours in every reign; Henry granted Ceredigion to Gilbert fitz Richard, whose military experience and ambition strengthened the Norman grip on central Wales. Descended from Count Gilbert of Brionne, the Clares were among the kindred of the dukes of Normandy; and though Henry dealt ruthlessly with his own brother Robert and his cousin, William of Mortain, he favoured blood ties whenever possible.

The kinsman who profited most from his generosity was his nephew, Stephen of Blois. He was the third son of Henry's sister Adela, the wife of Count Stephen of Blois and Champagne, and the most remarkable of the

---

[56] Orderic, vi. 277–9, 294–5; David Crouch, *The Beaumont Twins* (Cambridge, forthcoming).

[57] See below, pp. 79–80.

[58] *Liber Eliensis*, pp. 226, 413.

Conqueror's daughters. After the death of Count Stephen the county of Blois passed, not to his eldest son William (who for some reason was judged incapable), but to his second son Theobald.[59] Young Stephen, with no expectations of inheritance in his paternal lands, was brought up at the English court. Theobald became one of Henry's staunchest supporters in his Norman wars;, and possibly his services as much as Stephen's merits persuaded Henry to make magnificent provision for his nephew. In 1112 he made him count of Mortain and gave him some of the Mortain lands in Cornwall; later he added substantial fiefs in Suffolk and Lancaster. Stephen met with some reverses on the field of battle; but he may not have been as much to blame as Orderic Vitalis asserted for the defeat of the Norman forces at Alençon in 1118, and his uncle's favour continued.[60]

In 1125 Henry arranged Stephen's marriage with Matilda, the daughter and heir of Count Eustace of Boulogne. The marriage brought him a valuable cross-Channel honour in his wife's right; besides this, it meant that Stephen's children would be in the direct line of descent from the royal house of Wessex. Matilda's mother, Mary, was the sister of Henry's first wife, and a daughter of Queen Margaret of Scotland. Henry cannot have been blind to the implications of her ancestry; in 1125 the succession to the English crown hung in the balance. For although Henry had fathered more than twenty bastards,[61] he lost his first wife in 1118, and his only legitimate son, William Atheling, was drowned in 1120. Within a few weeks of the disaster Henry took a second wife, Adeliza of Louvain, but the marriage remained childless. His only legitimate daughter, Matilda, had been sent to Germany in her childhood to marry King Henry V; had she had children, their interests must have lain in Germany. The obvious heir was William Clito, son of Robert Curthose, and Henry's face was set against him. Only when his daughter Matilda was widowed in 1125 did the possibility of arranging a second marriage that might secure the descent of the kingdom in his own line become even remotely conceivable. In the years of uncertainty he may have contemplated making his nephew Stephen his heir if all else failed; or he may simply have wished to eliminate the danger of the heiress to Boulogne marrying William Clito. If Stephen was allowed to glimpse the possibility of a crown in 1125, the situation changed after the widowed Matilda was married to Geoffrey of Anjou. King Henry counted on the loyal support of Stephen to secure the crown for her descendants. In this he misjudged his man.

---

[59] Davis, *King Stephen*, pp. 3–6; Orderic, v. 346–7.
[60] Orderic, vi. 204–7.
[61] *Complete Peerage*, xi. App. D, pp. 105–21.

He did not misjudge his eldest and favourite illegitimate son, Robert of Caen, who was to prove the most faithful defender of the Angevin rights after 1135. In common with most of Henry's bastard sons, Robert was brought up at court and served in his father's household troops; he was rewarded with the hand of Robert fitz Haimo's daughter Sibyl, and in 1122 was created earl of Gloucester. Modern historians have sometimes suggested that he was a possible candidate for the succession; but in the twelfth century his illegitimate birth must have been recognized as an insuperable obstacle. A hundred years previously his grandfather, William the Conqueror, had been obliged to struggle for years against powerful lords who opposed his succession even to the duchy of Normandy because of his illegitimacy. Since custom had hardened still further in favour of the descent of fiefs to the children of lawful marriages, it was essential for a claimant to the crown of England to be born in lawful wedlock. In any case, Robert's loyalty to his half-sister was never shaken, and he used the wealth and influence he owed to his father in her cause.

King Henry's court provided careers open to the talents, both for the household knights who fought to earn fiefs and influential marriages, and for the household clerks, who rose through service to administrative offices and bishoprics. Even more than his brother, who had less time and perhaps less skill, he raised up the men who served him well, and withdrew his favours if they became slack or dangerous. Consolidation was his guiding motive. In Normandy, where he was harassed by frequent wars, he aimed chiefly at holding his frontiers and securing them by alliances, often by means of marriage alliances with members of his family.[62] In England which, after 1102, enjoyed internal peace for the whole of his reign, he used the wealth and patronage that he could control to preserve peace and order and the power of the king.[63]

Often this was done by means which, in later diplomacy, would have been called maintaining a balance of power. The death of a loyal supporter might bring in an heir who was less capable or less reliable; a counterpoise had to be found to prevent disturbance. Sheriffs might be used to hold the few surviving earls in check, as in the case of Geoffrey of Clinton and the earl of Warwick.[64] Geoffrey was one of King Henry's most trusted curial magnates. Coming from a small landed family in the Cotentin, with property at Glympton in Oxfordshire, he was made

---

[62] C. Warren Hollister, 'Normandy, France and the Anglo-Norman *Regnum*', *Speculum*, 51 (1976), 202–42.

[63] Southern, *Medieval Humanism*, pp. 206–33.

[64] D. Crouch, 'Geoffrey de Clinton and Roger, earl of Warwick', *BIHR*, 55 (1982), 113–24.

sheriff of Warwickshire soon after 1119. When Henry, earl of Warwick, died in 1119, his heir Roger was suspected of favouring William Clito. King Henry put pressure on him by raising Geoffrey to the rank of a great honorial baron in Warwickshire. He was granted a great estate owing the service of seventeen knights to Earl Roger, and was allowed to build a castle of his own at Kenilworth. Tenants of his from the Cotentin were brought in as vassals and settled in his English lands. His nephew, Roger, was made bishop of Coventry; Geoffrey was believed to have made a gift of 3,000 marks on the new bishop's behalf. But once the danger of William Clito had been removed in 1128, Earl Roger ceased to be a threat, and checks were put upon Geoffrey of Clinton. Charges of treason were brought against him. He succeeded in clearing himself and survived to serve the king until his death, but the meteoric rise of his family was halted. Nevertheless, in the critical years of the middle twenties he was one of the men used to guarantee the stability and loyalty of midland England. His family remained entrenched in the knightly class.

Geoffrey's career shows how, by adroit use of marriages, enfeoffments, and patronage of offices in church and state, King Henry secured a solid block of loyal supporters in the Midlands. He successfully held Warwick in check, and could rely on the support of the Beaumont earls of Leicester and his own brother-in-law, David of Scotland. David was made heir to the earldom of Huntingdon by marriage with a granddaughter of Judith and Waltheof. The security of Leicester was further underpinned by the elevation of Richard Basset, another of the new men, who enlarged his inherited estates and became, with Aubrey de Vere, joint sheriff of eleven counties by 1129. In other parts of England consolidation went on as local conditions required. In East Anglia the rise of Bigod continued, and Nigel of Aubigny's brother, William *pincerna,* secured an ample patrimony.

Shropshire, after the fall of the Bellême, provided rich fiefs for a Breton family that had been among Henry's adherents before his accession. Alan son of Flaald, the hereditary seneschal of the bishops of Dol, was rewarded with the hand and inheritance of Avelina, daughter and heir of Ernulf of Hesdin, who held land in ten counties. Although the disinheriting of Robert of Bellême did not involve his tenants, Alan fitz Flaald was given the honour of Warin the sheriff, after the death of Warin's son Hugh. Queen Adeliza was granted the comital revenues in 1126. In the absence of any new earl of Shropshire, Alan's son William became the principal magnate in the last years of Henry's reign; by 1138 he held the office of sheriff and was married to a kinswoman of Robert, earl of Gloucester. There was scope in the territorial reshuffle to bring in some new vassals of his own; but some great vassals from the earlier regime, including Pantulf and Corbet, remained there and throve in the region.[65]

Conditions in the north were far more fluid, and there was room for new families. The rise of Nigel of Aubigny, ancestor of the new house of Mowbray, shows how properties could be regrouped, new vassals enfeoffed, compact or scattered fees established as strategy demanded.[66] In many ways the settlement of the north in Henry's reign repeated a pattern that had appeared elsewhere in the aftermath of 1066. Some of the lands allocated to Nigel from the confiscated fees of the Stuteville family and others were former church lands, to which the previous owners retained claims. Some laymen too regarded themselves as disinherited. In this period and region, since feudal relationships of lord and vassal were still fluid, Nigel could move some of his own men from one fief to another with their full consent; but it was not always possible to reconcile the claims of earlier tenants with the needs of strategy. The letter in which the still childless Nigel made his brother William his heir, and instructed him to make restitution to named laymen and churches of lands to which they had a claim, indicates that he was aware of injustices in the settlement. For this Nigel himself must take some, but not all, of the blame.[67] On a small scale it repeats the evidence of the great land pleas in the Conqueror's reign; it shows too that the dispossession often stretched back to earlier holders. The history of Nigel's enfeoffment is one aspect of the consolidation of royal power in the north; feudally in the consolidation of a single lordship in the vulnerable Isle of Axholme and in the siting of castles in strategic places like Thirsk, and administratively in the appointment of Nigel himself as local justiciar in Yorkshire and Northumberland, with the custody of the royal castle at York.

Alongside the advance of feudal power went the advance of the church. The foundation of monasteries helped to anchor new families, strengthen their hold on their estates, and advance their influence into regions of disputed allegiance. In the secular church the strengthening of the hierarchy enabled Canterbury and York to increase their influence. The foundation of a bishopric at Carlisle in 1133, with its jurisdiction further secured by a territorial archdeaconry, was one stage in the severing of parts of Cumbria, which had once looked ecclesiastically towards Glasgow, from its Scottish dependence.[68] In Wales Henry recognized the value of ecclesiastical authority in the process of conquest. Here William Rufus had taken the first step by appointing the Breton clerk, Hervey, as bishop of Bangor in 1092. But the Welsh revolt shortly

[65] Eyton, *Shropshire*, vii. 211–41; Rees, *Shrewsbury Cartulary*, ii. 258–9; Malmesbury, *HN*, p. 3.

[66] Greenway, *Mowbray Charters*, Introduction, *passim*.

[67] Ibid., no. 3, pp. 7–10.

[68] Le Neve, ii. 21–3.

afterwards forced Hervey to retreat; by 1109 Henry had secured a new see for him at Ely. In 1120, when his Welsh campaigns restored some Norman influence in north Wales, he was able to make David the Scot bishop of Bangor with the agreement of Gruffydd ap Cynan.[69] In south Wales, where Henry's main efforts at colonization were concentrated, the impact of the Norman church came earlier in the reign. In 1107 he appointed as bishop of Llandaff the local archdeacon, Urban, who was prepared to make a profession of obedience to the archbishop of Canterbury.[70] The town of St Davids was at the centre of royal power after 1102, when Henry took the castle of Pembroke into his own hands. In 1115 he secured the election of Bernard, Queen Matilda's chancellor and chaplain, as bishop of St Davids. Bernard took a leading part in establishing territorial archdeaconries and developing parochial organization, while respecting traditional Welsh divisions. He too professed obedience to the archbishop of Canterbury on his election. After Henry's death, like the post-conquest Norman abbots in old English monasteries who quickly learned to champion the rights of their houses, Bernard took up the claims of St Davids and tried to secure archiepiscopal status for his see. The attempt failed; Canterbury successfully kept its *de facto* authority throughout south Wales, and a rearguard action fought by Gerald of Wales in 1200 was equally unsuccessful in securing a pallium for St Davids.[71] The running battle for the primacy fought between Canterbury and York did not prevent both archbishops from enlarging the sphere of their individual authority, and tightening their hold on their suffragans.

In all Henry's skilled manipulation of men and resources to stabilize and secure his realm he failed only in one thing: to provide for a smooth succession after his death. To have only one legitimate son was unquestionably a risk; with hindsight it might be called a gamble that failed. The advantages, had the son lived to have children, were manifest; no younger brothers to require great apanages or to dispute the right of the heir, as both Rufus and Henry himself had disputed the right of their older brother. Bastard sons could, like Robert of Gloucester, fight for their father and win the right to be established in great honours and married to heiresses. Alternatively they might be educated, like Roger of Worcester, for the church. Daughters could be married to powerful frontier magnates like Rotrou of Mortagne or King Alexander of Scotland, and to great border vassals like Eustace of Breteuil, in the hope of

[69] Barlow, *English Church 1066–1154*, p. 84.

[70] Ibid., pp. 80–1; Wendy Davies, *An Early Welsh Microcosm* (London, 1978), pp. 5, 139–59.

[71] Christopher Brooke, 'The archbishops of St Davids, Llandaff and Caerleon-on-Usk', *Studies in the Early British Church*, ed. N. K. Chadwick et al. (Cambridge, 1958), pp. 215–18; Richter, *Giraldus Cambrensis*, pp. 40–54.

stabilizing frontiers.[72] Henry's only legitimate daughter was a prize for the greatest in Europe; she was sent as a child to be the wife of Henry V of Germany. By 1120, when his son William had been knighted, the process of establishing him in England and Europe began. The English nobles did homage to him, and he left on a momentous visit to Normandy. King Louis VI, defeated at Brémule and outmanoeuvred elsewhere, agreed to abandon the claims of William Clito to Normandy, and received William Atheling's homage for the duchy.[73] So Henry secured recognition of his right in the duchy without himself doing homage. He had brought his long rivalry with Anjou temporarily to an end in 1113 by the betrothal of William to Count Fulk's young daughter Matilda. They were married in 1120, and Matilda brought Maine as her dowry. But as William was on his way back to England in the *White Ship* he was drowned; his young wife returned to France and took the veil at Fontevrault.

During the difficult years that followed Henry never contemplated recognizing the right of his nephew William Clito. He worked relentlessly for the destruction of the young man's hopes, first by securing the prohibition on grounds of consanguinity of his marriage to Fulk of Anjou's daughter Sibyl; and later when with the aid of Louis VI he had become count of Flanders, by subsidizing his enemies and assisting the rebels who defeated and killed him in 1128. Henry's first step to secure an heir was to take a second wife within a few weeks of his son's death. Adeliza, the daughter of Godfrey of Louvain, brought Henry valuable allies in Flanders, but she did not give him a son. His thoughts may have turned momentarily towards his nephew Stephen; but in 1125 the death of the Emperor Henry V opened up new possibilities. The Empress Matilda was brought home and recognized as Henry's heir. She was now available for remarriage, and once again he turned to Anjou. Fulk V's son and heir, Geoffrey, was unmarried; his father wished to hand over the county and pursue other ambitions in the kingdom of Jerusalem. Henry successfully overcame ecclesiastical opposition to a marriage between parties related in exactly the same degree as William Clito and Sibyl of Anjou.[74] His daughter, a reluctant empress betrothed to a mere count, became Geoffrey's wife in 1128. The marriage was personally wretched, but dynastically successful. In 1133 Henry, the first of her three sons was born; there was hope for a peaceful succession in the Anglo-Norman line. Henry's efforts were directed thereafter towards securing her succession by binding the greater barons with oaths of allegiance.

[72] Hollister and Keefe, *Journal of British Studies* (1973), 1–25.
[73] Orderic, vi. 290–1.
[74] J. Chartrou, *L'Anjou de 1109 à 1151* (Paris, 1928), pp. 21–2.

Her claim is stated most clearly by the strongly partisan William of Malmesbury. At a council held just after Christmas 1126, before her betrothal to Geoffrey, he 'deliberated long and deeply' on the question of the succession, and then bound his nobles of all England, and the bishops and abbots, by an oath

> that if he himself died without a male heir, they would immediately and without hesitation accept his daughter Matilda, formerly Empress, as their lady. He said ... that she alone had a legal claim to succeed him, since her grandfather, uncle and father had been kings, while on her mother's side the royal lineage went back for many centuries.[75]

Since some of the magnates disliked the Angevin marriage, and some, including Roger, bishop of Salisbury, alleged that they had taken the oath only on condition that the king did not give his daughter in marriage outside the kingdom without their consent, it was renewed on a later occasion. Even the anonymous author of the *Gesta Stephani*, who was Stephen's principal apologist among the chroniclers, mentioned an oath after the marriage, stating, 'King Henry in his lifetime had bound the chief men of the whole kingdom with a most stringent oath not to recognize as their sovereign after his death anyone but his daughter whom he had married to the count of Anjou, or her heir, if an heir survived her.' John of Worcester refers to two oaths, the first after Christmas 1126, and the second on 29 April 1128, shortly before her marriage to Geoffrey of Anjou, but after the betrothal.[76]

Certainly oaths were taken on at least two occasions; those who swore included David, king of Scots and earl of Huntingdon, Stephen, count of Mortain and Robert, earl of Gloucester. The oath to recognize her heir was particularly important; in both western Europe and the feudal kingdom of Jerusalem it was easier for a woman to transmit the crown than to succeed herself. In Spain Urraca, the widowed daughter and heir of Alfonso VI of Castile, Galicia and León, had been engaged in a bitter war against supporters of her son by her first marriage. In Jerusalem Melisende, daughter of King Baldwin II, was married to Fulk V of Anjou, and he succeeded as king on Baldwin's death in 1131.[77] Since Fulk was the father of Geoffrey of Anjou, Henry I cannot have been ignorant of events as they unfolded in Jerusalem; nevertheless his hopes were fixed on his daughter and any heir of her body, and he never contemplated leaving the crown of England to her husband, even before he quarrelled with him.

[75] Malmesbury, *HN*, pp. 3–5.
[76] *Gesta Stephani*, pp. 10–11; John of Worcester, pp. 22–3, 26–8.
[77] Orderic, vi. 406–9, 390–3.

Matilda at times found herself at loggerheads with her father, as strong willed and imperious as herself, particularly over the control of castles on the Norman frontier. There was violent friction between Henry and Count Geoffrey; and at the time of his death he was detained in Normandy by disturbances on the borders of Maine. But there is no reliable evidence that he ever changed his mind about his heir. When he died suddenly, at Lyons-la-Forêt on 1 December 1135, Matilda was occupied in frontier warfare in south-west Normandy, and her cousin Stephen was at Boulogne, on the Channel coast. Circumstances gave Stephen an initial advantage, which he seized decisively.

Stephen and Henry Plantagenet

On learning of his uncle's death, Stephen immediately crossed to England. Although the castles of Dover and Canterbury, which had been given to Robert of Gloucester, refused to admit him, he reached London and won the support of the citizens of London and some magnates. This was probably the occasion for the issue of his first 'charter of liberties', which was purely secular and witnessed only by his steward, William Martel.[78] He then proceeded to Winchester to secure the treasure and the crown. His brother, Henry of Blois, powerfully placed as bishop of Winchester, persuasively overcame all objections. Hugh Bigod swore that Henry on his death-bed had regretted forcing oaths on his vassals and, although Hugh was later accused of perjury, his word counted for the time being. William, archbishop of Canterbury, crowned Stephen king at Westminster on 22 December.[79] The fact of his coronation was his strongest claim to the crown; but he had to buy it with concessions. In particular he was indebted, perhaps reluctantly, to the church.

Stephen went further than promising to respect the liberties of his subjects; he applied to Pope Innocent II for confirmation of his right. Innocent's answer recited the arguments that persuaded him to approve the coronation:

> On the death of King Henry, religion in England was threatened and no just edict or law had any authority, so that shocking crimes went unpunished. Lest the people of God should be forced to endure further suffering, the prayers of pious men have been answered, as we have learned from the letters of our venerable brothers, the archbishops and bishops of the realm, and the letters

---

[78] *Regesta*, iii. 270 (p. 95) dates the charter *c*.22 December (the day of his coronation), but in the itinerary (p. xxxix) places it at the time of his first visit to London.

[79] Malmesbury, *HN*, pp. 15–16; *Gesta Stephani*, pp. 6–13.

of those friends of the holy Roman church, the glorious King of
France and the illustrious Count Theobald ... Divine mercy has
provided that you should be chosen king by the common assent of
the nobles and people, and consecrated by the prelates of the
realm.[80]

Although Count Theobald was thought by some chroniclers to resent
being passed over by his younger brother, and he gave only intermittent
and partial support to his cause, his readiness to write to Pope Innocent
on Stephen's behalf at the outset shows that he himself had no real
ambition to wear the crown of England.

Stephen's first so-called charter of liberties, issued at London, was not
properly speaking a coronation charter. It was a vaguely worded promise, addressed to his justices, sheriffs and barons, to preserve all the
liberties and good laws that King Henry had given, and that they had had
in the time of King Edward. At this stage there was no word about the
church. But he took an oath to preserve its liberties at the time of his
coronation, and his brother Henry can have left him in no doubt where
he must look for validation of his claim. At his Easter court at Oxford,
early in April 1136, he put into writing the promises made at his
coronation to restore and preserve the liberties of the church.[81] This
'Oxford charter of liberties' began by acknowledging that he had been
consecrated by William, archbishop of Canterbury and papal legate, and
confirmed by Pope Innocent. Next came a general promise of freedom to
the church. The following clauses spelled out in greater detail what this
involved: avoidance of simony, recognition that bishops had the right of
jurisdiction over the clergy and their property, confirmation of all ancient
customs, privileges and lands which the church had held indisputably at
the death of the Conqueror, with a promise to investigate claims to lands
lost before that date, and confirmation of later gifts. The king also
promised to restore to the church and kingdom lands afforested by King
Henry, to preserve peace and justice, to allow the chattels of deceased
prelates to be distributed in accordance with their wishes, and to entrust
vacant churches and their lands to the keeping of clerks or good men of
the bishopric. How much of his regalian right Stephen renounced by this
last promise is a debatable question. The view of Margaret Howell, that
it involved renunciation of the issues of vacant sees but not of the theory
that the bishop's barony was granted at the king's will, comes as near to a
satisfactory solution as the evidence allows.[82]

[80] Richard of Hexham in *Chronicles of the Reign of Stephen and Henry II* (RS), iv.
147–8.
[81] *Councils and Synods*, i. 762–6; Malmesbury, *HN*, pp. 18–20; *Regesta*, iii. 271.
[82] Howell, *Regalian Right*, pp. 29–31.

A general confirmation of all good laws and renunciation of injustice extended some benefits to all men, lay or clerical. Nothing was said about elections, though the rejection of simony and the recognition of the church's ancient rights carried implications to be worked out later. There were times when Henry of Winchester interpreted these rights far more rigorously than Stephen was prepared to do. But for the moment Stephen had been accepted by almost all the leading men of the realm. Though some hesitated at first, and Matilda launched an attack from Anjou on the Norman frontier castles, all but a handful of vassals in England had done homage within three months. There is a striking contrast between his hasty coronation in December, which took place according to William of Malmesbury 'in the presence of three bishops, no abbots and very few nobles', and the courts he held in late March or early April at Westminster and Oxford. The witness lists to charters issued in these courts read like a roll call of the Anglo-Norman nobles and bishops.[83] The only major baron to refuse to take an oath to him was Baldwin de Redvers, and he was soon driven out of the country. Shortly after Easter Robert of Gloucester, who had been hesitating in Normandy, decided that nothing could be done by force for the time being, as he could not even secure a base in his lands in England without submitting. He came to England and did homage: conditionally, he later alleged, on the king maintaining his rank unimpaired and keeping his agreements. The bishops also swore fealty to Stephen 'for as long as he should maintain the freedom of the church and the strict observance of its discipline'.[84] Many of those who later changed sides were able to put up some defence against charges of perjury.

If Stephen failed to maintain his position after a promising beginning, this was due partly to his own character and partly to the weakness of his title. He governed, as Stenton said, more like a count of Mortain than a king of England.[85] Open-handed, chivalrous and brave, if at times capricious and unreliable, he seemed unable to rule men. And many of those who held that once he was crowned king he was king indeed were not prepared to recognize his right to hand on the kingdom to his son. With help from Robert of Gloucester, Matilda kept alive a claim, at first for herself as lady of the English, and later for the succession of her son Henry. Certainly church support was necessary for Stephen to secure the succession in his line; and he alienated the church.

Besides this, the very speed with which he won recognition initially presented him with a task that was beyond his powers. He was the first

---

[83] Malmesbury, *HN*, pp. 15–16; *Regesta*, iii. 271, 944.
[84] Malmesbury, *HN*, p. 18.
[85] Stenton, *English Feudalism*, p. 221.

king to succeed simultaneously to rule in England and Normandy. Disturbances in the south-west, where Baldwin de Redvers raised rebellion in Exeter, and simultaneous invasions of his territory from the Welsh and Scots forced him to concentrate on England and leave Normandy, which looked to him to keep the peace and hold back the raids of Geoffrey of Anjou. He did not come to Normandy until the spring of 1137, by which time many parts were ravaged and impoverished by war; troubles in England forced him to recross the Channel in November. Normandy was left in the charge of William of Roumare and other justiciars, who were required, as Orderic bitterly commented, to 'do what he had failed to do himself: punish the malcontents and restore order for the wretched people.'[86] Stephen never returned himself. His failure in Normandy was fatal; too many barons had lands on both sides of the Channel, and they worked to restore their inheritance undivided under a single lord. Rebels like Baldwin de Redvers, when driven out of England, retired to raise rebellion in their Norman lands. Once Geoffrey of Anjou had conquered Normandy, and was in a position to hand it on to his son Henry, it became clear that, whatever might happen in Stephen's lifetime, the only satisfactory solution to the dilemma of these cross-Channel lords was the ultimate succession of young Henry in England also. But eighteen years of uneasy rule, interrupted from time to time by local risings or open civil war, had to pass before all parties accepted the principle of Henry's succession, and this happened only a year before Stephen's death.

The events of Stephen's reign help to bring into sharper focus the nature of feudal assumptions in this third generation after the conquest, and the degree of success achieved by church reform. Administrative development becomes clearer after Henry II's accession and the restoration of more effective royal power. Up to 1138/9 Stephen, in spite of local disturbances, maintained some degree of central control. He had to buy peace by concessions, and sometimes the price was high. King David of Scotland, who invaded the north immediately after Stephen's coronation, was bought off in February 1136 by the cession of Cumbria. The border was restored to its old place on the Rere Cross, to the bitter resentment of Ranulf, earl of Chester, who had claims in Cumbria.[87] But the alliance was precarious; there was no guarantee that David would not strike a blow for his niece Matilda, to whom he had sworn allegiance, if ever she should make a positive bid for the throne; and indeed he did so by invading again in 1138. Beaten back by the northern barons and the

[86] Orderic, vi. 494–5; Haskins, *Norman Institutions*, p. 127.
[87] Barrow, *Kingdom of the Scots*, pp. 144–8.

archbishop of York at the battle of the Standard, he still retained Cumbria, which was not recovered until the next reign.

In Wales too there were heavy losses. Revolt, which had been simmering when Henry I died, broke out openly in 1136, when the Welsh laid siege to most of the Norman castles, and burnt all they could capture. In the middle march they crossed the border into Shropshire, burnt Caus castle, and killed the sheriff, Pain fitz John. Stephen attempted to hold them back without intervening in person as he had done in Scotland, by using magnates with local interests to resist the rebels. This was not enough. Richard fitz Gilbert was killed in an ambush and his wife was besieged in Cardigan castle. Miles, castellan and sheriff of Gloucester and royal constable, who was sent to rescue her did so in one swift raid but attempted no more. Baldwin fitz Gilbert could penetrate no further than Brecon. Only the castellan of Pembroke Castle, which could be supplied by sea, held out and preserved some authority in the surrounding district. Elsewhere lands in the hard-won Welsh march were lost, and lands in Shropshire and Herefordshire were exposed to pillage. More seriously, some of the border barons formed or renewed alliances with individual Welsh princes, to whom they could look for military support should they ever decide to renounce their allegiance and rebel openly.[88] The Anglo-Norman realm, after two generations of expansion, was forced to contract, so adding disinherited vassals to the ranks of those whose ambitions were still unfulfilled. Stephen could hold their allegiance only by granting financial exemptions or parts of the royal demesne, or by creating offices for them. He was still able to put down any local rebellions but, as William of Malmesbury commented, always 'with more loss to himself than to his opponents, for after expending many great efforts in vain he would win a pretence of peace from them for a time by the gift of honours or castles. Finally he also established many as earls who had not been earls before.'[89]

Henry I had created only two new earls in his lifetime, and had allowed two earldoms to lapse; between 1136 and 1140 Stephen created more than a dozen. His gifts included the grant of Northampton to Simon of Senlis, Bedford to Hugh of Beaumont, York to William of Aumale, Derby and Nottingham to Robert of Ferrers, Pembroke to Gilbert fitz Gilbert and Hertford to his cousin, Gilbert fitz Richard, Worcester to Waleran of Meulan, Lincoln (later Sussex) to William of Aubigny and Cambridge (later Lincoln) to William of Roumare. These new earldoms,

---

[88] *Gesta Stephani*, pp. 14–23, 110, 172; Lloyd, *Wales*, ii. 469–80; for Pembroke see *Worcester Cartulary*, pp. xxxi–xxxiii.

[89] Malmesbury, *HN*, pp. 22–3.

R. H. C. Davis has suggested, were intended to be not just empty digni-
ties, but effective local authorities with control of sheriffs and castles.[90] If
so, Stephen was reverting to a type of administration that had serious
disadvantages for the royal power, and was the reverse of Henry I's
careful balancing of authority between sheriffs and established earls. And
if his attempt to take castles from the bishops who held them was part of
the same plan, it had the added disadvantage of bringing him into
sharper conflict with the church, just at the time when feudal disaffection
was preparing the way for open rebellion.

Feudally, the way was opened once Robert of Gloucester decided that
the time had come for a successful challenge to Stephen's rule. Whilst
campaigning in Normandy on Stephen's behalf in May 1138, he formally
renounced his homage. Stephen immediately confiscated his English fiefs,
and took possession of all he could occupy, but Bristol held out against
him and provided a base from which, in time, Robert could organize
resistance to Stephen and support for his sister.[91] Almost at once friends
of the Angevins took heart and rose in rebellion. Geoffrey Talbot seized
Hereford; William fitz Alan, sheriff of Shropshire, who owed everything
to Henry I and was married to a niece of Robert of Gloucester, rose with
the help of his uncle Arnulf of Hesdin, and held Shrewsbury against the
king. King David ended his truce and invaded Yorkshire. Stephen acted
with one of his rare bursts of speed and decisiveness; he himself captured
Hereford with the help of the citizens, and went on to take Shrewsbury,
where he hanged all the leaders of the revolt except William fitz Alan,
who managed to escape.[92] Heartened by his success here and the victory
of his northern barons over the Scots in the same week, and supported by
the papal legate Alberic, who arrived on a peace mission in the late
summer of 1138, Stephen attempted to assert his independence in his
dealings with his ecclesiastical vassals.[93]

In all Stephen's relations with the church his brother Henry, bishop of
Winchester, had up to that time played a leading part. One of the ablest
and most versatile of the princes of the church, Henry embodied many of
the reforming ideals of the older generation of Cluniac monks. He
worked whole-heartedly for reform as he knew it: clerical celibacy,
freedom of church elections from secular control, the strenthening of the
hierarchy. His personal ambition and ostentation were partly motivated
by his conception of the dignity of the church he represented.[94] To some

---

[90] Davis, *King Stephen*, pp. 129–44.

[91] Malmesbury, *HN*, 22–4; *Gesta Stephani*, pp. 56–7; Orderic, vi. 514–17.

[92] John of Worcester, pp. 49–50; Orderic, vi. 518–25.

[93] Tillmann, *Legaten*, pp. 38–9.

[94] For estimates of Henry of Blois see Voss, *Henrich von Blois*; Knowles, *Monastic Order*, pp. 285–93.

extent his reputation suffered from his temporary desertion of Stephen and support for the Empress in 1141, and from his active and successful involvement in organizing the defence of Winchester and the battle that restored Stephen to power once he had realized his mistake. Memories of that year clouded the narratives of later chroniclers, as they looked back to assess his character. Henry of Huntingdon's aphorism, witty but no more than a half-truth, stuck: 'a new kind of monster, compounded of purity and corruption, a monk and a knight'.[95] The bishop of Winchester was not in the habit of taking part in battle, though he was a practical statesman, a great builder and patron of the arts, and a first-rate financier; he was also a conscientious diocesan bishop and a very successful abbot. His actions cease to seem inconsistent if one accepts that, whatever his family pride, his principal motivation was a wish to further the interests of the church as he saw them.

Unfortunately his promotion by his uncle to the wealthy see of Winchester stood in the way of his ambition to lead the English church. When William of Corbeil died in November 1136, Henry hoped to succeed him as archbishop of Canterbury and papal legate. For translation to another see papal permission was necessary, and he set out for the papal court in the hope of obtaining it. He did not succeed. Pope Innocent II was then occupied in a struggle with the rival pope, Anacletus II; he may have temporized and proposed sending a legate at a later date.[96] Canterbury remained vacant until the schism ended with the death of Anacletus on 25 January 1138. Innocent II immediately despatched his legate Alberic to pacify England and settle the affairs of the English church. It must have become apparent to the legate that it would be impossible to secure a canonical election for a predetermined candidate. The prior and monks of Canterbury demanded their share in the election, as did the suffragan bishops; and the king normally expected his interests to be considered. The previous election had been contested and the monks of Canterbury had appealed to Rome; no one wanted a long tussle now. Accounts of proceedings come from later sources and are contradictory on some points. Certainly the legate presided over a meeting of diocesan bishops, and the monks of Canterbury were present at some stage; but the bishop of Winchester had been called away to carry out an ordination in St Paul's church. The outcome was the election on 24 December 1138 of Theobald, abbot of Bec, who was acceptable to monks and clergy alike, and was said to be favoured by the king and queen. Henry was deeply resentful, either of the election or the way it had

[95] Henry of Huntingdon, p. 315.
[96] Orderic, vi. 478–9; Saltman, *Theobald*, p. 8.

been hurried through in his absence.[97] Within two months Innocent II had shown confidence in him by giving him a legatine commission, and so placing the new archbishop in the impossible position of having to give precedence to one of his own suffragans.

Innocent's motives can only be conjectured; a reforming pope who had newly united the church after a debilitating schism, he is unlikely to have been guilty of the kind of casuistry with which he is sometimes charged. Probably he saw in Henry a valuable agent for reform, but was not prepared to sanction a translation to Canterbury that would almost certainly have rested on a disputed and uncanonical election. He may have looked to him to restrain his brother, and ensure that he kept his promises to the church. The Empress Matilda was known to be preparing a formal challenge to Stephen's right to the crown; when the second Lateran Council opened on 4 April 1139 she launched her appeal through her representative, Ulger, bishop of Angers, and accused Stephen of perjury and usurpation. The appeal was countered somewhat casuistically by Arnulf, later bishop of Lisieux, who alleged that Matilda was born of an unlawful union since her mother was a nun, and that King Henry had changed his mind on his death-bed. Innocent declined to change his first ruling and continued to support Stephen; but some of the cardinals, notably the later Celestine II, were sympathetic to the Angevins. After Innocent's death in 1143 opposition to Stephen at Rome became more vocal, and in the end prevented him from establishing his dynasty. The legateship held by Henry of Winchester was never renewed after it lapsed with Innocent's death; in or before 1150 it was granted to Archbishop Theobald.[98]

Meanwhile in England Stephen made the mistakes that led to his brother's temporary defection. His motive may have been to reorganize the administration of the country so as to have castles and offices in the hands of men he could trust. He may too have suspected that some of the bishops were waiting their time to declare for Matilda. Bishop Roger of Salisbury had been Henry's chief financial agent. Alexander of Lincoln and Nigel of Ely were Roger's nephews. In June 1139, while the court was at Oxford, Stephen used the pretext of an affray between the men of Count Waleran of Meulan and the bishops of Salisbury and Lincoln to arrest the two bishops and order them to hand over their castles. Nigel of Ely escaped, but later capitulated. The king took over Devizes, Malmesbury, Sherborne and Salisbury from Roger of Salisbury, and Sleaford and Newark from Alexander of Lincoln. Bishops had been arrested before on

---

[97] Gervase of Canterbury, i. 109; ii. 384; Diceto, i. 252; Saltman, *Theobald*, pp. 8–13; Voss, pp. 21–2.

[98] John of Salisbury, *Hist. Pont.* pp. 83–5; Chibnall, *World of Orderic*, pp. 199–201.

treason charges; the cases of Odo of Bayeux and William of Saint-Calais were remembered. But canon law had advanced greatly in clarity, subtlety and universality; the manner of the arrest in the king's court, without previous charges, was shocking; and all sources agreed on the brutality of the arrest and subsequent treatment of the bishops.[99]

Henry of Winchester used his new legatine powers for the first time to summon a council to Winchester to deal with the case. Stephen found some support for his demand to control the castles; Hugh of Amiens, archbishop of Rouen, who was present, asserted that bishops might have castles if they could prove by canon law that they ought to have them, but in time of danger they should put them at the disposal of the king. This was exactly what a previous archbishop of Rouen had done in 1119, when he allowed the king's troops to occupy his castle at Andely to hold back a threatened French invasion.[100] But the king's failure to restore the bishops' property before bringing charges against them was contrary to canon law. Finally the council broke up with mutual threats of appeal to Rome and of excommunication, which never went beyond a threat. Stephen may have agreed to do penance.[101]

Relations between the brothers, though seriously strained, were not broken. Henry remained with Stephen, and after Matilda landed in England openly claiming the throne he tried to make peace between the parties, which was one of the natural duties of a legate. He insisted, however, on the need for canonical elections, ruling out simony or forcible intrusion, though apparently ready to accept attempts to influence a chapter in the choice of a suitable candidate. There was open disagreement over the election to Salisbury when Bishop Roger died, an old and broken man, a few months after his disgrace. Henry would not accept Philip Harcourt, the candidate of Waleran of Meulan, whose influence over the king he distrusted. The long dispute over the York election, which began a year later, was not, however, due to any difference between the legate and the king; it began with an appeal by a minority in the chapter and dragged on for some years.[102] It was a foretaste of what freedom of election might involve in terms of prolonged litigation in and out of the papal court. But from 1139 it was plain to Henry that Stephen, raised (as he claimed) to the throne by the favour of the church, was not living up to the promises made in his Oxford charter. At the same time Robert of Gloucester's following was growing. Ranulf

[99] Malmesbury, *HN*, pp. 25–8; *Gesta Stephani*, pp. 72–81.
[100] Orderic, vi. 216–17.
[101] Malmesbury, *HN*, pp. 29–34; *Councils and Synods*, i. 781–7.
[102] For the complicated issues involved in this dispute see David Knowles, *The Historian and Character* (Cambridge, 1963), pp. 76–97.

of Chester and William of Roumare were veering to his side, and had allies among the Welsh princes.

When open war broke out, and Stephen was defeated and captured at the battle of Lincoln on 2 February 1141, Henry momentarily turned to the Empress. Archbishop Theobald was more cautious, and refused to abandon Stephen until Stephen himself, in his prison at Bristol, gave him and the other bishops permission to bow to necessity. On 7 April Henry presided at a legatine council which recognized Matilda as lady of the English and attempted to arrange her coronation.[103] Opposition from the Londoners, and Matilda's high-handed behaviour, prevented the ceremony taking place; and Henry soon saw that she had even less respect than Stephen for the liberties of the church. The election of William Cumin to the see of Durham took place at court, against the wishes of the chapter, and Matilda proposed to invest the elect with ring and staff. It is doubtful whether the election of Robert de Sigillo to the see of London was canonical, though he was allowed to take possession of the see, whereas William Cumin was excluded from Durham. Henry was disillusioned; he returned to his allegiance to the king and devoted his energies to defending Winchester against the Empress. In the course of fighting round Winchester Robert of Gloucester was captured; his exchange for Stephen followed, and in a further legatine council at Westminster on 7 December Henry endeavoured to undo and excuse the acts of his earlier council.[104]

Thereafter, though Stephen's treatment of the church aroused hostility at Rome, the English church as a whole loyally supported him. Even though Robert of Gloucester gained control of the west country and influenced some elections, this did not lead to schism. When Gilbert Foliot was consecrated bishop of Hereford in 1148 he immediately did homage to King Stephen, contrary to the wishes of the Angevin party. In John of Salisbury's words, 'although individual dignitaries followed different lords, the church as a whole recognized only one.'[105] But neither Theobald, archbishop of Canterbury and legate, nor Pope Eugenius III would consent to the coronation of Stephen's son Eustace.

There was far greater diversity in the loyalties of the magnates. The chief motive common to them all was family interest and ambition which, in the changing political fortunes of the reign, often pulled in different ways. Up to the time that Earl Robert renounced his allegiance

---

[103] Malmesbury, *HN*, pp. 52–6; *Councils and Synods*, i. 788–92; Matilda used the title 'domina Anglorum' in her charters for some years (*Regesta*, iii. p. xliv, no. 275); in two (one of which is probably spurious) she is called 'regina Anglorum' (ibid., 343, 699).

[104] For Henry's work as legate and insistence on freedom of election see Tillmann, *Legaten*, pp. 41–50.

[105] John of Salisbury, *Hist. Pont.* pp. 47–8.

there was no clear opposition to Stephen as king; Robert's defiance in 1138 produced a trickle of defections which increased the following year, when Matilda arrived in England openly claiming the crown. Individual case histories illustrate the motives that might determine loyalties in those difficult days. Brian fitz Count, the first to rally to the Empress, calls for no comment; his correspondence with Gilbert Foliot and Henry of Blois illustrates the honest conviction which determined his conduct. He could not bring himself to regard the oaths he had sworn to Matilda as anything but sacred; he was the first to rally to her cause and he ruined himself in her service.[106]

Miles of Gloucester is a much more complex and interesting case. He came from the family of Roger de Pitres which had been firmly established in the west Midlands since the conquest, and had produced sheriffs of Gloucester and royal constables. Henry I gave Miles as his wife the heiress Sibyl, daughter of Bernard of Neufmarché, lord of Brecknock, and he held the offices of sheriff, constable and local justiciar. But at the same time he was a vassal of Robert of Gloucester, from whom, in the semi-independent conditions of the march, he held Gloucester castle. At first his loyalty to the crown was greater than his loyalty to the Angevin line; he gave support to Stephen, who confirmed him in his offices, granted him the castle of Gloucester to be held from the king, and gave his son Roger the hand of another heiress, Cecily, daughter of Pain fitz John. She brought with her a weak claim to the inheritance of Hugh of Lacy, which Stephen recognized in December 1137. So Miles had a personal interest in supporting Stephen. He stood firm when Robert of Gloucester renounced his homage, and fought with Stephen against rebels in the Severn valley. But more ancient loyalties remained strong, and he may have felt insecure after the fall of his friend, Roger of Salisbury. The arrival of the Empress in the autumn of 1139 was decisive. He moved to her side and gave her strong support, so losing any hope of acquiring the Lacy inheritance. He was well rewarded; in 1141 Matilda made him earl of Hereford, and when he was killed in a hunting accident two years later his son Roger succeeded to his earldom. Stephen had, however, created a rival earldom of Hereford for Robert, earl of Leicester; and as Roger had to maintain himself precariously between the earls of Gloucester and Leicester his behaviour was subsequently even more equivocal than that of his father.[107]

Ranulf, earl of Chester, was perhaps in the most difficult position of

---

[106] Morey and Brooke, *Gilbert Foliot*, pp. 105–8; H. W. C. Davis, 'Henry of Blois and Brian Fitz-Count', *EHR*, 25 (1910), 297–303.

[107] David Walker, 'Miles of Gloucester, earl of Hereford', *Transactions of the Bristol and Gloucester Archaeological Society*, 77 (1958), 66–84; R. H. C. Davis, *Early Medieval Miscellany*, pp. 139–46.

all, though he did not change sides seven times as Round believed; after his initial rebellion in 1141 he remained, apart from one brief reconciliation with Stephen in 1146, uneasily on the side of the Empress. As the heir of a family who had been hereditary vicomtes of the Bessin he had very strong Norman interests, which were threatened early in the reign since the Cotentin and Bessin were disturbed by private war. His greatest English wealth lay in the honour of Chester, which included wealthy Midland estates; but he also cherished a claim to lands in Cumbria, recently restored to King David. His only hope of compensation in the north lay with Stephen; but to keep his Norman lands he needed to be on the winning side in Normandy. In England he particularly coveted the castle of Lincoln, which guarded the road to the north; he appears to have had some claim to one of the towers through his mother Lucy. To add to the difficulties of his position, his half-brother William of Roumare took Stephen's side vigorously at first, though his Norman interests were so strong that an Angevin victory in Normandy was bound to compromise his loyalty. And Ranulf's wife was a daughter of Robert of Gloucester. The unfortunate Ranulf stood to lose whatever the outcome; he leaned, however, more firmly towards the Angevin side and Stephen was probably right not to trust him even though he attempted to buy back his support in 1146 by granting him the castle of Lincoln and the Lancaster lands.[108]

The most successful of the magnates in maintaining and improving his position through all vicissitudes was Robert, earl of Leicester, with the slightly less effective assistance of his brother Waleran. Robert showed all the diplomatic skill of his father, who in the difficult early years of William Rufus had succeeded in keeping the trust of both Rufus and Robert Curthose. Although both the brothers had some lands on both sides of the Channel, and Robert's wife brought him the honour of Breteuil, the bulk of the Beaumont inheritance in England had gone to Robert, while Waleran secured the patrimony in Normandy and France. Stephen tried to strengthen Waleran's loyalty by making him earl of Worcester, though without providing any estates in Worcestershire, and attempting to arrange a marriage alliance. But it was almost inevitable that once Stephen lost control of Normandy Waleran would have to make his peace with Geoffrey of Anjou, and when in 1141/2 he contracted a marriage with a daughter of his Norman-French neighbour, Amaury of Montfort, it was plain that his future would lie in France. At least he and his brother were successful in looking after each other's interests in the region where they were dominant. Robert's loyalty to

---

[108] R. H. C. Davis, 'King Stephen and the Earl of Chester revised', *EHR*, 75 (1960), 654–60; Davis, *King Stephen*, pp. 93–7.

Stephen was rewarded in 1140 with a grant of the county of Hereford, once held by his wife's great-grandfather William fitz Osbern. Though Matilda replaced him by Miles of Gloucester a year later he remained outwardly loyal until the last year of the reign when, after a period of apparent neutrality, he changed his allegiance in time to welcome the Angevins.[109]

The government of England and Normandy at a time of such precariously balanced interests called for a skill in handling and ruling men that neither Stephen nor Matilda possessed. Open war in 1141 seemed briefly to favour the Empress; but her failure to secure the support necessary for coronation brought home to waverers the existence of a sacramental element in kingship. Stephen had been lawfully crowned and could not lightly be deposed. After his release his right to reign *de facto* in England was never seriously threatened, though between 1141 and 1144 Geoffrey of Anjou slowly gained control of Normandy, and rival magnates manoeuvred for power and privilege.[110] Attention was focused more and more on the next generation. Stephen attempted without success to win recognition for his eldest son Eustace, until Eustace died in 1153. As soon as young Henry of Anjou reached the age of fourteen in 1147 he made a bid for his inheritance. His first attempt was a fiasco; in 1149 he returned to the attack and showed his mettle by getting to the north of England to be knighted by his kinsman, King David, evading capture, and winning some local successes.[111] The same year his father Geoffrey invested him with the duchy of Normandy; it was as duke of Normandy that he invaded England for the third time in 1153. Although he could not defeat Stephen decisively, he fought him to a standstill and was able to establish his right to succeed. This was ratified in an agreement reached a few months before Stephen's death.

The last years of the reign have been characterized as the magnates' peace, in which we must include the bishops as magnates. In fact agreements between great lords to secure their interests began much earlier in the reign. One of the first was made between Robert, earl of Gloucester, and Miles, earl of Hereford in *c*.1141–3. Its principal provisions were renewed and clarified by their sons, William of Gloucester and Roger of Hereford after Earl Robert's death in 1147. The object of the treaty of friendship, or more accurately of 'conditional love', was to ensure that the two earls would further each other's interests and would not make a separate truce or peace in the war. It is all the more

[109] G. H. White, 'The career of Waleran, count of Meulan', *TRHS*, 4th ser., xvii (1934), 19–48; Le Patourel, *Norman Empire*, p. 105; Crouch, *The Beaumont Twins* (forthcoming).

[110] Haskins, *Norman Institutions*, pp. 123–55.

[111] *Gesta Stephani*, pp. 204–8, 214–19; A. L. Poole, 'Henry Plantagenet's early visits to England', *EHR*, 47 (1932), 447–52.

remarkable since the earl of Hereford was a vassal of the earl of Gloucester and both were outwardly supporting the Angevins; but Earl Roger at least showed himself ready to negotiate with Stephen in pursuit of his interests in Worcester, and made treaties of conditional love with both Stephen and the judiciously balanced earl of Leicester.[112]

The best-known treaty is that between the earls of Leicester and Chester, made some time after 1147, in the presence of their leading vassals and Robert, bishop of Lincoln. Its most important clauses limited the action each would take against the other in the service of his liege lord; neither was to bring more than twenty knights to a campaign, or allow his castles or land to be used as bases for attack. Each was to help the other against all men except his liege lord and one other named earl. They would not attack each other except after fifteen days' warning. Other detailed provisions concerned the recovery of castles and the protection of their mutual interests.[113] It was an attempt to secure stability in regions which they dominated, where they were more effective than their liege lord the king in keeping order.

Provisions such as these were respected by the royal justices when order was restored in the next reign. Clauses in the legal treatise of Glanvill, written c.1187–9, which refer to the support a vassal who had done homage to several lords might reasonably give to one of these against his liege lord, were probably prompted by the events of these years and the law suits generated by them. They were not a recognition of normal rights of private war which, outside the marches at least, had never been regarded as lawful by the Normans in England, but which came dangerously near to being recognized in these years.[114] Other treaties of friendship are known through references in charters; and individual charters show the same preoccupation with securing claims to disputed castles, offices and patrimonies. In 1146 an agreement made between Robert of Gloucester and Philip, bishop of Bayeux, shows Robert's concern to secure the bishop's protection for the Norman lands claimed by his son-in-law, Ranulf, earl of Chester. Bishop Hilary of Chichester negotiated with the count of Eu for the restoration of lands lost to the church earlier in the reign.[115]

If the situation is to be described as anarchy, it is a modified anarchy; a type of regionalism more characteristic of France at a slightly earlier date. The rights claimed by patrons of monasteries, which sometimes amounted to extortion, were more like the rights of advocacy exercised

---

[112] Davis, *Early Medieval Miscellany*, pp. 139–46; Davis, *King Stephen*, p. 113.

[113] Stenton, *English Feudalism*, pp. 249–55, 286–8.

[114] Glanvill, ix, 1, 8 (pp. 104, 112).

[115] R. B. Patterson, *Earldom of Gloucester Charters* (Oxford, 1973), no. 6; King, *TRHS* (1984), 141–3.

in France or the Low Countries than the restricted patronage prevailing in Normandy and England. Territorially, Stephen retained control over a central core of the kingdom; but the Angevins dominated the south west and, thanks to Hugh Bigod, Norfolk also. In the Midlands and the North the great earls of Leicester, Chester and Lincoln, and lesser lords such as Robert of Stuteville in Yorkshire, maintained some steady government in their own regions. Baronial coins were struck in the outlying provinces; Matilda and her son Henry are known to have issued coins from mints at Bristol, Cardiff, Oxford, Wareham and probably also Hereford, Gloucester, Malmesbury and Sherborne. Some second-rank men like Henry of Neufbourg and Eustace fitz John struck coins at Swansea and York.[116] Control of the coinage was one of the most tenaciously guarded royal rights; this weakness is revealing. Stephen's administration had continuity in the parts of the country fully controlled by him; there was some development in the form of writs, and the techniques of central accounting were never lost. Thanks to the recognition still accorded by the church, the bishops accepted him as their lord, even if the need to take care of their temporal interests forced them to negotiate with the local earls. Even in Wales the subjection of the church of St Davids to Canterbury was never broken. But in whole regions Stephen had little more effective control than the kings of France could exercise in Normandy. The magnates made themselves responsible for the preservation of the peace and the safeguarding of their mutual interests. Their private ambitions were expansive, and within the general framework of mutual support each endeavoured to extend his power and influence. Their methods included castle building and the foundation of religious houses under their patronage in areas of disputed lordship.[117]

During these years young Henry, duke of Normandy, promised in his charters to restore the patrimonies claimed by the recipients when he came into his inheritance. When finally he and Stephen made their peace at Winchester in 1153, and Stephen accepted Henry as his heir, Henry was realist enough to promise restitution to the disinherited. According to Robert of Torigny, 'it was sworn that lands which had fallen to intruders should be restored to their former and legitimate possessors who had held them in the time of the excellent king Henry.'[118] There were bound to be difficulties since, quite apart from the hazards of war, there had been disputed inheritances at the end of Henry I's reign; but the undertaking was essential to win the support of the magnates. It also contributed to the theory of which the new king made much during his

[116] Yver, *BSAN* (1965), pp. 189–94; King, *TRHS* (1984), 147–52.

[117] See for example Edmund King, 'Mountsorrel and its region in King Stephen's reign', *Huntington Library Quarterly*, 44 (1980), 1–10.

[118] *Regesta*, iii. 44, 180, 272; Robert of Torigini (RS) iv. 177.

reign: the legal nullity of the reign of Stephen. What was lawful was what had been accepted or held on the day that Henry I was alive and dead, just as to William the Conqueror the rights to which he claimed to succeed were those existing under Edward the Confessor, and the interlude of Harold's rule was ignored. This legal fiction was, however, easier to uphold when the interlude had lasted nine months than when it had lasted nineteen years.

When Stephen died on 25 October 1154, Henry's accession was remarkable in several ways. For the first time since the coming of the Normans the succession was assured. It had been agreed the previous year at Winchester, and Henry did not have to hurry to England to seize the royal treasure and have himself crowned. He was at Torigny in Normandy when the news of Stephen's death reached him, and he waited to put his affairs in order there before coming to England to be crowned with his wife at Westminster on 19 December. So, as Henry of Huntingdon relates, 'for about six' (actually over seven) 'weeks England was without a king, but by the grace of God peace remained undisturbed, through either love or fear of the future king.'[119] The charter that Henry issued at his coronation was a simple confirmation of the good customs enjoyed by all in the reign of his grandfather; it was no more than a ratification of the promises he had made before his accession.[120]

Besides the greater security and order of his succession, his reign was remarkable for establishing the union of England with Anjou and Poitou. Whether either his grandfather Henry or his father Geoffrey had intended this is a debatable question.[121] Geoffrey had two younger sons; he was still relatively young when he invested Henry with the duchy of Normandy. But he died suddenly on 7 September 1151; Henry was immediately invested with Anjou and Maine, and he never gave them up, though his younger brother Geoffrey twice rebelled unsuccessfully. Then in March 1152, King Louis VII of France obtained the dissolution of his marriage with Eleanor of Aquitaine, who had failed to give him a son. Within two months, on 18 May 1152, Henry married Eleanor without the king's permission. So, though the nature of his authority varied in different regions, he was lord of lands from the Channel to the Pyrenees before he secured the realm of England. His *imperium*, or empire, was bound to be different from that of his grandfather.

Nevertheless, as far as the two older parts of the Anglo-Norman realm were concerned, the emphasis was on continuity. There was no sudden influx of Angevins into England, and the foundation by his vassals of one

[119] Henry of Huntingdon, p. 291.

[120] *Councils and Synods*, i. 828–9.

[121] Le Patourel, *Feudal Empires*, ch. 9; Hollister and Keefe, *Journal of British Studies* (1973), 1–25.

or two small cells of the Poitevin abbey of Fontevrault in England was not comparable to the planting of dozens of alien priories in England after the Norman conquest. Geoffrey of Anjou is said to have told his son not to transpose customs from one province to another; and Henry deliberately chose to respect the customs and methods of administration that he took over in England. True to the traditions of his Norman forebears, his first concern was to recover the lost territories. By 1157 he had won back Cumbria and Northumberland from King Malcolm of Scotland, secured Malcolm's homage for the earldom of Huntingdon, and persuaded the Welsh princes to acknowledge his suzerainty, though the situation in Wales was not entirely clear.[122] A readjustment of relations with them and the marcher lords was necessary before he could strengthen his position in south Wales sufficiently to attempt a new enterprise: the invasion of Ireland in 1171. To obtain the consent of King Louis VII to his investment as duke of Normandy he had been compelled to surrender the Norman Vexin, and it took him ten years of negotiation and some fighting to recover it. But by 1164 the old Norman frontiers were restored.[123] Relations with the French king, however, entered a new phase. He did formal homage to Louis in Paris after being crowned king of England; for the first time a Norman king of England did homage elsewhere than in the marches. Henry I had never consented to do homage at all. Vassalage was in time to bring great problems, but for the moment the contrast between the restricted demesne of the French king and the wealthy provinces of his most powerful vassal was remarkable. Walter Map told a story of a jesting remark made to him in Paris by King Louis: 'Your lord the king of England has men, horses, gold, silk, jewels, fruits, game and everything else. We in France have nothing but bread and wine and joy.'[124]

So Henry II's reign in some ways marked a new beginning; but the opening years were also the time when the changes resulting from the Norman conquest and the amalgamation of Norman with English customs began to appear most clearly in society. These changes were also part of wider European movements from which England had never been isolated. Developments in canon law, the influence of increasing literacy on government, changing patterns of trade, increased productivity and population growth, all played their part in shaping the realm that the Normans had held for a hundred years. The changes were very far from complete; but they had reached a stage when it begins to be possible to discern them.

---

[122] William of Newburgh (RS), i. 105–6; *Chron. Hoveden*, i. 216; Lloyd, *Wales*, ii. 495–9, 512–13.

[123] Warren, *Henry II*, pp. 71–7.

[124] Walter Map, pp. 450–1.

PART II

Wealth and Government

4

From Domesday Book
to the Pipe Rolls

The first century of English feudalism also saw the rise of administrative kingship in England. Both were European movements; what is unique is their timing and interplay in the development of the English realm. It would be a crude generalization to say that mature feudal elements emerged rather later, and administrative centralization rather earlier than in the neighbouring regions of France or Flanders. Nevertheless there is a certain amount of truth in this.

The administrative change can be seen most clearly in the great records surviving from the first century after the Norman conquest. In common with most successful conquerors, including their Norman cousins in southern Italy, the followers of Duke William took over the institutions they found on arrival, and governed through them during the first phase of settlement. They found so much of value that they preserved a great deal whilst introducing some change. Both Duke William and King Edward had governed their domains, collected revenue, and dispensed justice by means of a perambulating court and household and fixed local officials. Both had revenues in cash and kind, in which cash made up a significant proportion of the whole. Both had household clerks who, in England at least, formed a rudimentary writing office, capable of drafting and preserving whatever documents were required in the course of administration. Whatever the state of society at large, the central core of government was rapidly becoming both literate and numerate on both sides of the Channel. But the English administration was superior in several ways which the Normans quickly recognized. First of all, the king's revenues included the geld, a nation-wide tax originally imposed to buy off the Danish invaders and protect the kingdom against new raiders. It was assessed on property, estimated in units called hides or carucates, and collected through a network of shires and the smaller administrative units known as hundreds and wapentakes, in which royal officers, the sheriffs, were in touch with local estate officials and men from the village communities.[1] Second, there was an efficient instrument in the sealed writ for the exercise of royal authority. Whilst a substantial number of charters were issued in the name of the Norman dukes, these were usually written by the beneficiaries, and were not sealed. The terse English executive writ, addressed to particular officials or other individuals and conveying royal commands, had far greater potential as an instrument of government than the solemn diploma, which recorded a grant made or a decision reached in the ducal court.[2] Third, the English coinage was superior to any in north-west Europe at the time. The Norman dukes enjoyed control over their own coinage; but it could not compare in purity of standard with the English, nor did it yield an income equivalent to the profits of the English mints. Many Englishmen were dispossessed by the Normans, but the mints were wisely left in the hands of the families who had controlled them under Edward the Confessor and Harold. Early attempts to introduce an additional new money tax were abortive and unnecessary.[3]

The unique record that has provided a focal point for all later studies of the Conqueror's England is Domesday Book. The Domesday inquest was carried out in 1086 as the climax of twenty years of reconstruction and settlement. It was noted by contemporary chroniclers because of its extent and thoroughness, and by those writing slightly later because it produced a written record kept permanently in the treasury, which has survived in a central repository of government documents to the present day.[4] But it did not come as a bolt from the blue. Behind it lay the experience and records amassed in the course of government. There were first of all the rolls of the English kings relating to geld and its assessment; and second the records of royal demesne administration and the private experience of estate management, particularly on the great ecclesiastical

---

[1] Stenton, *Anglo-Saxon England*, pp. 644–8. The hide (or carucate in some areas of Danish settlement) had an agrarian meaning as the basic unit of land sufficient to support a very large family group; it varied in size according to the fertility of the soil and the prevailing local customs. The virgate was a subdivision of the hide. The hide occurring in eleventh-century assessments was a fiscal unit used to calculate various public burdens; it was more artificial and standardized, but never wholly divorced from the value of the agrarian unit.

[2] Bishop and Chaplais, pp. ix–xv; Bates, *Normandy*, pp. 154–5; Chaplais, *Fécamp*, i. 93–5.

[3] For an introduction to the English coinage see Dolley, *English Coinage*; Bisson, *Conservation of Coinage*, pp. 14–28.

[4] The Record Edition of Domesday Book was published in four volumes between 1783 and 1813. Translations county by county are provided in the *Victoria History of the Counties of England* (VCH). Important general works on the survey are Maitland, *Domesday Book and Beyond*, and Galbraith, *The Making of Domesday Book*, and *Domesday Book: Its Place in Administrative History*.

estates. To these should be added the more recent experience of the great land pleas initiated by royal writs, and carried out under the presidency of Norman magnates (both ecclesiastical and lay) on the testimony of sworn local inquest juries, in the shire courts or specially convened courts of several shires.

Few records of Anglo-Saxon government have survived. They were written in the vernacular, and although old English was used in some royal writs and geld rolls for a few years after 1066, Latin rapidly took over after 1070 as the language of official documents.[5] Apart from one or two brief lists known as burghal and county hidages, surviving fragments of assessments were chiefly those copied into the cartularies of monasteries, and kept because they related to the monastic estates. The Abingdon cartulary has one of the clearest references in a document headed: 'Concerning the hundreds and concerning the hides of the church of Abingdon in Berkshire, as the writings in the king's treasury record them, divided among the various hundreds'. The reference cannot be to Domesday Book, because a second extract, which reproduces the Domesday statistics in abbreviated form, follows and is described as being 'in the other book of the treasury, written in the time of King William, who conquered England'.[6] It is almost inconceivable that a land tax capable of raising more than £20,000, and frequently producing over £10,000, could have been levied fairly regularly without generating at least a rudimentary survey. This is borne out in other countries; and indeed historians have made the assumption that earlier administrative records existed in Sicily when the Normans, who certainly kept general surveys in their financial department, first settled there towards the middle of the eleventh century.[7] Whatever their form, earlier English records would have been rendered obsolete by the violent changes in land tenure that accompanied the Norman settlement. New geld surveys were undoubtedly made by William I in the course of his reign. The earliest fragment of a geld roll from Northamptonshire, drawn up some time in the 1070s, is evidence of the continuity of administration, since the language was English and the basis of the assessment was still the same as in the time of King Edward.[8] Although the *Anglo-Saxon Chronicle* refers to gelds being taken only when they were abnormal, for instance when the rate was raised from 2s. to 6s. a hide, the geld was becoming an

[5] Clanchy, pp. 13, 129, 165.

[6] Printed, C. C. Douglas, 'Some early surveys from the abbey of Abingdon', *EHR*, 44 (1929), 618–25. Other early records are described by S. Harvey, 'Domesday Book and its predecessors', *EHR*, 86 (1971), 753–73.

[7] D. Clementi, 'Notes on Norman Sicilian Surveys', in Galbraith, *Making of DB*, pp. 55–8.

[8] *Anglo-Saxon Charters*, ed. A. J. Robertson (Cambridge, 1939), pp. 230–6.

annual levy in the closing years of William's reign. The last of his geld rolls date from a time very near the Domesday survey; historians have argued a case for both 1084 and 1086, and the surveys may have been piecemeal, or revised in certain localities.[9] They were based on shires and hundreds or wapentakes within the shires; but since part of the liability for collection lay on the lords of estates, some knowledge of estates underlay the geld assessments.

The estates had their own methods of administration; on the largest, and particularly on the royal estates, these were producing their own records. The king held lands in almost every county in England, and the administration had advanced far beyond the stage when their principal function was to provide his court with produce as it travelled round the country. Household provision remained a necessary part of government; but the revenues from the royal demesne, though still expressed as the farm of a specified number of nights, were translated into cash values. The liability for the collection of revenues and the upkeep of the estates fell on the sheriffs, and made up an important part of the fixed payment, the 'farm of the shire' for which each sheriff was responsible. His work consisted in supervising the men who ran the separate estates; often these were individual farmers, though the practice of sometimes letting out individual manors collectively at farm to the men who cultivated them appears early on the royal estates.[10] Farm contracts could be oral; they were usually of the stock and land variety, and the farmer, who paid a fixed sum (the *firma* or farm) annually, took any surplus profit himself and was responsible for restoring the estate as fully stocked with beasts and men and sown with corn as when he took charge of it. The witness of the court in which the transfer was made, and the keeping of tallies or notched sticks recording the numbers of animals kept and acres sown, made possible some check on efficiency in a largely illiterate village community. But a large estate needed some central record, however rudimentary.

Traces of such records exist in twelfth-century references which point to much older documents. In Henry II's reign the documents preserved in the treasury included a *rotulus exactorius* or roll of demands, which contained a note of the 'king's farms arising from each county, of which the sum cannot be reduced, but is frequently augmented by the devoted labour of the justices'.[11] The volume now known as the Herefordshire Domesday, compiled *c*.1160–70, included a statement of the farm of Herefordshire in the time of Henry I, together with the details of the

[9] The discussion is summarized by Galbraith, *Making of DB*, pp. 87–101, 223–30.

[10] *PR 31 H.I*, pp. 6, 23, 24.

[11] *Dialogus de Scaccario*, p. 65.

stock on various demesne manors and the total of danegeld for the county.[12] The details of stock must have been copied from earlier rolls. They are of the kind required when a manor was handed over to a farmer on any great estate in the early twelfth century.[13] Fragments from pre-conquest surveys of ecclesiastical estates show that information on manorial dues and rights was being preserved in writing. Some written evidence of the actual resources of the royal demesne manors on which the farms were based must have existed among the records that were accumulating before the Domesday survey.

Whether the great estates kept written records is more doubtful. The Anglo-Saxon treatise describing the duties of the reeve stated that he should know every detail of his lord's property, down to the last mouse-trap or peg for a hasp, and expected him to undertake all the duties later divided between several officers.[14] But even in the mid-eleventh century a large estate needed a steward above the local manorial overseer, and even if he found tallies an adequate check on the honesty and capability of his reeves or farmers he needed some more permanent central record. Whatever Orderic Vitalis may have meant when he said reproachfully in his description of the unruly household of Earl Hugh of Chester that 'he kept no account of what he gave or received', he certainly assumed that a great lord ought to have some record of whether or not he was wasting his resources.[15] The same assumption was made by the royal officers who gathered facts for the geld assessment and the Domesday survey; they could not have completed any general survey in a matter of months if they had not been able to rely on the great lords to provide much of the information for checking in the local courts.

The important land pleas of the Conqueror's reign gave the Norman rulers experience of how to obtain information about land tenures and customs through the use of sworn inquisitions in the local courts. Such inquisitions had been used in King Edward's time to resolve disputes about lands and rights. One early case (c.1053–5) settled the boundaries of the fen between the abbeys of Ramsey and Thorney by the sworn testimony of a number of old neighbours, mostly fishermen, who were acceptable to both parties and knew the traditional limits of their fishing rights.[16] Sworn recognitions were available in the shire court if the king's writ ordered an investigation into disputed rights to lands. William I had to consider many complaints from churchmen that Normans had occupied property rightly belonging to abbeys and bishoprics. Sometimes

[12] *Herefordshire Domesday*, pp. xxi, 75.
[13] *Leges Henrici*, 56, 3 (p. 174).
[14] T. F. T. Plucknett, *The Medieval Bailiff* (London, 1958).
[15] Orderic, ii. 260–3.
[16] Van Caenegem, *Writs*, pp. 69–71; Harmer, *Writs*, pp. 252–5.

spoliation had begun before the conquest, and the process of conquest involved much violent seizure. Within a decade many of the dispossessed churches were in the hands of Norman abbots who had the king's ear. To settle the pleas that arose, William used the traditional machinery of royal writ and local court, presided over by his own followers. One of the most famous land pleas, instigated by Archbishop Lanfranc to investigate the lands of Canterbury, was held on Penenden Heath and presided over by Geoffrey of Coutances.[17] Another plea involving the claims of Ely led to prolonged litigation before Geoffrey of Coutances, Robert of Mortain, and at times Lanfranc himself. Some of the proceedings took place in a joint meeting of the four shire courts, specially convened at Kentford, and attended by the sheriffs of Suffolk and Norfolk, Cambridgeshire, Huntingdon and Essex, with a number of trustworthy French and English knights and thegns. The last stage of the investigation almost coincided with the Domesday inquest, and was initiated by a writ addressed to Lanfranc, ending:

> Make enquiry by the bishop of Coutances and bishop Walchelin and others to discover who had the lands of St Etheldreda recorded and sworn to, in what way the oaths were taken, and who took them, and who heard them, and what the lands are, and of what kind, and how many, and how they are named, and who holds them, and have these things severally noted and written down. See to it that I am quickly informed of the truth of the matter by your breve, and let the abbot's messenger bring it.[18]

The whole process of feudal and territorial administration was generating written records in increasing numbers for a generation and more before the Domesday inquest, and prepared the way for it.

At Christmas 1085 King William held his court at Gloucester and had 'deep speech' with his magnates about the danger to the realm. It was a time of crisis, when Cnut of Denmark was threatening invasion, and exceptionally large numbers of knights were being assembled in preparation for an attack that never in fact took place. But the danger acted as a catalyst, and initiated the great enquiry into the resources of the kingdom and how they were distributed. The accounts of contemporaries emphasize its comprehensiveness. The *Anglo-Saxon Chronicle* noted that the survey recorded every hide and virgate of land and every cow or pig. Robert Losinga, bishop of Hereford, inserted an entry for 1086 in his copy of the chronicle of Marianus Scotus, which gives the best-informed concise statement:

[17] Bates, *BIHR* (1978), 1–19; Le Patourel, 'Penenden Heath', pp. 15–26.
[18] *Liber Eliensis*, pp. 206, 426–32.

In the twentieth year of his reign, by order of William king of the English, a survey was made of the lands of the several provinces of England, of the possessions of the individual magnates, of their fields, and manors, and men both servile and free (including both those who dwelt in cottages and those who possessed houses and lands), of ploughs, and horses and other beasts, of the service and rent of all men throughout the land. Other commissioners followed the first, and men were sent into provinces which they did not know and where they were unknown, so that they could check the survey of the first investigators, and denounce any who were guilty to the king.[19]

The terms of reference are known from a note in a private document of the abbey of Ely, the *Inquisitio Eliensis,* compiled in the course of the enquiry. The king's barons made the inquest 'by oath of the sheriff of the shire and of all the barons and their Frenchmen, and of the whole hundred, of the priest, the reeve and six *villani* of each village'. They asked the name of the manor; who held it in the time of King Edward, and at the time of the inquest; how many hides there were, how many ploughs on the demesne, how many among the men; how many *villani* and cottars and slaves; how many freemen and sokemen; how much wood, meadow and pasture; how many mills and fisheries; how much had been added or taken away; how much it was and is worth; how much each freeman or sokeman held. All this information was to be given for three dates: in the time of King Edward, when King William gave it, and at the time of the inquest; in addition, they asked if more could be taken from it than was being taken.[20]

Both the Domesday survey and part or all of a survey to reassess the geld were carried out in the same year. For convenience the country was divided into seven or eight circuits;[21] it did not include Durham or the north, where Norman rule was less effective, and the great cities of London and Winchester were omitted also, possibly because of the complexities of tenure. Where the names of the commissioners are known they were certainly lay or ecclesiastical magnates whose principal interests were in other counties. For instance, the four barons who conducted the inquest in Worcestershire were Remigius, bishop of Lincoln, Walter Giffard, Henry of Ferrers, and Adam, brother of Eudo Dapifer. The bishop of Durham was a commissioner in the south-western circuit. Samson, later bishop of Worcester, was one of the royal clerks deeply

[19] Stubbs, *Charters,* p. 95.
[20] Stubbs, *Charters,* p. 101; Galbraith. *Making of DB,* p. 60.
[21] See below, Map 9.

involved in the survey, and may have been responsible for the compilation of Domesday Book itself.[22] A convincing outline of the probable procedure has been put forward by V. H. Galbraith; it was in four or five phases.[23]

First of all the principal tenants-in-chief were required to supply details of the estates they held. They sent in written accounts, prepared in advance by their stewards, manorial officers and scribes, and forwarded to the sheriff. Much of this information must already have been collected for their private needs. Some great landholders may have sorted their tenants into hundreds as a result of earlier assessments for geld liability; and their returns, or breves, would have included the subdivision of holdings by hundreds. This stage may have produced estate documents such as the Battle Abbey returns and one of the fragments from the abbey of Evesham.

Next came the holding of sessions of the shire court, presided over by the circuit commissioners, and attended by juries of mixed French and English from every hundred or wapentake, with the priest and reeve. These checked, hundred by hundred, the written information available in the breves, with help from the geld rolls for each region, to ensure that nothing had slipped through the net. When disputes about lands broke out they were noted, and possibly recorded as *clamores, invasiones,* or *terrae occupatae.*

In some places where there were special difficulties an early draft of the returns, or part of them, may have been made locally. The *Inquisitio Comitatus Cantabrigensis* may represent this stage; the details are recorded hundred by hundred, as testified by named jurors in each hundred. Because the Cambridgeshire region contained so many small freemen and sokemen, and villages were frequently divided between several manors, a framework of the returns from the great estates would have missed a great deal.

In the south west a different social structure and background of local administration produced a different type of solution. Many of the hundreds of Somerset, Dorset, and Cornwall corresponded with great 'manors' comprising numerous dependent hamlets, mostly of royal origin.[24] As a result the basic unit of administration was seignorial in structure. The preliminary draft for this circuit is the volume known as

[22] Galbraith, *EHR* (1967), 86–101.

[23] Galbraith, *Domesday Book,* pp. 37–46; *Making of DB, passim*; for other recent literature see S. Harvey, 'Domesday Book and Anglo-Norman governance', *TRHS,* 5th ser., 25 (1975), 175–93; H. R. Loyn, 'Domesday Book', *Anglo-Norman Studies* 1 (1979 for 1978), 121–30; E. King, 'Domesday Studies', *History,* 58 (1973), 403–9.

[24] H. M. Cam, '*Manerium cum hundredo*', *Liberties and Communities in Medieval England* (Cambridge, 1944), pp. 64–90.

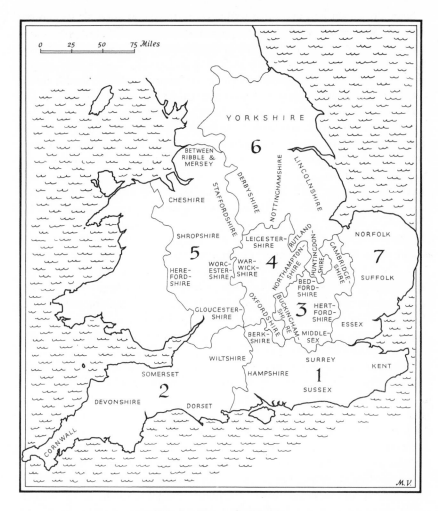

MAP 9   Domesday circuits
(conjectural: Yorkshire and Lincolnshire may have made up a separate, eighth circuit)

Exon Domesday, where the evidence is feudally arranged, and there is lack of concern with the hundred. There are even summaries of the total fiefs of the count of Mortain and a few other great tenants-in-chief in three or four counties. It cannot be assumed that preliminary drafts of either kind existed for all circuits; but they indicate the great variety of tenure, status and administration that lay behind the specious uniformity suggested by the terms of reference.

In the fourth phase the information collected by the commissioners, whether or not it had gone through a preliminary circuit draft, was then sent to Winchester, and some effort was made to abbreviate and standardize the heterogeneous returns. The returns from East Anglia never went beyond this stage. Possibly they arrived late, because of the difficulties of collecting evidence in an area with so many small free tenants; and work on the returns must have been interrupted when the king died only twenty-one months after he had ordered the survey. So the final volume for Norfolk, Suffolk and Essex is the so-called 'Little Domesday', in which the returns were copied in several different hands and were never standardized. It contains a wealth of detail, particularly of stock on the manors.

The final draft, the Exchequer Domesday, comprises all the other circuits, and was achieved mainly by discarding a mass of detail and preserving only the facts likely to be useful to the administrators. It was written on quires, later bound into a book, and was the work of a single scribe. His hand can also be detected in two corrections in the *Exon Domesday*. The probability that this work was supervised by a single able official, whether or not he actually wrote the volume, is very strong. But whether the mastermind behind the draft was that of Samson of Bayeux or another person remains uncertain. Ranulf Flambard is another possibility; he was to prove his ability in organization in the next reign, but he was still relatively young in the king's service.

In all the debate on the purpose of Domesday Book, the best summary of its multiple use comes from the pen of the master of Domesday studies, V. H. Galbraith. 'Within a generation', he wrote, 'it was thought of above all as a book of hides or hidage, invaluable for settling the incidence of geld ... But it was also invaluable as a guide, however imperfect, to the great honours and baronies created by William I, and to the details of "royal demesne".' Preserved in the treasury at Winchester, it was a constant source of reference for the royal administrators whose task was to tap all the sources of wealth available to the king. Whilst from time to time local attempts to bring it up to date were made, and produced such fragmentary surveys as those for Worcestershire, Leicestershire, Lindsey and Northamptonshire, it continued to provide a great mass of data of permanent value.[25] The hide remained the basis of assessment for most of the aids and gelds levied in the next seventy years. Not until the reign of Henry II and the feudal returns of 1166 did taxation come to be concentrated more on the knight's fee.

The Domesday inquest, indeed, was not concerned with knights' fees, which were not yet conceived as fiscal units; its interest was in tenants-in-chief. These in their turn were concerned with their own tenants, the

[25] Round, *Feudal England*, pp. 169–224.

freemen and sokemen they found established on the lands granted to them, and the knights they had enfeoffed with estates varying greatly in size. Some knights were recorded in their breves, and figure largely in some of the records they made for their own use, like the feudal book of Abbot Baldwin of Bury. Many of them are named incidentally in the returns of the great fiefs in Domesday Book. But the Worcester chronicler was quite wrong when, writing probably in the early 1120s, he said that one of the questions asked in the inquest had been 'How many enfeoffed knights?' By 1120, when some older ministerial tenures were being converted into knights' fees on the Worcester estates, the question might have been more important fiscally than it would have been a generation earlier.[26] When William sent out his commissioners he and his household were still in the early stages of relating feudal tenures to territorially assessed taxation.

This period saw a depletion of the royal demesne. Kings had to reward their followers with lands no less than with offices; and though lands came to them by escheat and forfeiture, most were regranted, often to loyal kinsmen of the dispossessed. It was important for them to ensure that in parting with the lands they did not also sacrifice the profits accruing from them. That William II and Henry I at least succeeded is shown by comparing the figures in Domesday Book with those in the 1130 Pipe Roll, in so far as they are comparable; the demesne lands shrank in extent, but the royal revenues apparently increased.[27] This was achieved by exploiting all the resources, both royal and feudal, to which the king was entitled. William I's successors were well aware of the need, and their ablest servants such as Ranulf Flambard, Roger, bishop of Salisbury, and the men who came after them in the royal household were equal to the task of devising expedients for converting unwanted services into revenue without losing their grip on traditional English levies. The exact nature of the various gelds, aids and other taxes to which the chroniclers and charters refer is often uncertain. Various expedients were employed, and we cannot assume that any tax mentioned is necessarily an early example of a familiar later levy such as scutage for the commutation of military service. Some demands proved unacceptable and were later dropped or substantially modified.

For a century after the conquest gelds assessed on the hide continued to be levied intermittently. Liability was apparently calculated on the hides and carucates of Domesday Book, with some later adjustments both up and down. Assessments could vary by changing the rate from the normal

[26] FW, ii. 18; Dyer, *Lords and Peasants*, pp. 46–7.
[27] J. A. Green, 'William Rufus, Henry I and the Royal Demesne', *History*, 64 (1979), 337–52.

2s. on the hide up to 6s. in a time of real crisis; and they might occasionally vary from county to county. The tax was flexible; exemptions could be granted out of favour or need, and these did not necessarily become permanent. Analysis of the earliest Pipe Rolls has shown that the geld did not wither away because permanent exemptions had made it hardly worth collecting. At any time of firm government, exemptions could be varied from year to year. In 1129–30 the geld actually collected made up just over 10 per cent of Henry I's total revenue for the year.[28] And even though exemptions or pardons reduced the amount actually paid to about half the amount originally demanded, they were still very valuable as a source of patronage. The tax was, however, unpopular, and Henry I promised the following year not to levy it again for seven years. But Henry II took it in 1155–6 and in 1161–2, and attempted unsuccessfully to take it again between 1173 and 1174. When collected in his reign it amounted to some 20 per cent of a diminished revenue. It was never abolished, and an assessment based on ploughlands reappeared briefly in the carucage of Richard I's reign; but it certainly aroused resentment, and unless Henry II was prepared to make an issue of it he had to find other means of supplementing the shrunken royal revenues. The decade of the 1160s, with the last levy of danegeld and the 1166 investigation into the enfeoffment of knights, was the period when royal finances definitely moved away from the hide towards the knight's fee as an acceptable basis for the assessment of a substantial part of the royal revenue, and also saw the first tentative imposition of a tax on movables with the 1166 levy for the relief of the Holy Land. But the full development of taxes on movables still lay in the future; and, as A. L. Poole has suggested, the thirteenth of 1207 rather than the earlier levies was 'the true forerunner of the tenths and fifteenths of later times'.[29]

Before the end of the eleventh century the question of how to assess obligations of vassalage in terms of cash was beginning to make itself felt. Enfeoffments of both tenants-in-chief and a rising number of their knights, and the movement of custom from more general family inheritance of land towards primogeniture inheritance of fiefs, brought about a change in the nature of vassalage.[30] Holders of fiefs might be unable or unwilling to carry out military service in person. It was more convenient for lords to insist on substantial reliefs and aids, to take over rights to the

[28] Green, EHR (1981), 241–58; Green, BIHR (1982), 1–17; her figures for Henry I's receipts from danegeld are £2,489 5s. 11d., out of a total of £22,864 10s. 4d.

[29] Poole, Domesday Book to Magna Carta, pp. 419–20; for the carucage of 1198 see Chron. Hoveden, iv. 46.

[30] See below, ch. 6.

wardship of minors from kinsfolk, and to allow castle guard and military service to be commuted to cash when the heir to a fief was incapable of performing them. There are some signs that William Rufus, who maintained a large force of stipendiary household knights in addition to any service he might expect from his vassals, pressed some claims beyond what was acceptable. Certainly the church chroniclers whom he alienated accused him posthumously of extortion.

The sparse sources for the administrative activity of his reign suggest, however, a genuine concern to find an acceptable method of assessing the obligations of his subjects without loss to the royal treasury. An isolated, but significant, writ addressed to the bishop of Lincoln, Ranulf Flambard, Haimo Dapifer and Urse d'Abitot, instructed them to 'assess Thorney Abbey for geld and scot and military service and all customs as leniently as any honour is assessed in England which has the same amount of land. If anything more has been taken from the abbey, let it be restored.'[31] Thorney did not owe feudal military service, but the customary obligation to provide soldiers for defence lay on the land, and there may have been some attempt to raise an aid to support knights. Evidence of Ranulf Flambard's activity in the Fens in about 1094 suggests that he was devoting his keen intellect to the problems of relating the obligations of vassalage to ancient territorial dues, and had provoked a protest from Thorney.

The amount of reasonable relief had not yet been settled by custom; there was still an arbitrary element in the 'gifts' that might be demanded; and knights ready to serve in person might not be ready to pay taxes for defence as well. When Henry I promised in his coronation charter that the demesne lands of knights who held by military service should be exempt from all gelds, so that they could provide themselves with arms and horses, his motive may have been to ensure that he had adequate forces to meet any threat of invasion from his brother Robert; indeed, when Robert invaded England in 1101, Henry called out the army of his whole realm, as the Abingdon chronicler related.[32] But he was also promising not to exploit the double obligations of some enfeoffed knights to feudal service and to the payment of any general land tax based on the hide. Vassalage did not become territorialized without some problems of adjustment. But in fact both scutage and geld were collected as a matter of course from some fees later in the twelfth century.[33]

[31] *Regesta*, i. 422; Southern, *Medieval Humanism*, pp. 190–1.

[32] Stubbs, *Charters*, p. 119; Green, *EHR* (1981), 246; *Chron. Abingdon*, ii. 128; Bigelow, p. 75.

[33] See *Rufford Charters*, ed. C. J. Holdsworth (Thoroton Society Record Series, 29, 30, 32, 34 (1972–81), no. 719.

When Henry I took an aid for the marriage of his daughter Matilda to Henry V of Germany it was assessed on the hide.[34] The exact nature of a 'knights' aid' which has left traces in the records of his reign is uncertain. In the reign of William Rufus Shrewsbury Abbey had been exempted by a charter of Earl Hugh of Shrewsbury (1094–8) from the 'geld of knights'. A similar geld was sometimes taken by Henry I. A letter of Richard of Belmeis written shortly before 1127 testified that the monks of Shrewsbury had never paid knights' aid;[35] and in the 1130 Pipe Roll a number of entries refer to payments of the residue of 'old knights' aid' by about fifteen tenants. They included the bishops of Durham, Lincoln and Exeter, the abbot of Crowland, Baldwin de Redvers, Robert of Bampton, eight knights in Carmarthen, and two or three small lay tenants in Cornwall, Surrey and Essex.[36] The abbot of Crowland, the only monastic tenant, did not owe military service, but had acquired some land from which service was due. The knights of Carmarthen and Durham were in unsettled regions, where it is likely that any service due would be performed in person. The aid was certainly not scutage. It is a reminder that Henry I levied various gelds and aids from towns, counties, and other groups and individuals, and was trying to find the best way of ensuring that no one slipped through the net of interlocking old and new customs. Possibly it was the imposition of new types of aid that caused resentment at payment of the old geld to build up. But not until the reign of Henry II was a satisfactory new basis of assessment securely established. And at all times the conditions that persisted were not unlike those described by Evelyn Jamison in southern Italy. There the two types of service, in person and in money, 'were separate, not alternative, ways of rendering military service, and were present side by side'. The use made of them by the king varied, depending on whether his greater need was for men or for money.[37]

There was certainly an increase in demand for cash in the reigns of William Rufus and Henry I, both of whom supported large contingents of permanent household troops, and could raise reserves of trained stipendiary knights from Flemish or Breton allies no less than from the portionless or dispossessed sons of their own Norman vassals. In the first years of Henry's reign his existing stipendiaries and active vassals may not have been enough for his needs in holding the kingdom and reconquering Normandy, and he worked hard to build up an elite household

[34] ASC (E), 1110; Regesta, ii. 942, 946, 959, 963, 964, 968.
[35] Rees, Shrewsbury Cartulary, i. 9–10 (no. 4); ii. 318 (no. 353); the translation 'scutage' in Regesta, ii. 1473 is misleading.
[36] PR 31 H.I, pp. 49, 58, 84, 89, 114, 130, 132, 153–4, 159.
[37] 'Additional work by E. Jamison on the Catalogus Baronum', Bullettino dell' Istituto Storico Italiano per il Medio Evo e Archivio Muratoriano, 83 (Rome, 1971), 6.

force that would be at least as strong as that of Rufus and better disciplined. The bitter complaints of the English chroniclers about the devastation left by the passing of William's retinue on its travels continued for the first few years of Henry's reign. A royal writ addressed to all the sheriffs and ministers of England, ordering them to restore to Abbot Faritius of Abingdon all the men who had left his land of Wallingford 'because of giving lodgings to my court or for other reasons', belongs to this period.[38] The *Anglo-Saxon Chronicle* lamented in 1104 that 'always wherever the king went there was complete ravaging of his wretched people caused by his court, and in the course of it often there were burnings and killings.' But after that year the *Chronicle* made no more complaints of this kind. This suggests that Eadmer was not exaggerating the benefits of Henry's reforms in 1108, when the king put an end to the worst abuses of his servants and retainers by insisting that any proven offenders should be blinded and mutilated.[39] And Walter Map's description of Henry's court, though written in the reign of his grandson and tinged with nostalgia, reinforces Eadmer's evidence: 'He arranged with great precision, and publicly gave notice of, the days of his travelling and of his stay, with the number of days and the names of the vills, so that everyone might know without the chance of a mistake the course of his living, month by month.' The result was that merchants hurried with their wares from all over England and abroad, so that the court was always well supplied with provisions.[40]

These arrangements for provisioning the court coincided with the last stage of converting the renders from royal demesne lands, for which the sheriffs were responsible, from food to cash. Walter Map's contemporary, Richard fitz Nigel, described the change according to the traditions of his day. He himself knew persons who had seen food and forage being brought at fixed times to the court from the crown lands, and the wages and rewards of knights and other necessary expenses were met with the profits of jurisdiction and various other levies. 'But in process of time', he added, 'when King Henry was engaged in suppressing armed rebellion in distant places overseas, coined money became of the utmost necessity to him for that purpose.' Since he was beset with vociferous complaints about the inconvenience of bringing victuals from great distances, he had the renders valued and the sheriffs charged with a fixed sum of money in their place.[41] Fitz Nigel's account is oversimplified, and the traditions he knew were not always reliable; but he was

[38] Van Caenegem, *Writs*, no. 110; *Regesta*, ii. 856.
[39] Eadmer, *HN*, pp. 192–3. The ravaging of William II's court is described by Barlow, *William Rufus*, p. 135.
[40] Walter Map, pp. 471–3.
[41] *Dialogus de Scaccario*, pp. 40–1.

right in pointing to the reign of Henry I as a time when a significant step was taken in the conversion of any food farms that still survived into cash, and the growing importance of stipendiary military service.

In the course of these changes, the possibility of landed knights performing more and more of their services in cash was increasingly recognized. As Stenton pointed out, the early charters of enfeoffment almost invariably spoke not of a knight's fee, but of the service or services of a knight. These services were miscellaneous; they included the important duty of castle guard and sometimes escort duty, as well as the provision of miscellaneous aids and service in the host. Limited services for fragmented tenements could be expressed in terms of fractions of the service of a knight. It was accepted that part of the service would take the form of cash. A charter of King Stephen granting Gervase of Cornhill, citizen of London, leave to hold Berkesdon by the service of half a knight, to be rendered annually in money, was unusually explicit, but it illustrates the trend.[42] At the same time, the concept of a knight's fee developed as a necessary way to describe an estate charged with the service of a single knight. The slow, but never total, standardization of obligations involved some movement in the direction of a standard size, at least as a desideratum, for a knight's fee. Charters record grants and promises of property to make up a knight's fee of a specified amount. Fees yielding an annual revenue of £10 (expressed as 10 librates of land) were often regarded as adequate, though larger amounts might be provided, and many smaller or larger early fees remained in existence. Standards might vary between honours. In Holderness, where the fixing of a standard fee was not attempted until the end of the twelfth century, eight carucates was adopted, whereas the neighbouring Gant honour had settled for seven.[43] In many honours it is possible that nothing approaching standardization was ever attempted.

The possibility of personal service was always an alternative to payment, particularly for those who held a whole knight's fee or more. But as various aspects of the service were defined more precisely in terms of money, so the length of service which a vassal was bound to give, either in the field at his own expense or as castle guard, became more clearly limited, even if it was never standardized over the whole country. Forty days' field service or its equivalent in cash, if required, became normal in the course of the twelfth century, replacing the much more fluid personal service given as an obligation of vassalage and in the hope of further reward that had characterized early Norman society, both before and after the conquest. Castle guard, because it was a more continuous early

---

[42] Stenton, *English Feudalism*, pp. 154–9; *Regesta*, iii. 244.
[43] Stenton, *English Feudalism*, pp. 163–5; English, *Holderness*, pp. 141–3.

need, had been defined at different levels in individual fees, and continued to be more variable; even the king's demands from his tenants-in-chief varied between the different honours.[44] At least it became possible to calculate the service or cash equivalent that could reasonably be demanded in any particular case.

The financial changes were accompanied by changes in the court and household that were at the heart of the royal administration. A difficulty in describing them arises from the lack of a technical vocabulary, inevitable in a time of growth and change, when new institutions were only half formed and imperfectly defined. Contemporaries used a variety of words, some of which later acquired a technical meaning they did not have in the early twelfth century. The treasury was a storehouse of treasure, in the sense that survives in the twentieth-century cathedral treasury; it was a repository for valuables, not a department of state. A justiciar was a royal justice, who might be acting on an *ad hoc* or more general commission to try pleas of the crown; even a 'justiciar of all England' was not the same as the viceregal chief justiciar who emerged in the reign of Henry II. The chancellor was in charge of a writing office, and when it became appropriate to describe this as a chancery is a problem on which historians at present differ in writing of both royal and private chancellors and their clerks. Sometimes earlier appointments and arrangements seem to foreshadow the later developments; but looking for prototypes can too easily turn into a kind of historical determinism. Some expedients were tried and abandoned; and sometimes those that survived did so only because they were acceptable compromises for the time being.

Nevertheless the Norman kings, grappling with the problems of government common to the feudal principalities of western Europe, succeeded in devising methods of centralized administration that were remarkable for their precocity. In their finance and administration of justice they were at least a generation ahead of France or Flanders or Catalonia; and not behind even Norman Sicily, with its Byzantine inheritance.[45] That they could not have achieved this without their English inheritance goes without saying; but the practical difficulties of governing dominions divided by the Channel were also decisive in hastening the emergence of more tightly organized departments of government that the king could control even during periods of absence overseas.

---

[44] Hollister, *Military Organization*, ch. 5.

[45] For comparisons see Bisson, *Conservation of Coinage*; Hollister and Baldwin, *American Historical Review* (1978), 867–905; Bruce Lyon and Adriaan Verhulst, *Medieval Finance* (Bruges, 1967).

Early administration was centred in the household, which travelled with the king. When he was overseas in Normandy, much business followed him, but a viceregent had to deal with some affairs in England. William I often left Queen Matilda as his representative in Normandy; in England a number of trusted magnates and kinsmen looked after the affairs of the realm in his absence. William fitz Osbern held a key role in the first few years, and Odo of Bayeux afterwards, until his disgrace. Lanfranc played an important part in transmitting the king's orders; and both Robert of Mortain and Geoffrey of Coutances frequently acted on *ad hoc* bodies for important pleas.[46] William Rufus was less frequently overseas until the later years of his reign, when he governed Normandy during his brother's absence on crusade. It was then that an administrator of a new type appeared: Ranulf Flambard, one of the ablest clerks to rise in the royal household at the end of the Conqueror's reign. Rufus respected his shrewd and ruthless efficiency, and entrusted more and more initiative in administrative work to him. His success as a financial agent exploiting both new and old sources of revenue won him the reward of the bishopric of Durham in 1099, and also accounts for his great unpopularity.

Henry I on his accession dismissed and imprisoned Flambard for appropriating revenues that should have gone to the royal fisc. Though he escaped to Normandy, and within a few years had made his peace with the king, Henry left him to exercise his talents in his northern bishopric, and did not readmit him to his own inner circle of *curiales*. Chroniclers referred to him by various titles when he was the principal agent of Rufus.[47] Orderic called him 'justiciar and chief manager of the king's wealth'; Florence of Worcester used the terms *exactor* and *placitator*, and William of Malmesbury referred to him as *causidicus*. His duties were financial and judicial. 'Justiciar' at that date was a term widely used for both shire justices and justices with *ad hoc* commissions. *Placitator* and *causidicus* suggest that he may have been initiating actions to defend royal rights, like the unpopular ducal advocates in Normandy.[48] *Exactor* recalls the *rotulus exactorius*: the roll of fixed revenues kept in the treasury. These titles epitomize the administrative changes then taking place. The 'roll of demands' belonged to the financial organization of the eleventh century and the Domesday survey, largely dependent on the accountability of stewards and farmers of fixed demesnes, which was gradually giving way to a more centralized accounting procedure. The

---

[46] D. Bates, 'The origins of the justiciarship', *Anglo-Norman Studies*, 4 (1982 for 1981), 1–12.

[47] For his career see Southern, *Medieval Humanism*, ch. 10; Malmesbury, *GR*, ii. 369; FW, ii. 46; Orderic, v. 310.

[48] Orderic, iv. 242–3; and see below, p. 201 n.30.

fiscal officers used by Rufus and Henry I in England, efficient as they
were in swelling the royal revenues by judicial actions, were often
oppressive, and became so generally hated that they had no lasting
influence in England. The justiciar was, however, to develop in Henry II's
reign into a great officer of state, who combined the functions of early
viceregents with the duty of presiding over the exchequer account.

Specialization of function became a little clearer during the long reign
of Henry I. The king was absent in Normandy for longer periods; and
though his household and court accompanied him and some magnates
and household officers were active on both sides of the Channel, Hollister
has traced the emergence of small groups of individuals who were chiefly
associated with work in either England or Normandy.[49] One group
became closely involved both in regency judicial duties and in the regular
accounting that took place in England round the new exchequer board in
the treasury. Henry's queen, Matilda, was the official regent during her
husband's absence; but Roger, bishop of Salisbury, gradually took over
more and more of the viceregal duties under her. After the death of the
queen in 1118, and that of the heir to the throne, William Atheling, in
1120, Roger emerged visibly and not merely effectively as second to the
king in the kingdom. With him were frequently associated, both before
and after 1118, Robert Bloet, bishop of Lincoln, Richard Belmeis, bishop
of London, William of Courcy, Adam of Port, Walter of Gloucester, and
Ralph Basset. A number of these men acted as justices in pleas heard
during the king's absence. And all of them appear in the earliest detect-
able exchequer court, when it began to emerge from obscurity about
1110.

The origins of the Exchequer are bound up with the early history of the
treasury.[50] Money needed for current expenses was carried with the king
by the household officers who accompanied him; but well before the
conquest a permanent repository for the bulk of the royal wealth had
been fixed at Winchester. Responsibility for the treasure store, both fixed
and mobile, was placed on one or two chamberlains, or on an officer
called the treasurer, who had charge of the keys and was not equivalent
to the great court treasurer of the twelfth century. Henry the treasurer
was active in 1086, and Herbert the Chamberlain occurs in Domesday
Book as the holder of a small estate in Hampshire. In the first half of
Henry I's reign there were two treasury chamberlains. Herbert suffered
forfeiture for treachery in 1119 and was replaced by Geoffrey of Clinton.
Robert Mauduit, whose estates included Porchester (an important base

[49] Hollister and Baldwin, *American Historical Review* (1978), pp. 870–80.
[50] Hollister, *EHR* (1978), 262–75; Emma Mason, 'The Mauduits and their chamberlainship of the Exchequer', *BIHR*, 49 (1976), 1–23.

for shipping treasure to Normandy) was drowned in the *White Ship* in 1120; his lands and treasury chamberlainship passed to his son-in-law, William Pont de l'Arche. These men, even when they were rising *curiales* like Geoffrey of Clinton, were all household officers, and could not be described as great officers of state. The emergence of a court treasurer came in the course of the reign, but before then the accounting and its associated judicial activities had taken shape at Winchester.

A momentous innovation took place in the early years of the twelfth century. This was the decision to hold annual accounts at one and the same place in one and the same curial session. The actual name of the Exchequer came from the table covered with a checked cloth like a chess board, on which the calculations were made during the regular rendering of account.[51] It was an abacus, on which calculations were made by moving counters in columns corresponding to thousands, hundreds and scores of pounds, and pounds, shillings and pence. It was intelligible even to the illiterate, and by the use of an empty column overcame the weakness of the Roman system of numeration (where zero is lacking) so effectively that it remained in use long after the system of Arabic numeration was widely known. Together with the tallies, the notched sticks representing sums of money paid, which were split to act as receipts, it made possible the rapid development of a sophisticated system of accounting from the late eleventh or early twelfth century. Robert of Lorraine, bishop of Hereford from 1079 to 1095, was familiar with it, and it was coming to the notice of sheriffs about 1100, when Adelard of Bath was teaching at Laon and wrote a treatise on the abacus. Another short treatise on the abacus was written by a royal clerk named Thurkil, and addressed to his colleague, 'Simon of the rolls' some time before 1117.[52] The examples of multiplication and division cited by Thurkil were thoroughly practical: 'What is the product when twenty-three knights owe you six marks each?'; 'Divide £800,137 among 1,009 knights'; or '200 marks are to be divided among 2,500 hides, which is the total number of hides in Essex, as Hugh of Bocland says.' 200 marks was the amount Essex paid as a *donum* early in Henry II's reign, and Haskins suggested that it represents a supplement to danegeld. These problems were the kind facing clerks who had to adjust old assessments made for various purposes to new methods of raising money. The abacus made it possible to use the information stored in Domesday Book and the geld rolls more effectively for the changing needs of everyday government, and to safeguard the royal revenue. It would be wrong to think that the

---

[51] The workings of the Exchequer are described by Poole, *Exchequer*; for the abacus see *Dialogus de Scaccario*, xxxv–vii, 6–7.

[52] C. H. Haskins, 'The abacus and the king's *curia*', *EHR*, 27 (1912), 101–6.

continued use of Roman numerals retarded the development of numeracy among the trained officers who handled the royal finances.

However, the great innovation was the regular holding of a central receipt, in curial sessions round the exchequer table. Twice a year, from the early years of Henry I, separate groups of administrators met at the Winchester treasury and the Norman treasury, and heard the accounts of sheriffs and vicomtes. The business inevitably had a judicial side, and the earliest references to it are as much judicial as financial. It dealt with pleas for exemption from aids or gelds, and coerced defaulters. A writ addressed to the 'barons of the Exchequer' in 1110 proves that the abacus was in use by that date;[53] but many of the early sessions of the court are described simply as 'in thesauro'. It was not yet either a 'permanent financial bureau' or a 'central organ of government'; it was simply an occasion, and the group of barons sitting at the Exchequer could vary in composition from court to court. In practice Roger of Salisbury presided; he was not called treasurer, but was a great administrator exercising curial control. By the mid-1120s the title of treasurer was beginning to be applied to his nephew, Nigel, a *curialis* who was active in England and Normandy, supervising both treasuries, and who might not unreasonably be called the first court treasurer, though he remained a member of the household. His son, Richard fitz Nigel, who wrote the famous *Dialogue of the Exchequer*, learnt the business of the Exchequer from him, and held the office of treasurer for thirty years under Henry II (1158/9 to 1189).

The biennial sessions at the Exchequer were the first regular curial meetings normally held without the king, and in a fixed place. For most purposes court and household still followed the king. Treasure needed for his daily expenses was carried with him, in the care of a household chamberlain. Until the main treasury was moved by slow stages to Westminster towards the end of Henry II's reign, the most convenient port for sending valuables to Normandy was Southampton. The Mauduit family held Porchester, a convenient staging post, as part of the inheritance that went with their treasury chamberlainship. Perhaps because the royal castle at Falaise (in a part of Normandy traditionally loyal to Henry I) was a convenient storehouse for treasure needed by him on his campaigns, the harbour at Barfleur was frequently used for his crossings to Normandy. Treasure passed to and fro with the army. When the *White Ship* was wrecked on a return journey to England in 1120 the treasure chest was recovered, but the treasury chamberlain, Robert Mauduit, went down with the ship.[54] It was useful, however, to have

[53] *Regesta*, ii. 963.
[54] Le Patourel, *Norman Empire*, pp. 166–76; Orderic, vi. 304–7.

repositories in several places, and there are traces of subsidiary treasuries in London, both at the Tower and at Westminster, and occasionally elsewhere before the financial centre, both for treasury deposit and accounting at the Exchequer, settled down at Westminster.[55]

Systematic records of the annual accounts, the great Pipe Rolls, began to be kept in the reign of Henry I. A solitary roll for the year 1129–30 survives from his reign; it shows the exchequer system already working on much the same lines as when Richard fitz Nigel described it half a century later. Entries of debts going back mainly to the period 1125–9 indicate that similar records had been kept for several years at least. Nothing remains from Stephen's reign; but an almost continuous series of Pipe Rolls from the beginning of the reign of Henry II indicate that the central accounting had not wholly lapsed even during the intervals of civil war. A few sheriffs still made payments in weighed coin on the 1129–30 roll; but as a result of reforms initiated by Roger of Salisbury most paid in assayed coin to ensure that the king's revenues did not suffer from any imperfections in the silver content of the coinage. The rolls contain a systematic record of the sheriffs' farms, comprising revenues from royal manors and some royal boroughs, and fixed payments from shire and hundred courts. Other items included various gelds and aids, the profits of royal justice, forest revenues, and payments to the king for office or release from office. Various exemptions were entered, making the rolls incidentally a record of royal patronage.[56] In the development of this systematic control of finance the English kings and their servants had advanced beyond the less elaborate domanial finance that had existed when the Domesday survey was made, and still prevailed over most of western Europe. The French king did not achieve a similar central account with systematic records until the last decade of the twelfth century. Possibly, since judicial accompanied financial growth, it also contributed to the precocious development of English law.

The men who carried on the royal government were trained partly in whatever European schools were available in each generation, and partly in the royal household and chapel. Some of them had had previous experience in the households of bishops or other great lords. Odo of Bayeux sent his promising young clerks to the schools at Liège and elsewhere; two of them, Thomas of Bayeux and his brother Samson, were taken into the king's chapel.[57] Thomas was quickly promoted to be

---

[55] R. A. Brown, '"The treasury" of the later twelfth century', *Studies presented to Sir Hilary Jenkinson*, ed. J. Conway Davies (Oxford, 1957), pp. 35–49.

[56] Kealey, *Roger of Salisbury*, pp. 52–5; S. L. Mooers, 'Patronage in the Pipe Roll of 1130', *Speculum* 59 (1984), 282–307.

[57] Orderic, iv. 118–19.

archbishop of York; Samson did sterling service at the time of the Domesday survey, and subsequently became bishop of Worcester. Ranulf Flambard, the ablest of the younger clerks who were chosen by William I, appears to have had no early patron to place him in the schools; when chroniclers called him 'almost illiterate' they probably meant that he had never formally studied the liberal arts. His apprenticeship was served in the royal household under the chancellor Maurice; and he learned there, among the rolls and tallies, the basic skills which he later perfected in financial and judicial administration. He earned the normal reward of promotion to a bishopric, the wealthy and important, if somewhat turbulent, see of Durham in 1099.

Normandy at this time was a fertile breeding ground of clerks; Henry I found some of the talents he needed among the Norman clerks he had known as an ambitious younger son, when he built up his own household before securing the crown. One of these, John, archdeacon of Sées, was educated in the bishop's schools at Sées and, according to Orderic Vitalis, was 'well taught in various disciplines, both secular and ecclesiastical. Because he was a fluent speaker, with a talent for reasoning, he was promoted to the office of archdeacon, took his seat among the justices examining legal cases, and for many years conducted ecclesiastical business with intelligence and skill.' Henry made him bishop of Lisieux in 1107, soon after winning control of Normandy; his work lay mostly in the duchy, where he organized the Norman exchequer and presided over the king's judicial business, but as a leading *curialis* he was in close touch with all Henry's magnates.[58] Roger of Salisbury, the man most active in shaping the English exchequer, came of more obscure origins. A priest from the diocese of Avranches, he attracted Henry's notice before his accession; and in 1102 Henry made him bishop of Salisbury. He may have studied in schools at Caen;[59] wherever he acquired his basic learning he was quick to adapt, and showed original and constructive talents. When he appointed a *magister scholarum* in his cathedral of Salisbury in 1107, he wrote to the learned Hildebert of Lavardin, bishop of Le Mans, to ask for a recommendation. Hildebert sent him his own precentor, Master Guy of Etampes, who had studied at Laon before joining the bishop's household.[60]

Laon came to the fore as a school for ambitious young clerks just before the turn of the century. Anselm of Laon, who taught there, provided a practical pastoral training for priests. The *Sentences* compiled

[58] Orderic, vi. 142–5; Haskins, *Norman Institutions*, pp. 87–90, with corrections by Le Patourel, *Norman Empire*, pp. 223–8.

[59] Gibson, *Lanfranc*, p. 104.

[60] Migne, *PL*, clxxi. 219; Edwards, p. 18; Kealey, *Roger of Salisbury*, pp. 91–2.

in Laon were designed to provide sound moral advice on everyday problems; they gave a grounding for advance in the reformed church, where there was a demand for clergy who could carry out their pastoral duties efficiently and aspire to become conscientious bishops rather than theologians.[61] Other teachers there gave training in computation and the use of the abacus, which the clerks of the royal household were to put to such good use. No wonder the little town of Laon was overflowing with students, who flocked from as far afield as Pisa, Milan and Germany as well as England. Henry I's interest was so keen that he secured the election of his chancellor, Waldric, to the bishopric in 1107: an achievement all the more remarkable since Laon was outside his dominions, and the worldly Waldric had to be hurriedly ordained subdeacon and made a canon of Rouen to make him acceptable to the reluctant cathedral clergy. Although his rule, unwillingly accepted by Anselm of Laon, was hated by the citizens, and he was murdered in a communal riot in 1112, the presence of an English bishop tightened the links with England.[62] Master Anselm consented to accompany Waldric on a visit to England, and the school at Laon became a Mecca for English scholars. They included Roger of Salisbury's nephews, Alexander and Nigel, later bishops of Lincoln and Ely; Gilbert the Universal, bishop of London; Robert, bishop of Exeter; Robert Bethune, bishop of Hereford; and Archbishop William of Corbeil. When the canons of Laon travelled across England in 1113 to raise money to rebuild their cathedral after a disastrous fire, they were welcomed by alumni all along their route.[63]

Movement across all the dominions of the English kings and even further afield continued in the twelfth century; but secular clerks had a choice of a number of good centres of study in England too. In the secular cathedrals like Salisbury most bishops appointed a *magister scholarum*, who often supervised the secretarial work of both bishop and chapter, and came increasingly to be called chancellor. Guy of Etampes enhanced the reputation of Salisbury; Albinus of Anjou, whom the chronicler Henry of Huntingdon called 'my master', was probably *magister scholarum* at Lincoln, where Huntingdon himself was trained. A school at St Paul's, London, was organized early in the century under Master Durand, and Exeter had a high reputation. Apart from the cathedral schools, Oxford, with its learned canons at St George's in the castle, and

[61] V. I. J. Flint, 'The "School of Laon"; a reconsideration', *Recherches de théologie ancienne et médiévale*, 43 (1976), 89–110; R. W. Southern, 'The School of Paris and the School of Chartres', *Renaissance and Renewal in the Twelfth Century*, ed. R. L. Benson and G. Constable (Cambridge, Mass., 1982), pp. 115–17.

[62] H. W. C. Davis, 'Waldric the Chancellor of Henry I', *EHR*, 26 (1911), 84–9.

[63] Kealey, *Roger of Salisbury*, pp. 48–50; Morey and Brooke, *Gilbert Foliot*, pp. 54, 69; Smalley, *Becket and the Schools*, pp. 20–2.

the Augustinian canons at Oseney and St Frideswide's, became an important centre of study and teaching in the reign of Henry I, though it did not emerge as a *studium generale* until the 1190s. Northampton enjoyed a temporary importance in the middle years of the century.[64] Schools such as these provided basic teaching; those who wished to pursue the higher studies such as theology frequently went abroad, above all to Paris. Law, both civil and canon, became more desirable as a training for ambitious administrators from about the middle of the century, and then the attraction of Bologna increased although other schools had much to offer. Thomas Becket picked up a little legal knowledge at Auxerre as well as Bologna during a year of study abroad. Clerks travelled abroad not only to learn; some Englishmen went to teach. Robert Pullen, who had begun teaching probably at Exeter and Oxford, taught in Paris from 1138 until he was called to Rome to become a cardinal and serve as papal chancellor. Robert of Melun taught at Paris for over forty years before his appointment as bishop of Hereford in 1160.[65] One of the best known of the peripatetic scholars and administrators was John of Salisbury, who wrote his own record of his prolonged and varied studies in Paris before he joined the household of Archbishop Theobald. For four years, from 1148 to 1152, he acted on behalf of Theobald in the papal court; thereafter he was prominent in Theobald's learned circle at Canterbury, writing many of his letters and applying his administrative experience to the needs of the household.[66] His support of Becket cut him off from all hope of the advancement he might have expected in England, even after Henry II's penance and submission; when he finally achieved a bishopric it was at Chartres, in the domains of the king of France.

This freedom of movement for the ablest scholars through the best schools of western Europe stimulated and did not stifle the continued practical training of administrators in royal and episcopal households. Open to new learning whenever it was appropriate, these centres of apprenticeship both developed new techniques of government and trained the staff necessary to apply them. Richard fitz Nigel learned his letters at Ely; he owed his professional training to his father, Bishop Nigel, and gained experience by sitting at the exchequer board. He wrote

[64] Edwards, pp. 18, 182; C. R. Cheney, *English Bishops' Chanceries 1100–1250* (Manchester, 1950), pp. 23–39; for Oxford see R. W. Southern's chapter in *The History of the University of Oxford*, ed. J. I. Catto (Oxford, 1984), 2–12.

[65] Smalley, *Becket and the Schools*, ch. 2; D. E. Luscombe, *The School of Peter Abelard* (Cambridge, 1969), pp. 281–98.

[66] For his life see Christopher Brooke, 'John of Salisbury and his world', *The World of John of Salisbury*, ed. Michael Wilks (Studies in Church History, Subsidia 3, Oxford, 1984), pp. 1–20.

his own treatise in the form of a dialogue between master and pupil, to explain the workings of the Exchequer to young clerks who would find no such aids in the academic schools elsewhere. The great household officers and barons of the Exchequer were themselves actively engaged in improving their techniques and did so, not by setting up a school, but by inviting experts to sit with them. The Norman kingdom of Sicily, with its Byzantine and Arab inheritance, seemed to have something to offer, and this accounts for the appearance in England of Master Thomas Brown. 'He was a great man at the court of the great King of Sicily' (Roger II), Richard fitz Nigel records, 'a prudent counsellor, and almost at the head of the king's confidential business.' But after Roger II's death in 1154, his son William I removed many former favourites from office, and Thomas left the country. In Fitz Nigel's words:

> There were many kingdoms in which he would have been received with honour. But as he had frequently been invited by our noble King Henry of England, and since report cannot compare with the plain truth, he preferred to return to his native land and his hereditary liege lord. The king received him as befitted them both; and because Thomas had held a great position in Sicily he is appointed here also to important duties in the Exchequer.[67]

He arrived about 1158 and sat at the Exchequer for over twenty years, had his own clerk, and kept his own roll; for a number of years he held the office of king's almoner. His presence there left traces of two interesting experiments in record keeping. One was a fertile initiative: his roll, apparently of the *regni iura regisque secreta*, was of a kind that later developed into the Memoranda Roll. The other, an attempt to bring Domesday Book up to date for the county of Herefordshire, where he had property, was never quite completed. The book tried to provide the information about knights' fees that had become necessary in the century since the Norman conquest, but would have been meaningless in 1086 when knight service was still far from being rooted in the individual fee. Also it brought up to date the names of tenants and subtenants in the county. In the words of V. H. Galbraith, 'In the twelfth century the quintessence of the Domesday inquest was to be found in the tenancy of the honours, in the hidage of the individual manors, and in the annual *valet*. All the rest had gone more or less out of date.'[68]

Thomas Brown's book belongs to a series of measures that have left traces in such transitory records as Master Thurkil's little treatise on the abacus, with its mathematical calculations relating county hidages to the

[67] *Dialogus de Scaccario*, pp. 35–6.
[68] *Herefordshire Domesday*, pp. xxii–xxxii; Poole, *Exchequer*, p. 119.

obligations of knights, or Rufus's command to Ranulf Flambard to investigate whether Thorney abbey was being overcharged in gelds, scots and military service in comparison with other honours of the same size. All this led up to the emergence of the knight's fee as a fiscal unit for purposes of assessing scutage and taking reliefs at an accepted 'reasonable' figure. In cases where the standard charges proved very oppressive, some attempt might be made to bring the size of the holding up to an acceptable level; but the size was never more than a rough and ready rule, applied when demand was sufficiently vociferous. The permanent record of financial achievement that emerged and provided a model for centuries to come was the great series of Pipe Rolls.

The rolls provide a commentary, very important though not quite complete, on the revenues and expenses of the realm, on the king's patronage exercised through exemptions and the sale of offices, and on the cash stipends payable to some of the king's servants. But, as the description of the household of Henry I preserved in the Constitutio domus regis shows, part of the reward of resident members of the household consisted of food and candles.[69] Many household clerks were rewarded with prebends and church offices. And not all the duties of vassalage were convertible into cash; some, by mutual agreement, were performed in person. Thomas Keefe has pointed out that the great earls of Henry II who seemed favoured by tax exemptions served in many ways: they travelled on the king's business, acted as justices, supervised the maintenance of castles, attended courts and, when need arose, led contingents of the king's armies. Some of the exemptions granted were personal favours for life only: Reginald, earl of Cornwall, Henry II's uncle, owed £370 for scutage, which the Exchequer made no attempt to collect but which was collected by the royal custodians of the Cornwall estates after Reginald's death.[70] Some rewards in the form of outright gifts and the hands of wealthy heiresses went to magnates with heavy responsibilities for keeping the peace on a sensitive frontier. Some reading between the lines of the Pipe Rolls is necessary to understand the interplay of feudal lordship and territorial kingship in the first century after the Norman conquest.

During this period the king's court and household were meeting places for great magnates, both lay and ecclesiastical, and skilled administrators rising partly by favour and family influence, but much more by sheer ability. The royal service offered careers open to the talents no less than to birth and wealth, though these counted. Few passages from the

---

[69] Constitutio Domus Regis, in Dialogus de Scaccario, pp. 129–35.
[70] Thomas Keefe, 'Henry II and the earls', Viator, 13 (1981), 191–222; J. E. Lally, 'Secular patronage at the court of King Henry II', BIHR, 49 (1976), 157–84.

Ecclesiastical History of Orderic Vitalis have been more distorted by citation out of context than his comment on the men whom Henry I 'raised from the dust' and 'stationed above earls and famous castellans' and 'made formidable even to the greatest magnates'; men such as Geoffrey of Clinton, Ralph Basset, Hugh Buckland or Rainer of Bath. Orderic had personal knowledge of the spectacular careers of all these men. But he also said that Henry rewarded his loyal supporters with riches and honour; and he went on to describe how Robert of Beaumont, count of Meulan, became earl of Leicester and 'outstripped all the magnates of the realm in wealth and power'. Modern scholars have restored the balance, of which Orderic himself never ceased to be aware, by showing the importance of magnates among Henry's *curiales*.[71] There was a similar mixture of ecclesiastical princes and rising young clerks of promise. Influential bishops like Roger of Salisbury and Richard Belmeis of London, who had risen by their ability, built up ecclesiastical dynasties that lasted through the century; even reforming monk bishops of good birth, like Henry of Blois or Gilbert Foliot, took it for granted that they would use some of their patronage to advance their own kinsfolk. But they also found room in their numerous households for poor scholars of promise and administrators of skill who lacked family backing. This was one of the strengths of Anglo-Norman government at this time. French administration was to develop along different lines, with a more separate administrative class.

Apart from the biennial sessions of the English and Norman exchequers, court and household remained ambulatory with the king, even when the appointment of *ad hoc* commissions became more frequent and regular. Charters and writs that expressed the king's will and pleasure, and set judicial enquiries in motion, originated in the *curia regis*. It is extremely unlikely that pre-conquest dukes of Normandy ever used a seal on privileges; as kings of England they took over the sealed writs of their Anglo-Saxon predecessors, and developed them to meet the changing needs of central government, in Normandy no less than in England.[72] William I kept the services of Regenbald, who had been chancellor under Edward the Confessor and Harold, and some of the English scribes, introducing Normans gradually as they became accustomed to the existing forms of administration; his sons preserved continuity in a similar way on their accession. Chancellors were important household officers

---

[71] Orderic, vi. 16–21; Hollister, *Viator* (1977), 63–81; Hollister, 'Henry I and the Anglo-Norman magnates', *Anglo-Norman Studies*, 2 (1980 for 1979), 93–107.

[72] Fauroux, pp. 45–7; Bates, *Normandy*, pp. 154–5; cf. a reference in a charter of William I to St Stephen at Caen (*c*.1081–87), to the summoning of an expedition 'per brevem meam' (L. Musset, *Les actes de Guillaume le Conquérant et de la reine Mathilde pour les abbayes caennaises* (Caen 1967), no. 4a bis (p. 64).

who frequently earned promotion to bishoprics; they were responsible for the writing chamber (scriptorium) and probably drafted the writs.[73] But increasingly the routine work was taken over by the master of the writing chamber, who was also keeper of the king's seal. Ranulf Flambard, the protégé of William I's chancellor, Maurice, held this office from about 1085; one of the best-known stories of his early career is the Durham chronicler's account of his capture by pirates in the Thames estuary, when he saved the seal from capture by throwing it into the sea. Richard de Capella held office under Henry I until he became bishop of Hereford in 1131. The salary and emoluments of the master of the scriptorium were subsequently more than doubled by Henry for Robert de Sigillo: an indication of his increasing duties and status.[74] But there was no clearly organized chancery as an office of state, and chancery records did not begin until the end of the twelfth century. The secretarial work of administration was carried out by a number of clerks and chaplains who served in both writing chamber and royal chapel. Indeed the royal secretariat that we call, for convenience, the chancery, was frequently referred to in the early twelfth century as the chapel.[75]

The scribes and chaplains did not all travel with the king. Some were sent out with the justices, or were occupied in keeping accounts at one of the treasuries; some were left with the viceregent when the king was in Normandy. Many of them were on the way to advancement as archdeacons, canons or bishops; some were rewarded with substantial estates. A relatively large number of hands of chancery scribes occurs in royal charters up to the later years of Henry II; T. A. M. Bishop identified ten in the period 1135–41, and sixteen in the early years of Henry II (1155–61). Besides these, a number of charters were drafted by the beneficiaries themselves, and taken to the king for sealing.[76]

Bishops' households too in this period were frequented by a large number of clerks, serving as they were needed without specialized appointment, and hoping to earn some advancement by their ability. The career of one of Henry I's clerks, Bernard the Scribe, shows how an Englishman from a good family whose fortunes had declined as a result of the conquest climbed back to high favour by working in the royal chapel and scriptorium. He succeeded in recovering some of the family's lands with the aid of powerful royal servants, including Geoffrey the

---

[73] *Regesta*, i. pp. xv–xvi; ii. pp. ix–xi; Barlow, *William Rufus*, pp. 146–8.

[74] Simeon of Durham, ii. 135–8; *Dialogus de Scaccario*, p. 129.

[75] T. A. M. Bishop, *Scriptores Regis* (Oxford, 1961), pp. 23–4. Fitz Stephen said that Becket as chancellor employed fifty-two clerks on his own and the king's business (Cheney, 'William Fitz Stephen', p. 143).

[76] Orderic, vi. 174–7; P. Chaplais, 'The seals and original charters of Henry I', *EHR*, 75 (1960), 260–75.

Chancellor, Robert de Sigillo, and William the Almoner, amongst whom his working life was spent. The witnesses to the legal decisions in his favour show that a strong *esprit de corps* already existed in the chancellor's staff, and that the chancellor himself looked after his own.[77] If the chancery still barely existed as a distinct office, it was on the way to becoming a separate department of state. It was rapidly adapting itself to the demand of more literate forms of government. By contrast with the chancery of King John, with its letters close and patent and its great series of central records, the organization even of the early Angevin chancery was rudimentary. But a significant step in the 'rise of administrative kingship' had already taken place in the development of writs and exchequer rolls, and their use to exercise central control of justice and finance.

[77] J. H. Round, 'Bernard, the king's scribe', *EHR*, 14 (1899), 417–30; Southern, *Medieval Humanism*, pp. 225–8.

5

The Wealth of England

Rural England

When England is examined in its European setting we can see that 1066 was relatively unimportant in the broad economic changes of the period. From about the tenth century a slow rise in population, well attested if only partly explained and impossible to chart with precision, affected the greater part of western Europe. It continued for some three centuries and was accompanied by further advances of cultivation into woodland and waste. The changes affected both England and Normandy throughout the eleventh and twelfth centuries, becoming more rapid in the last three decades of the twelfth century. Both regions experienced a stimulus to trade; both had flourishing ports and markets; and it would be true to say of Normandy as of England that 'elements of a money economy had penetrated deep into society.'[1] The assessment for danegeld levies speaks for itself in England. In Normandy there was a proliferation of rural 'bourgs', and cash revenues were a not uncommon element in ducal and seignorial gifts to monasteries.[2] Yet this does not alter the fact that both regions were then, and were to remain for some centuries, pre-industrial in the sense that, in spite of numerous (often highly skilled) local crafts and industries, and tenuous lines of both interregional and international trade, the basis of the economy was agrarian. The major stimulus to expanding production and a higher level of surplus wealth came from the advance in the frontiers of land under cultivation, and the possibility of supporting a growing population that included elements significantly above subsistence level.

Domesday Book makes it possible for us to put twenty years of social and economic development in England under the microscope, in a way

---

[1] Miller and Hatcher, pp. 25–6.
[2] L. Musset, 'Peuplement en bourgage et bourgs ruraux en Normandie', *Cahiers de civilisation médiévales*, 9 (1966), 177–208.

not possible elsewhere in Europe at the time or in England for many years afterwards. The period was one of adjustment after the disruption of conquest and the devastation of some regions subjected to the ravaging of armies and the suppression of rebellion. So it is not surprising that the statistics collected by Welldon Finn from the great survey have been cautiously interpreted by him to suggest that in 1086 England had not yet recovered economically from the shock and damage of the military occupation.[3] But this does not mean that in the longer term the conquest should be regarded as an unmitigated disaster for the English, leading to the economic depression of the greater part of the peasantry. Such a view, though still leaving some traces in general histories, no longer holds the field. It would be more appropriate to look at the twenty years from 1066 to 1086 in parallel with the years of Stephen's reign, when disturbances of a very different kind once again caused disruption, affecting local economic and social development dramatically for a short time but rather less spectacularly in the long run.

One of the questions asked by the Domesday commissioners in their various circuits from Yorkshire to Kent, from East Anglia to Cornwall, was 'Who holds this manor?' The term, applied to a wide variety of economic and juridical units, must have been as baffling to many of the men of whom it was asked as it has been to historians ever since; yet it came near enough to an overall reality to be answered in concrete terms, in spite of great regional variations. Maitland's probing analysis, though a little too heavily weighted on the side of geld, still has much to teach us. He offered as one suggested definition, 'A manor is a house against which geld is charged', but admitted that the house had disappeared in some places. If we widen the description to take in more than geld, and see the manor as a centre for the payment of dues in cash, kind and service, we are near to Miller's prudent definition of it as 'equivalent to the rights that a lord had on land and men round his residence'; and this is probably as near to a comprehensive definition as we can ever hope to come.[4] For the manors of Domesday Book range over extremes of size and organization. They include at one end of the scale enormous manors like Leominster, with sixteen members rated at eighty hides, having thirty teams of oxen on demesne and 230 teams owned by the men; or Taunton, said to be worth £154 1s., with land for 100 teams.[5] At the other extreme were the tiny manors of thirty acres or less, particularly

---

[3] R. Welldon Finn, *The Norman Conquest and its Effects on the Economy: 1066–86* (London, 1971), pp. 3–6.

[4] Maitland, *Domesday Book*, pp. 108–20; E. Miller, 'La société rurale en Angleterre (x^e–xiie siècles)', *Agricoltura e mondo rurale in occidente nell'Alto Medioevo* (Settimane 13, Spoleto, 1966), pp. 111–34.

[5] DB, i. 180, 87b.

common in Suffolk and Essex, which a free man could manage with one team and the help of a bordar or two. Some manors had detached berewicks: little centres of dependent demesne cultivation, or outliers of lands held by men in the soke of some lords. Such units of lordship were a survival from a system that had probably been widespread in a great part of England two centuries earlier, and has been called 'extensive lordship'.

The characteristics of this system, most strongly marked in northern and eastern England by the eleventh century, but with discernable traces in many parts of the west, have been summarized by Geoffrey Barrow.[6] Scattered groups of peasants and petty dependents owed suit of court, rent and often labour services of some kind to the manorial centre where the lord resided, at least intermittently. They were described as being 'in his soke'. A system of royal government through local units of hundreds in Wessex and Mercia and wapentakes in the Danelaw was super-imposed upon this in many districts. Soke meant far more than juris-diction. In East Anglia and the northern Danelaw, where most of the centres had English names, the system was older than the tenth-century Danish conquest. Regional variations developed; but attempts to explain them by race have never proved satisfactory, and there were underlying similarities. In parts of the south east (West Suffolk, Cambridgeshire, Hertfordshire and Middlesex) the duties of sokemen included a fixed cash payment, carting or carrying services, acting as bodyguard for the lord or the king when he was in the county, some hospitality, provision of fodder for the lord's horses, mowing the meadow, sometimes making deer hedges, paying suit of court to the three-weekly hundred court, and contributing to the sheriff's aid. They have a very close resemblance to those of the geneat, the honourable companion or retainer described in the pre-conquest treatise known as the *Rectitudines singularum person-arum*.[7] And they are very close both to those of the sokemen in the Danelaw and the radmen or radcnihts of the West Midlands in Domesday Book. A comparable system prevailed in the 'shires' of Northumbria. The whole system must have implied the existence of domestic slaves or demesne serfs for arable cultivation, at the same time as a ministerial or service group of horse-owning sokemen and geneats.

The most important groups of estates organized to provide for the needs of a great ambulatory household in 1066 were the royal estates. Like the great Carolingian estates, these had been organized at an early date to provide for the maintenance of the royal court during a specified number of days. The unit in which the liability was expressed was the

[6] Barrow, *Kingdom of the Scots*, pp. 9–27; see also *The Kalendar of Abbot Samson of Bury St Edmunds and related Documents*, ed. R. H. C. Davis (Camden 3rd ser., 84 (1954)), pp. xl, xlv–xlvii.
[7] Liebermann, i. 444–53; translation in *EHD*, ii. 813–16.

'farm of one night' or, less frequently, of one day. Because the productivity of the land might vary over a period for many reasons, and the size of the estates fluctuated when old properties were given away or new lands acquired, these farms were reorganized from time to time. The requirements of the king in cash or kind varied in different parts of his domains, and there was an overall movement in the eleventh century towards payments in cash. The Domesday record for 1066 preserves traces of a long period of historical change, in ancient renders and dues shaped by earlier organization or regional characteristics. Unlike geological fossils, the fossilized remains of custom are not here deposited in successive strata; up to 1066 they are all in the same layer of documentation, but attempts to date them have yielded some valuable results.[8] They bear the traces of active reorganization after the kingdoms of East Anglia and Mercia were acquired by Wessex, and of much greater intensity of organization in some of the Wessex shires nearest to the heart of royal government in the eleventh century.

Responsibility for the revenues from the royal estates lay with the sheriff, though officials under him were more directly concerned with the management of individual properties. In Wiltshire, Somerset and Dorset the royal lands were grouped most neatly to provide the farm of one night, on a scale that might genuinely have supported the royal court. Arrangements elsewhere were more variable, though in Oxfordshire, where the county as a whole rendered a farm of three nights, the farm seems already to have become a unit of valuation for assessing the total value of the shire. Other variations occur, such as those in the shires north of the Thames where dues combined money payments, including some renders associated with hunting, with renders in kind, particularly honey. The payments of the sheriff for Warwickshire in 1066 were estimated at £65 and thirty-six sextars of honey or £24 8s. Cambridgeshire manors owed a similar mixture of cash payments and dues expressed in farm units of honey, corn and malt, many of which were in the process of commutation to cash payments. The Domesday figures for 1086 show further changes in the organization of demesne management, some of which were certainly a continuation of the movement away from kind to cash that had already become important in many of the royal estates before 1066. Others suggest a tightening control of more of the shire dues and renders, together with the pleas of the county, in a single sheriff's farm.

Administrative needs and economic change bore in different ways on

---

[8] P. A. Stafford, 'The "Farm of One Night" and the organization of King Edward's estates in Domesday', *Economic History Review*, 2nd ser., 33 (1980), 491–502; Lennard, *Rural England*, pp. 128–30, 142–6.

the prosperity and freedom of the peasants and lesser gentry. But it was extensive lordship of the kind exemplified on most early great estates no less than on the royal estates, and not the mythical 'free village community' visualized by nineteenth-century historians, that underlay much later manorialization, even though other factors were at work. The most basic characteristic of manorialization was the development of a demesne to which peasant holdings were tributary: in its simplest form it was the home farm giving rise to labour services, both week works and boon works. Ploughing services were of great importance. But lordship extended beyond the arable fields to the waste and pasture. Whatever rights the free peasants, who were settled in varying numbers in the majority of villages and owed only occasional dues or services to a lord, may have enjoyed in the woodland and waste appendent to each village, the lower strata of peasantry owed rents and services such as grassearth for grazing or pannage for turning pigs into the woods. These reflect the economic subordination of the different kinds of dependent holdings to the lord's demesne. All these types of services and dues were widespread in the early part of the eleventh century, as the duties of the substantial working tenant known as the gebur in the *Rectitudines* illustrate; and some manorialization spread even into the regions where extensive lordship was most persistent.

Manorialization came about in various ways. Sometimes a group of settlements making up a soke or northern shire lost outlying members, which became more intensively cultivated. The formation of new manors might result from the division of property between heirs and the dowering of daughters, according to local inheritance customs. T. H. Aston has shown how, in the period long before Domesday, family arrangements providing for division between co-heirs had contributed to the break-up of lordships into smaller units, and sometimes to the formation of several manors within a single village. He has also shown the opposite process at work, when outgrowths from a discrete manor led to the establishment of new manors. Sometimes settlements, such as those round temporary pasture lands, came into existence with a manorial structure from the start. Elsewhere a substantial new settler moving into previously uncultivated land might attract a group of poorer men willing to accept the obligations of manorial lordship in return for small holdings of their own.[9]

Another influence was economic pressure: increased taxation or population growth might lead to more intensive cultivation of the land and greater concentration of peasant settlement. A third factor was the settlement on the land of military dependents who had once lived in the

[9] Aston, *Social Relations and Ideas*, pp. 20–5, 29–30, 37–9.

lord's hall. This had begun in the pre-conquest period; from the ninth century thegns were taking root in the English soil, and eleventh-century housecarls were holding lands in the reign of Edward the Confessor.[10] After the conquest the gradual enfeoffment of knights had the same effect of producing large numbers of resident lords of manors: men of middling means interested in the cultivation of their home farms for the support of their families. They had a more permanent interest in the properties than the earlier farmers on the great estates, though some of the farmers succeeded in establishing a hereditary claim to the estates they administered. Stenton has shown how part of a soke might be converted into an estate of the manorial type, as in the village of Norton Disney. In 1086 it had no demesne; there were seven sokemen and eleven villeins with five teams, and it was sokeland of the Countess Judith's manor of Stapleford. By the mid-twelfth century Robert, son of Turketin, who held it, confirmed to the abbey of Newhouse ten ploughlands of his demesne in Norton and four acres of demesne which his man Hyngolf held of him and had given with his consent.[11] Robert typifies an important gentry element in society, ready to create demesnes in regions where they did not find them ready made.

Even if villein services existed on many manors where arable demesne lands were cultivated, eleventh-century lords could choose whether to take them in cash or labour. Their choice depended on whether they wished to feed their own households for all or part of the year with the produce of particular manors, and what their requirements were. The needs of monasteries, bishops, great lay lords, knights or the administrative servants and others who held small estates of their own varied very greatly; so did their capacity to oversee and manage their demesnes. They were influenced too by the availability and cost of labour and, increasingly as time went on, by the attractions of the market. The lord's requirements, conditioned partly by economic factors, partly by political change, set up a chain reaction which affected the peasantry at every level. One cannot expect to find any constant ratio between the size of demesne arable lands and the week works demanded from the villeins. Conditions varied between regions and between estates; fluctuations in the size of the demesne might have totally different consequences in the late eleventh century and a hundred years later.

Any large arable estate needed a core of permanent farm servants: the *famuli*, of whom ploughmen and stockmen were the most important.[12]

[10] For housecarls see N. Hooper, 'The housecarls in England in the eleventh century', forthcoming in *Anglo-Norman Studies*, 7 (1985 for 1984).

[11] Stenton, *Danelaw Documents*, p. cviii.

[12] M. Postan, 'The *Famulus*: the estate labourer in the twelfth and thirteenth centuries', *Economic History Review*, Supplement no. 2.

In many manors described in Domesday Book the ploughmen were slaves, living in the lord's house. But death, emancipation, and the low birth rate normally found in any slave economy mean that slavery can be profitable only if there is a constant supply of new slaves through trade, war, raiding or penal loss of freedom. As internal wars became less frequent, and the church set its face against the enslavement of Christians by their fellow Christians, the slave trade was gradually stamped out and the economic basis of slavery undermined. The serf ploughmen of Domesday Book were already a declining class; many demesne ploughs were driven by smaller tenants called bordars or *bubulci* who were former slaves. These hutted serfs, by whatever name they were known, held their own few acres and in return gave one or two days' ploughing service every week to their lord; many of them worked for him on other days in return for wages. Some probably worked for the more prosperous villein or free tenants if the demesne requirements were small; their own few acres would neither support their families nor occupy all their time. Other sources of labour were provided by the villeins themselves; one or two might serve for a year or two as *famuli*, paid in cash and weekly food liveries, and by the remission of various customary dues. At such times their wives and children, with the aid perhaps of paid labour, must have worked their own holdings. A third type of *famuli* were the wage labourers, paid and fed entirely by the lord. The disappearance of the class of slaves did not cause the collapse of the demesne economy; lords had a choice of other ways of cultivating the lands they wished to exploit directly. Evidence of the increase in some peasant services in the Domesday returns suggests that at that date there may have been a shortage of men, and lords met increased demands for gelds and other levies by a more ruthless exploitation of the works and dues they could claim from their peasants. As population increased they were more ready to commute services and pay wage labour; the population boom of the late twelfth century left them unusually free to choose what they would demand.

The arrival of the Normans brought new settlers of knightly status who helped to speed up the process of manorialization. In so doing they certainly depressed the status of some of the peasantry. In places, particularly in Yorkshire and Staffordshire and part of the Welsh border, the armies ravaged the land and left it waste for a time. But not all the 'waste' of Domesday Book was barren and uncultivated; the term might also be applied to lands that for any reason were not paying geld,[13] and the most fertile of the devastated regions were resettled within a generation. Larger units of cultivation, as individual Norman magnates took

---

[13] Green, *EHR* (1981), 252.

over the lands of many thegns, generated greater capital resources. The lords of great estates, whether lay or ecclesiastical, had the capital necessary to restock and bring under cultivation both lands that were temporarily waste and others that had never known the plough. They could afford to drain marsh and fen land, and to build new mills. Settlement could expand into woodland and on heavy soils where more equipment and labour were necessary. In the long run assarting in difficult regions, as well as expansion in poorer, upland areas where the soils were marginal, more than offset the lands taken out of cultivation by castle building or by the restrictions on agriculture produced by the Norman kings in the forests they protected for their hunting. Indeed, cultivation was permitted in the forests outside the coverts for game; licences to assart became a valuable new source of royal revenue, and acres of scrub or rough woodland were brought under the plough.[14] And the settlement on assarted lands of new peasant families stimulated a rise in population that was already perceptible in the early twelfth century, though it did not gather speed and have dramatic effects on inflation and labour conditions until the later years of Henry II.[15]

The demands a great lord made on his manors depended on their place in the administration of his honours. Domesday can never give a complete picture, because many of William I's greatest vassals held cross-Channel estates. Part of their residence was on their Norman lands, and for part of the year they followed the king's court, wherever it happened to be. The concern of the first generation after the conquest was to establish a firm base in their English honours, with castles at points that were strategically necessary; and to make provision for supporting their households intermittently at least in any castle or other residence chosen as the caput of an honour. The existence of a large demesne at a suitable strategic point may have helped to determine the location of a castle; if necessary the demesne would be enlarged, or other provision made for supplying the household. Ancient or newly developed markets could be exploited; cash renders might be preferred to demesne produce. Provision had to be made for knights, either in the household or in houses nearby, or on lands of their own. All but enfeoffed knights with sufficient lands for their support received stipends and many were partly fed in the lord's court. Methods of military organization must have had their impact on estate management, though the details are often difficult to discover. The Montgomery-Bellême family had exceptionally large cash revenues from their lands in Normandy and France; but Roger of

[14] Young, *The Royal Forests*; *Dialogus de Scaccario*, p. 57.
[15] P. D. A. Harvey, 'The English inflation of 1180–1220', *Past and Present*, 61 (1973), 3–30; J. C. Russell, *British Medieval Population* (Albuquerque, 1948).

Montgomery found it convenient to have two very large demesnes at Singleton and Harting, near to his castle of Arundel, and this was only one side of demesne production favoured by his family. Robert of Bellême brought horses from Spain to breed on his Shropshire estates, an important step providing war horses for his military needs.[16]

Richard of Clare greatly increased the sheep flocks on his English lands, thereby both improving their fertility and providing cash revenues. Ernulf of Hesdin was praised by William of Malmesbury for his 'wonderful skill in agriculture', and the increased values of his Domesday manors prove that this was no empty rhetoric.[17] On the other hand, many lords were interested more in cash revenues than in increasing demesne production. But the suggestion that they were 'foreign lords ... who used their English lands simply to fund Continental adventures' is very wide of the mark.[18] Even if many of the first generation of Normans thought of their Norman lands as the patrimonial inheritance to pass on to their heirs, they were working to make their English acquisitions into new patrimonies. The next generation thought even more clearly of the family lands, wherever they might be, as a single inheritance. Some branches of a family became more firmly settled in England, others in Normandy; many held and acquired possessions in both regions. They became denizens, not foreigners, on both sides of the Channel. Some resources went to the maintenance of military households and to wars, particularly in the Welsh marches and on the Scottish border; some were used to finance crusades and pilgrimages, or to endow religious houses.

It might occasionally happen that a lord left the running of his English honours largely to his household officers. For example Stephen, count of Aumale and lord of Holderness, rarely came to England and then mostly followed the royal court. He drew cash revenues from England, some of which he granted to St Martin of Auchy in 1115. But in his lifetime the coast defended by the castles of Holderness was not threatened. And the leading vassals of the honour such as Fauconberg, St Quentin and Ros, who had made their homes in the lordship under his predecessors, built up their wealth both in Holderness and in the neighbouring counties by marriage alliances. They founded lasting families.[19] Stephen's relation to Holderness was that of a lord of many honours, who maintained his military obligations in all of them, but resided most frequently in some; and those favoured residences, which did not include the bleak, oat-growing lands of Holderness, were the collecting points for any surplus

[16] Harvey, *Social Relations and Ideas*, pp. 55–7; Giraldus Cambrensis, *Itinerarium Kambriae, Opera* (RS), vi. 143.

[17] Lennard, *Rural England*, pp. 210–12.

[18] Harvey, *Social Relations and Ideas*, p. 70.

[19] English, *Holderness*, pp. 14–16, 145–56.

revenues. But his son, William le Gros, put down lasting roots in Yorkshire.[20]

There were sound general reasons for maintaining a balance between demesne cultivation and cash renders, and they were economic rather than political reasons. At the time of the Domesday survey and for some decades afterwards the balance tipped slightly in favour of cash renders. One reason may have been a shortage of manpower; the ravages of war and famine had to be made good before the population rise became significant. A second was the absence of a sufficiently strong market incentive. Markets were numerous and were increasing in numbers both in manorial centres and in new towns. But they met the needs primarily of the immediate locality, providing outlets for the surplus produce of small landholders as much as great lords, and feeding the inhabitants of castles and towns, very few of which had more than 3,000 or 4,000 inhabitants.[21] By the thirteenth century population growth had driven up prices, making production for the market attractive and labour abundant and cheap, quite apart from the resources that could be wrung out of villein obligations. The lords of Domesday lived in a different world. They acquired demesnes of varying size and potential; individuals chose different ways of exploiting their resources, but relatively few of the great lay tenants had any immediate incentive to increase any arable demesnes other than those that supplied their chief residences, provided they could find the resources to maintain their way of life and pay their taxes by any other means. Undoubtedly the increasing demands of the kings for aids, gifts and gelds in cash contributed to their need to increase the value of their estates. This was done most easily by letting the demesnes out for higher farms, taking the profits of mills, raising the rents of rent-paying tenants, and exploiting all possible seignorial and judicial dues to which they were entitled. In many places this led to increased burdens on the peasantry; but wherever woodland, waste or upland was available there was a possibility of increasing profits by settling rent-paying tenants on new holdings. Even at this date there was a marked difference between the condition of the peasants on colonizing and non-colonizing manors.[22]

Peasant assarting was often encouraged by lords with an eye both to increasing their available labour force and swelling their rent rolls, and these men tended to enjoy a greater measure of economic independence.

[20] The Meaulx Abbey Chronicle speaks disparagingly of soils capable of growing only oats (*avena*, incorrectly translated by English, *Holderness* as 'wild oats'). *Chronica monasterii de Melsa*, ed. E. A. Bond, RS (1866–8), i. 90–8; cf. Kapelle, pp. 214–30.

[21] Reynolds, *Medieval Towns*, pp. 36–7.

[22] See J. Z. Titow, 'Some differences between manors and their effects on the condition of the peasants in the thirteenth century', *Agricultural History Review*, 10 (1962), 1–13.

For example, numerous relatively free peasants settled in the Arden region of Warwickshire during a phase of post-conquest colonization. The growth of freedom, which T. H. Aston saw as complementary to the growth of the manor in the Old English period, continued after the conquest, and for much the same economic and social reasons.[23] The interest of the lords consisted as much in the increased rents paid both by new settlers and by the farmers of thriving manors as in the direct exploitation of their demesnes. In the twelfth century a number of lords, like the monks of St Benet of Hulme or the canons of St Paul's, London, included in their farm leases provision for an increase in rent after some years, or, if the lease was for two or three lives, on the succession of a new life.[24] Others, particularly some of the newer religious orders, favoured acquisitions in unsettled areas; some chose to combine demesne cultivation by wage labour with the establishment of a rent-paying peasantry. The Cistercians, best known for these enterprises, were by no means alone; another striking example is the establishment by the Templars of a thriving community at Temple Bruer in the heath-lands of Lincolnshire during the reign of Henry II.[25]

For much of the century after the Norman conquest the men who had the closest interest in demesne cultivation were the honorial barons and knights, like Robert son of Turketin, and the farmers holding individual manors or groups of manors on the great estates. Some of these men added to their original holdings by purchase, inheritance, or marriage; later royal records or private surveys indicate the outline of their properties. They left, unfortunately, no direct accounts of their methods of estate management. But their careers illustrate the degree of social mobility that was possible, at least for those who could place one foot firmly on the ladder of advancement. Private, no less than royal, service offered almost unlimited opportunities for gain to the members of the ministerial class. In the early twelfth century a great household, like that of the abbot of Ramsey, employed in addition to its steward, chamberlain, constable and marshall, a multitude of cooks, masons, ostlers, and a baker, brewer, cordwainer, glazier, vintner and interpreter.[26] Men such as these might be settled on lands appropriate to their status, in the same way that household knights were enfeoffed, except that their tenure was usually not by military service. This gave them the initial stake necessary to attempt the gamble of territorial advancement. If the retired harpist

[23] R. H. Hilton, *The English Peasantry in the Later Middle Ages* (Oxford, 1975), pp. 122–3; Aston, *Social Relations and Ideas*, pp. 1–43.

[24] Lennard, *Rural England*, pp. 182–4.

[25] B. A. Lees, *Records of the Templars in England in the Twelfth Century* (British Academy, Records of Social and Economic History, 9 (1935)), pp. clxxxii–clxxxiii.

[26] J. A. Raftis, *The Estates of Ramsey Abbey* (Toronto, 1957), p. 51.

was prepared to settle happily on a cottage tenement others, particularly the greater stewards, were more acquisitive. And the farmers of manors, whatever their initial wealth and status, might if they were appointed and reappointed over a long period learn to know the estates and help to improve their productivity. For them the next step was to secure a hereditary right.

Most agreements were verbal at the time of Domesday. Written farm contracts came into existence in the course of the twelfth century. Records of customs make it plain that stock and land leases were common.[27] These could be either for a term of years or for one or two lives. The Normans appear, initially, to have taken over the leases as they found them; their own leases in the duchy tended rather to metayage, a form of crop sharing. But the strengthening of principles of tenure that resulted from the conquest had its influence here too. The ambition of many farmers was to convert their lease into a hereditary fee farm. In principle the two were distinct; the *Leges Henrici primi* distinguished between the farmer who held his farm in fee and had done homage for it in the lord's court from the farmer who was not his lord's feudal man and was answerable in the manor court.[28] But practice may have been less clear cut, particularly if a farmer held some other tenement on feudal terms, and time often ran in his favour. The disorders of Stephen's reign in particular gave opportunities to the ambitious. When the *curia regis* rolls begin in the late twelfth century they reveal many lords in litigation with farmers who claimed to hold their farms in fee. The abbey of Bury St Edmunds had to give way after long litigation to farmers who had entrenched themselves in the manors of Semer and Groton during Stephen's reign.[29] The abbess of Caen succeeded in buying off the claims of Simon of Felsted's family only at considerable expense in land and money. Almost every substantial religious house had similar problems.

The career of Simon of Felsted is an interesting case of social change.[30] In the reign of Henry I he held an eight-acre tenement in the abbey's manor of Felsted in Essex for 8*d*. rent and regular week works. Unless he held other lands outside the fee of the abbess, of which there is no evidence, he was then a man of humble status, who was employed to farm the manor on behalf of the abbess of Caen. Owing to difficulties in communication between Normandy and England during the wars of Stephen's reign, he took over the administration of all the abbey's other English manors, situated in Norfolk, Gloucestershire, Wiltshire and Dorset. Over a period of some twenty years he steadily entrenched

---

[27] Lennard, *Rural England*, pp. 195–6.
[28] *Leges Henrici*, 56. 1, 2 (pp. 174–5).
[29] See below, ch. 6.
[30] Chibnall, *Charters and Custumals of Caen*, pp. xl–xlii.

himself, particularly in Felsted and Minchinhampton, by bringing new land under cultivation, establishing his own tenants there, and clearing woods without regard to the long-term interest of the abbess. When communications were restored, it was not possible to dislodge him. He obtained some property outside the fee, including a tenement in London which he held by charter of Queen Eleanor, had his Essex holdings confirmed by Henry II, and claimed to hold all the abbey's manors by hereditary fee farm. Ultimately the abbess succeeded in buying off the claims of his son William to the fee farm, and took her principal manors back into demesne; but William was left in possession of a new manor in Felsted so substantial that he was able to marry into a great feudal family and establish his descendants as knights of the shire.

Since Felsted was a colonizing manor with opportunities for bringing former woodland under the plough, the aggrandizement of its farmer did not lead to a general economic depression of the peasantry. Services were more exactly defined rather than increased; there were opportunities for the more prosperous to enlarge their holdings and set up their children. The manor had more free tenants than a hundred years previously, as well as a continuing core of villeinage and a demesne that was soon restored through new assarting to its former size. By contrast, some farmers and lords were undoubtedly oppressive, especially in their demands for increased rents and renders. And wherever men were scarce lords tended to press their demands for labour services to the limit that custom allowed. The greatest change came slowly in the legal condition of the *villani*, but that was part of a great transformation of the law and its application in the courts.[31]

Towns

Eleventh-century England was well placed to share both in the Scandinavian and North Sea trade (which included the northern Viking route to Ireland and thence across the Irish Sea), and in the cross-Channel trade with Normandy and northern France, the Low Countries and the Rhineland. About the year 1000 London was already visited regularly by traders from Rouen and elsewhere in Normandy, the Isle de France, Ponthieu, Flanders, the towns of Huy, Liège and Nivelles, and parts of Germany.[32] External trade and internal colonization stimulated the growth of urban centres. There was an abundant supply of good silver currency, strictly regulated by the crown; over eighty mints, all situated

[31] See below, pp. 187–91.
[32] Reynolds, *Medieval Towns*, p. 39.

in towns, were active during the tenth and eleventh centuries. At a conservative estimate, at least 5,000,000 silver pennies to the value of £25,000 must have been in circulation at any time. Since the silver content of British ores was low, the silver mines of Derbyshire, the Mendips, Wales and elsewhere cannot have met more than a fraction of the demand. Silver must have been a major import; probably the supply came from Germany, and was paid for with wool exports.[33]

The scale of urbanization must not be exaggerated; at the time of the Domesday survey although, according to Darby's calculations, over 100 places were called towns or included burgesses among their inhabitants, only seven towns had populations much above 4,000, and only thirty-two had over 1,000.[34] The numerous smaller places would have been little more than villages by modern standards; but the figures stand up to comparison with those in most parts of northern Europe at the time.

The Norman conquest had some effect on the topography and scale of urban settlement through the building of new castles, monasteries and cathedrals. Administrative changes affected the prosperity of towns that were active centres of government, and ports that were involved in the increased cross-Channel traffic. Ports were enlarged to meet increased shipping in many commodities, ranging from the Caen stone that was in great demand for building cathedrals and churches to the herrings that some Norman lords exported from English fishing ports to their continental lands. Castle building in an existing town necessitated the demolition of houses on the site, as in York, Lincoln, Norwich, Shrewsbury and elsewhere; yet the need to supply the castle must often have led to house building in a new quarter. Where castles were built or monasteries founded in the country, as at Tutbury or Battle, urban settlement normally sprang up at their gates. The new abbey of Shrewsbury stimulated the growth of a flourishing suburb, across the river from the castle.

The Conqueror's new abbey of Battle immediately attracted settlers; a reference to twenty-one tenants (*bordarii*) in 1086 reveals the nucleus of a community, and within twenty years the abbey's first rental listed 115 tenants of burgages in the town. Some were ploughmen and oxherds, occupied with agricultural work; but they included smiths, cooks, cobblers, bakers, brewers, carpenters and stewards, and a cordwainer, leather-worker, weaver, bell-founder and goldsmith. Bury St Edmunds, a pre-conquest foundation, built 342 houses between 1066 and 1086 on former arable land.[35] New and expanding settlements attracted some Normans and other immigrants, the Frenchmen of Domesday Book. The

[33] Dolley, *English Coinage*; P. H. Sawyer, 'The wealth of England in the eleventh century', *TRHS*, 5th ser., 15 (1965), 145–64.

[34] Reynolds, *Medieval Towns*, pp. 36–7.

[35] *Battle Chronicle*, pp. 53–9; Reynolds, *Medieval Towns*, p. 41.

Battle chronicle recorded that, as the building of the new abbey church progressed, 'a great number of men were recruited, many from the neighbouring districts and some from across the Channel.' Some 40 per cent of the first burgesses had continental names.[36] But skilled English craftsmen were valued everywhere; knowledge of a craft was one of the surest ways for an English family to survive and even to prosper. In particular, William I left the mints in the hands of the experienced moneyers who were already working; until the major changes of Henry II's reign most of the moneyers came from families of English or Danish descent.

Battle was a relatively simple example of a small seignorial borough owing its existence to the foundation of an abbey. Some trading and military settlements like Newark, which were not described as boroughs in Domesday Book, had a sizeable community of burgesses and grew rapidly as urban centres.[37] Many influences contributed to the emergence of new towns. Some gained importance through improvements in river navigation. Trade, industry and defence all played a part alongside seignorial interest in the growth of Lynn towards the end of the eleventh century. Salt making was an important and long-established industry along the coasts of eastern England; Domesday Book recorded salt-pans in thirty-four Lincolnshire and sixty-three Norfolk villages, with some important concentrations around the shores of the Wash. A group of small settlements round the estuary of the Gaywood river, where the port of Lynn was later established, had seventy-two salt-pans. There was multiple ownership in the growing town, as in the salt-making centres of the west country, where numerous lords and religious houses acquired small shares in the salt-works of Nantwich and the bishop of Worcester's thriving town of Droitwich.[38] Ralph of Tosny, the lord of Rising and the abbot of Bury all had holdings in Lynn, but the dominant interest was that of the bishop of East Anglia, shortly to establish his seat at Norwich. The need to defend the vulnerable east coast estuaries led to the siting of William of Warenne's castle at Rising; this with his new Cluniac priory at Castle Acre stimulated the market economy of the hinterland. The trade, both export and internal, in salt and salt herrings from the local fisheries as well as corn from the extensive area drained by the Ouse and other rivers of the Wash, encouraged the growth of the port. Overseas merchants from Scandinavia, Germany and Flanders were attracted in larger numbers to Lynn no less than to the older ports of Boston and Yarmouth.

[36] Clark, *Anglo-Norman Studies* (1980), 28–9.
[37] For Newark see *Documents relating to the Manor and Soke of Newark-on-Trent*, ed. M. W. Barley et al. (Thoroton Society Record Series, 16, 1956), pp. xvii–xix.
[38] H. C. Darby, *The Domesday Geography of Eastern England* (Cambridge, 1952), pp. 69–72, 134–6; Dyer, *Lords and Peasants*, p. 32; *VCH Shropshire*, ii. 63, 72.

The bishop played his part in securing market privileges and encouraging settlement. But at a time of general economic growth, established industry and potentially important trade routes, both local and international, were as influential in the rise of Lynn as any changes in the pattern of defence and ecclesiastical organization resulting from the Norman conquest.[39]

The town of Lynn emerged slowly from a cluster of villages and hamlets; small towns were still half rural in outlook. At Battle the craftsmen lived alongside the farm servants, and almost all the holders of burgage tenements had to spend a day mowing the meadow and another making malt, as well as repairing the mill. Even when we study the larger towns we find that we have, as Maitland observed, fields and pastures on our hands.[40] The larger towns, however, had a more complex economic structure, and were more affected by the changes in the nerve centres of government. Winchester, London, York and Lincoln were influenced in different ways by the aftermath of the conquest.

Winchester was omitted from the Domesday survey, but a survey was made c.1110 and another in 1148. The publication of these surveys and an intensive archaeological study of the site conducted by Martin Biddle have made it possible to examine the Norman city in the process of change.[41] Winchester, the ancient capital of Wessex, was a royal, fortified borough, in which the bishop had a well-established interest. At the time of the conquest it was still the seat of a royal palace and the place where much of the treasure was kept; it had a royal castle, ancient monasteries and a cathedral. It was near to the port of Southampton, and to what became, after the making of the New Forest, a favourite hunting ground. William I put the seal of his succession to the Anglo-Saxon kingdom by taking over the court ceremonial of Winchester, which was continued into the early part of Henry I's reign. The king wore his crown there at Easter, the greatest festival in the Christian year, whenever he was in the kingdom. He enlarged the royal palace, and the bishop rebuilt the cathedral on a scale that was more than half as large again as King Edward's abbey at Westminster. The castle too was greatly enlarged; the treasure had been moved there by the end of the eleventh century, and soon afterwards the living apartments were extended. Although building work involved some demolition of existing houses, recovery was very rapid, and the impressive investment in public works, which continued for about fifty or sixty years, soon brought prosperity. In 1130 the figures

[39] For the early history of Lynn see D. M. Owen, *The Making of King's Lynn* (British Academy, Records of Social and Economic History, new ser., 9, 1984); Owen. 'Bishop's Lynn', *Anglo-Norman Studies*, 2 (1980 for 1979), 141–53.

[40] F. W. Maitland, *Township and Borough* (Cambridge, 1898), p. 9.

[41] See Biddle, *Winchester*.

of contributions owed to the borough aid show Winchester (120 marks) second only to London (180 marks); next came Lincoln (90 marks), York (60 marks) and Norwich (45 marks).[42]

The town's importance as a centre of the court and of financial administration meant that a number of lay magnates and also some household officers, like Ranulf Flambard and Roger of Salisbury, had houses there. Their presence attracted a solid core of prosperous trades-people, and in addition there was a growing cloth manufacture. Al-together some forty trades were represented, including goldsmiths; the tanners and shield-makers had their own streets. The moneyers were prominent; as elsewhere most if not all were English. Eleven out of sixteen definitely had Old English names, and the others may have been of mixed descent or have owed their names to changing baptismal fashions. The presence of the court and the royal officials did, however, bring an exceptionally large proportion of Normans into the city; 61 per cent of all citizens in the 1110 survey had continental names, and though this is not definite proof of origin the presumption is that many of them were Normans and that most had at least one continental parent.

The prosperity of Winchester was affected by the gradual disengage-ment of the court and administration from the city. This was beginning in Henry I's reign; after 1108 he only once (in 1123) wore his crown at the Easter court at Winchester, and thereafter no king spent Easter there until 1176. After William Rufus built his great new hall in Westminster, the royal palace there increased in importance as a place of residence. During Stephen's reign the bishop steadily gained in importance as the king receded. Henry of Blois took over the old palace at Winchester and fortified it; it was burnt during the siege of 1141, and the materials were used to enlarge the episcopal palace at Wolvesey. The royal withdrawal was gradual; the treasure remained in the castle, and the exchequer sessions were still held there in the early years of Henry II. In addition, Henry of Blois's wealth, importance and patronage of the arts partly compensated for the diminishing royal presence. But political importance had declined, and London was fast rising commercially at the expense of Winchester; it even acted as a magnet for population as far westward as Hampshire.

York was another regional centre involved in political change.[43] For the great northern city, one-time capital of a Viking kingdom and still the established seat of the northern archbishopric, the conquest meant at first diminished stature and a decline in prosperity. The wars and rebellions in

[42] Ibid., pp. 487, 501.
[43] For its history see A. C. Dickens and E. Miller, 'Medieval York', in *VCH Yorks.*, *The City of York* (1961), pp. 25–54.

which York suffered during the first years of Norman rule, and the building of substantial fortifications within the city, both had a catastrophic effect on the population which was probably reduced by half to between 4,000 and 5,000. A symptom of economic decline was the reduction of the number of licensed moneyers from twelve, which equalled London, to four. But Thomas of Bayeux, elected archbishop in 1070, was typical of the Norman episcopate in the energy he devoted to restoring the cathedral and establishing a well-endowed, well-housed cathedral clergy. The interest of the archbishop helped to revive trade and bring back craftsmen to the city; the tolls collected show that by the end of the century trade was creeping up again. Within a few decades William of Malmesbury could describe York as a 'very great town and a metropolitan see', though it still bore the scars of conquest, and the Norman kings preferred lands south of the Humber.[44] This was accurately observed, for Henry I visited it only four or five times; good relations with Scotland enabled him to leave the north to the care of his deputies and the northern barons. In the 1130 borough aid its contribution was only half that of Winchester.

York's greater national prominence began to return in Stephen's reign. With Scots rule temporarily restored in Cumbria and Scottish armies threatening Yorkshire, the city was in the front line of defence and on the main route to the north. Stephen, as his impotence to rule effectively in large areas of the west country increased, attached great importance to holding the loyalty of the north. He visited the city in 1142 and again in 1149, when he was warmly welcomed by the citizens. As a result of increasing regional autonomy under his weak rule the activities of local mints increased. There were signs of anarchy in the loss of contact with the die cutters of London, and in the issues of baronial coins by such barons as Eustace fitz John and Robert of Stuteville.[45] These, however, were temporary disturbances. York was climbing back to a position of wealth and political importance.

In the early years of the twelfth century Lincoln enjoyed greater wealth than York. At the time of the conquest it was an important trading centre and mint town, with a population of over 6,000, actively involved in trade with Norway and elsewhere.[46] In spite of some disturbances caused by the building of the minster and castle, the establishment of a bishopric increased its importance. A community of Jews settled there, as at York, and engaged in financial business. Many of the leading notables remained undisturbed throughout the period, particularly the lawmen and the

[44] Malmesbury, *GP*, pp. 208–9, 'urbs ampla et metropolis'.
[45] King, *TRHS* (1984), 150–1.
[46] See Hill, *Medieval Lincoln*, chs 2, 3.

moneyers, who continued to bear English or Scandinavian names. Some citizens acted as bankers; one, probably the wealthy moneyer Arcil, was believed to be looking after the deposited treasure of King Magnus of Norway and acting as an agent to purchase supplies for his household.[47] The strategic importance of the city, which dominated the route to the north, made it a battle ground between the king and Earl Ranulf of Chester, son of the great Lincolnshire heiress Lucy, during Stephen's reign. The citizens took the king's side; in their wish to be independent of magnate sheriffs and castellans who claimed office as a hereditary right their interests were at one with his. After the battle of Lincoln in 1141 the forces of the earls of Chester and Gloucester took vengeance by killing and burning. But the set-back was temporary. Like the other regional centres at Exeter, Norwich and Bristol,[48] Lincoln enjoyed an important place in the economic life of the province that ensured its rapid recovery from war and looting.

Only one English town was developing on a scale that would make it comparable in population, wealth and diversity of occupations with the great cities of Flanders and northern Europe, and that was London. Its safe harbourage drew ships of all nations. The road system marked it out as the commercial centre of the country, and it was steadily becoming the main centre of government. Before the end of Henry II's reign, Fitz Stephen, in an account of London that glows with rhetoric, could describe it as 'the capital of the kingdom of the English'. There are no reliable population figures; 15,000 to 20,000 is little more than a speculative guess, though the figure of nearly 1,000 for the city militia, given in *Gesta Stephani*, is a plausible one.[49] But its potential for growth in wealth, financial expertise, international contacts, and internal trade that was more than merely regional, was immense. Important aspects of civic life continued to be dominated by the great feudal families who held Baynard and Montfichet castles and struggled to secure a hereditary right to the constableship of the Tower; but alongside them a class of wealthy citizens was rising and demanding a controlling voice in city politics.[50]

Edward the Confessor made a significant move when he built his great abbey church at Westminster, and from the time of Harold Westminster was the place of crowning for the kings of England. One of William I's first acts, even before his coronation, was to send a party ahead to London to raise a castle in the city; and once crowned he completed the fortifications in London 'to contain the restlessness of its vast and savage

[47] Orderic, vi. 48–51.

[48] For Bristol and Norwich see *The Atlas of Historic Towns*, ed. M. D. Lobel, vol. 2 (London, 1975).

[49] *EHD*, ii. 956–62; *Gesta Stephani*, pp. 128–31.

[50] For the growth of London in this period see Brooke, *London*.

population. For he saw it was of first importance to hold down the Londoners', as William of Poitiers wrote.[51] His principal castle, the Tower of London, was built just to the east of the city; other early fortifications included Baynard and Montfichet castles. His son, William Rufus, completed the building of the White Tower; he also took another step towards London and away from Winchester when he built the great hall at Westminster. Henry I's reign brought active reorganization and greater centralization of government; and in Henry II's reign the exchequer account was held with increasing frequency at Westminster. This was followed by the establishment of regular judicial sessions in London before the end of the century. More and more of the leading churchmen and magnates acquired houses in the city; and in Fitz Stephen's words, 'in them they live and spend largely, when they are summoned to great councils by the king or by their metropolitan, or drawn thither by their private affairs.'

All this contributed to the wealth of the prominent citizen families, which was drawn from such varied sources as rising town rents, trade, financial dealings and minting. There were twelve licensed mints in London which in the late eleventh century produced about a quarter of the coin of the realm.[52] Moreover London had by then become the centre for the control of dies whenever a new issue was made. It earned this prominence through its importance as a centre of international trade. Even in Stephen's reign, when the official die cutters lost control of mints in some outlying regions, no irregular or baronial issues were associated with London itself. As elsewhere, minting was left in the hands of the established English families, and in the greatest, like that of Deorman, the privilege was handed on through several generations.[53] In Winchester and Lincoln the moneyers were the most important group after the royal officials; and this probably came near to being the truth in the more complex society of London. They were closely associated with the goldsmiths. A steady profit accrued from the mints, and their wealth was augmented by associated activities, such as exchanging coins and money lending. Contacts with great lords enabled them to acquire property and influence outside the city. Deorman and Brihtmaer of London figure among the knights of Canterbury; it may be that they served with their money rather than their swords. Later they may have given service in the lower offices of the Exchequer; in the twelfth century this was often rewarded by land held in petty serjeanty. And Deorman was apparently

[51] William of Poitiers, pp. 236–8; see also R. A. Brown, *The Tower of London* (London, 1984), pp. 5–15.

[52] See Dolley, *English Coinage*, pp. 12–14.

[53] For Deorman and his family see Nightingale, *The Numismatic Chronicle* (1982), 34–50.

descended from an English thegn, and retained or recovered his family's land.

Minting was only one source of civic wealth. A merchant family such as that of Gervase of Cornhill contained both English and Norman elements, and built up both mercantile and landed wealth.[54] Gervase had property in Essex and Suffolk as well as London; his wife Agnes was the granddaughter of Edward of Southwark, a wealthy Englishman. He lent money and acquired some land through mortgages; his enemies accused him of usury. One of these was Gilbert Becket, father of Archbishop Thomas, a member of a once prosperous family that had suffered losses. His contacts illustrate the links between Norman and English financiers and merchants. Most of the wealthiest citizens of Rouen and Caen dealt in finance, and helped to ensure the smooth running of the government by handling some money transactions.[55] Early in the century they may have provided bridging loans, though money was regularly shipped between England and Normandy in Henry I's reign. From the middle of the century they certainly lent to the royal family. It was William Trentegeruns, a leading citizen and vicomte of Rouen, who provided young Henry II with loans that enabled him to plan his invasion of 1149, and so to avoid the fiasco of his first rash attempt in 1147, when he had to borrow money from King Stephen to pay his way back to Normandy. There were commercial and financial as well as family contacts between these Normans and some of the London families.

Gilbert Becket's family originated in Rouen, possibly in the cloth manufacturing suburb, where they dealt in city rents and properties.[56] With his wife, who came of a mercantile family in Caen, he settled in London, where he prospered and became sheriff. He had the misfortune to lose much of his property by fire; but he had connections with rich citizens and one of these, Osbert Huitdeniers, gave young Thomas Becket a start in life as a sheriff's clerk. Like Deorman, Osbert held land by knight service outside London, as well as being an important citizen. On the whole, although these men were on the fringes of commerce and industry, they appear to have been chiefly financiers and property owners. Some of the merchants of Rouen handled the lucrative wine trade; but any connection the Becket family may have had with cloth was probably a minor one. When evidence for the cloth trade becomes more adequate about the middle of the century, the main export trade appears to have been chiefly in the hands of Flemings like William Cade of Saint-Omer,

[54] Reynolds, *History* (1972), 346–7.

[55] L. Musset, 'Y a-t-il eu une aristocratie d'affaires commune aux grandes villes de Normandie et d'Angleterre entre 1066 et 1204?', *Annales de Normandie*, 28 (1978), 347.

[56] R. Foreville, *Thomas Becket dans la tradition historique et hagiographique* (London, 1981), ch. 10, pp. 438–48; Brooke, *London*, pp. 212–13.

or the Jews, who first settled in London under the protection of William the Conqueror.[57]

Whilst it is plain that in the early decades of the twelfth century city government was a mixture of traditional and newer institutions, the details are far from clear. The ancient court of husting, meeting weekly, had become the most important organ of local government. Aldermen presided over the wards of the city but, as Susan Reynolds wrote, they were probably merely 'a social and legal elite within the city's courts', with no functional connection with the husting court before the middle of the century. The royal officials – sheriffs, portreeves, and later justiciars – controlled the government of the city, and the sheriff was responsible for the farm of about £500 until the city secured its first charter about 1133.[58] During Stephen's reign the aspirations of the citizens became more articulate. The accounts in the Gesta Stephani and Historia Novella, both of their acceptance of the king in 1135 and of their negotiations with the Empress in 1141, make it clear that they had some form of communal organization, with many of the characteristics of the communes that were so prominent a part of civic life on the continent at that time.[59] But though they wished to appoint their own officials and showed open hostility to the great feudal lords entrenched in the city, like Geoffrey de Mandeville who briefly recovered his father's office of constable of the Tower, they recognized their common interest with the king, and believed that they were entitled to a voice of some kind in the acceptance of a new monarch. After the capture of Stephen in 1141 the citizens were momentarily persuaded to give a grudging acceptance to the Empress as their lady, and to allow preparations for her coronation to begin. However, they quickly reacted against her cavalier treatment of them and the favour shown to their enemy, Geoffrey de Mandeville. Returning to their old allegiance, they drove her out of the city and sent their militia to help Stephen's queen at the siege of Winchester. The chronicles of the reign regularly refer to them as magnates or barons; and a generation later Fitz Stephen confidently asserted, 'The inhabitants of other towns are called citizens, but those of London are called barons.'

To both Fitz Stephen and his contemporary, Jordan Fantosme, praise of London was essentially an element in their praise of the glorious saint and martyr, Thomas Becket, who was the son of a citizen; nevertheless their words, stripped of a little rhetoric, ring true. Jordan stressed the

---

[57] Hilary Jenkinson, 'William Cade, a financier of the twelfth century', EHR, 28 (1913), 209–27, 731–2.

[58] There are doubts about the date of earliest charter; see C. N. L. Brooke, G. Keir and S. Reynolds, 'Henry I's charter for the City of London', Journal of the Society of Archivists, 4 (1970–3), 561–4.

[59] Gesta Stephani, pp. 4–7, 120–7; Malmesbury, HN, pp. 54–7.

loyalty of London and its barons: 'Never did they fail to be first in coming to the support of their liege lord in his moment of need.' To him they were the most loyal of all the realm during the rebellion of 1173, and the villain was their enemy, Gilbert of Montfichet.[60] Since Jordan's chronicle was designed to show how Henry's penance for the murder of Becket coincided with the capture of the king of Scots and the collapse of the rebellion, he was able to present the power of the saint, the virtues of the king and the loyalty of the Londoners as a harmonious whole. This is not pure fantasy; the most recent research on this period suggests that there was a continuing community of interest between the king and the wealthy barons of London, and that Henry II did not repress the development of the internal government of the city, as was once believed.[61] They provided an important element in the wealth of the kingdom that underlay the successful growth of a more centralized financial government. They were able to supply the credit needed in any sudden crisis until great international financiers emerged towards the end of the twelfth century.

[60] *Jordan Fantosme's Chronicle*, ed. R. C. Johnston (Oxford, 1981), pp. 68–9, 120–1, 142–5.

[61] Reynolds, *History* (1972), pp. 344–5.

PART III

Law and Society

6

Towards a Common Law

The century and a half between Cnut's codes of law and the legal developments and treatises of Henry II's reign was the great formative period in English customary law, out of which, under the influence of administrative centralization, the common law was slowly created.[1] Some of the changes had much in common with the customs of France and Normandy and Scandinavia, and indeed of the greater part of western Europe. But there was also much that was peculiar to England. As Milsom has noted, only twice have the customs of European peoples been worked up into intellectual systems; these two developments, separated by a millenium and a half, were the Roman and the English.[2] The English development led to the emergence in the thirteenth century of a common law of such strength and vitality that it continued along its customary lines when most other European systems underwent a reception of Roman law and all were profoundly influenced by it. The process by which this took place is one of the most important chapters in the first century of Norman rule. In studying this change it is important to avoid reading back into the twelfth century abstract concepts such as property or freedom, which were formulated later by analysis. Writers of customaries in the reign of Henry II, such as the writer known as Glanvill who had picked up a smattering of Roman law, were apt to apply tags from the language of Roman lawyers to developments that owed nothing directly to them. This gives their treatises the appearance of precocious legal thinking, and has misled many later historians. To understand how custom crystallized into law and how law changed it is necessary, as far as the sources allow, to look at it through its workings in society.

Certain general developments were common to both England and Normandy before the conquest. In both regions a system of social

[1] For these developments see in general, Pollock and Maitland; Milsom, *Historical Foundations*; Milsom, *Legal Framework*; van Caenegem, *Writs*.
[2] Milsom, *Historical Foundations*, p. 1.

relations in which kinship and lordship both had an important place was being modified by the increasing importance of lordship. This was to influence the descent of property and the methods of law enforcement and peace keeping, and to weaken the legal position of women, who had often enjoyed a more central place in earlier tribal organization. Within the families the older kin groups, where theoretically at least all the sons had some rights of inheritance, were tending to become fragmented and give way to lineages. The integrity of the family holding was preserved by the descent of property in a single line, or several single lines if the family had extensive lands. Since properties were usually centred on a chief residence toponymics began to appear, making descent more readily traceable in the documents. Many families which were old cannot be traced before the early eleventh century.[3] This was the time when, in Normandy, great families such as Beaumont and Brionne were emerging, with Clères at a lower level in society. This process, accompanied by the greater importance of lordship, appears to have gone a little further in Normandy than in England before 1066, and to have affected customary law in different ways. Another difference was that in England local communities had a more effective share in the maintenance of order and the apprehension of wrong doers.

The principal sources for the study of Old English law are the legal codes, supplemented by wills, diplomas and landbooks.[4] Cnut's laws are the last of an important series of vernacular legislative pronouncements. The codes were recorded by ecclesiastical scribes, and their survival depended in part on the chance preservation of ecclesiastical archives, notably those of Rochester and Worcester, but there is no reason to suppose that any later codes were lost. After the conquest, when Norman administrators tried to record Anglo-Saxon customs, they used nothing later than Cnut. The laws were promulgated in the most important assemblies of the great lay lords and bishops of the kingdom, gathered in the king's court on one or other of his great estates.[5] The court had much in common with other royal courts of western Europe and was peripatetic with the king. Its name of witan, or 'wise men', implies not an institution but an occasion for discussion, decision, and making known through promulgation.

The work of law-giving consisted chiefly in recording and reconciling

[3] For Normandy see Bates, *Normandy*, pp. 111–14; for England, Holt, *TRHS* (1982), 193–212; (1983), 193–220; (1984), 1–26; (1985), forthcoming.

[4] For translations of codes see Whitelock, *EHD*, i. 327–564; for wills, Whitelock, *Anglo-Saxon Wills*; Sheehan, *The Will in Medieval England*.

[5] For the composition of the king's councils see Simon Keynes, *The Diplomas of King Aethelred 'the Unready' 978–1016* (Cambridge, 1980).

local customs, and adapting them to the needs of a more effective royal power and an evolving lordship that slowly replaced some of the obligations of the kindred. Each series of laws included and adapted many provisions from earlier codes. They were particularly concerned with criminal matters, such as fixing the wergild or blood-price of men, on which the scale of compensation was based; they defined the cash compensation to be paid for all except the bootless crimes punishable by death, and placed responsibility for bringing offenders to justice on kindred, lord, or tithing group of ten adult men. They also included many provisions relating to the rights of the church and the status of the clergy. But they were silent on a number of important matters; they did not deal specifically with the descent of land, or attempt to define the normal rights of kindred and lord. Regulations dealt with crimes leading to forfeiture, not with what happened when there was no crime. They were concerned with the consequences of a man's violent occupation of land that was not rightly his, not with the nature of the right he was held to have violated. There were a few regulations of widows' rights, and of payments according to rank that a lord might claim as a heriot on the death of one of his men. There were also, in the laws of Alfred and Cnut, one or two general regulations concerning the transfer of bookland.

The nature of bookland has given rise to much discussion; if we describe it as land held by the book we have at least a convenient starting point for studying it.[6] Landbooks or diplomas appeared from the seventh century onward to confer special status on land. At first they were records of royal grants, and were written in Latin. Often the purpose was to free land from some of the rights of kinsmen, so that it could be given to a church in perpetuity. But some landbooks ensured hereditary tenure for an otherwise revocable grant, or freed land from specified public burdens. They should as far as possible be interpreted against the background of customary law governing the rights of the kindred and the special status of royal demesne lands; these, unfortunately, are hard to discover. Certainly a distinction, widespread in Germanic societies, existed between inherited property, which was inalienable from the kin, and acquired property which could be disposed of more freely. Patrimonies were freed from hereditary claims only with great formality and the backing of royal authority. Alfred's code stated that if a man had bookland which his kindred had left him with a properly written and

---

[6] On bookland see H. R. Loyn, *Anglo-Saxon England and the Norman Conquest* (London, 1962), pp. 170–9; Stenton, *Latin Charters*, pp. 60–5; Patrick Wormald, in Campbell, *The Anglo-Saxons*, pp. 95–7; Maitland, *Domesday Book*, pp. 226–58; and for Germanic customs cf. Karl Leyser, 'The crisis of Medieval Germany', *Proceedings of the British Academy*, 69 (1983), 426–39.

testified prohibition of alienation he was not to dispose of it outside the kindred.[7] So a provision designed partly to make possible the granting of land to the church had the side effect of turning many ninth-century monasteries endowed with bookland into family monasteries ruled by hereditary abbots from the founding family.

Certain royal rights which overrode any lord's claims appear in the provisions of Cnut's code. If a coward had treacherously deserted his lord or his comrade in a land or sea engagement, his lord was to seize the goods and the land which he had given; but if the man had bookland it was to pass into the king's hands.[8] Here the concern appears to be with acquisitions rather than patrimonies, or perhaps with land granted from the king's own patrimonial demesne, with special rights of reversion. Sometimes alienation took place by stages. Land could be leased for a period of two or three lives, followed in some cases by more permanent establishment. As King Alfred wrote in his preface to St Augustine's *Soliloquies*, 'Every man hopes when he has built a dwelling-place on land loaned from his lord that he may rest on it for a time and hunt and hawk and fish and get a living somehow for himself from that loan ... until through his lord's kindness he has earned perpetual possession.'[9]

In addition to the solemn diplomas which guaranteed the status of land, other written records of transfers had become more numerous by the early eleven century. Most important were the vernacular writs, recording grants of land or rights made by the king to a beneficiary. Like the Latin landbooks, they were kept by the recipient and used as title deeds. Both landbooks and writ-charters were proof of the right of an individual to sell or give land, as when a thegn 'who had the right of selling to whom he would' sold land in a Worcestershire manor to the abbot of Evesham, and made the transfer by means of a charter placed on the altar with the witness of the county. But documents still had a very small place in land transfers, which took place most commonly with the witness of shire or hundred. Although written testaments were some-times made by men and women, these were only records of oral declarations before witnesses. A prudent landholder safeguarded his rights by combining oral and written proofs. In the time of Cnut the wife of a Herefordshire thegn disinherited her own son in favour of her kinswoman, Leofflaid, wife of Thurkil the White. After the case had been proved by witness of the shire court in favour of Thurkil's wife, Thurkil rode 'with the permission and witness of all the people' to Hereford

---

[7] Alfred, 41 (*EHD*, i. 379).

[8] II Cnut, 77 (*EHD*, i. 430); *Leges Henrici*, 13.1; 13.12 (pp. 116–18).

[9] Cited Stenton, *Latin Charters*, p. 62.

cathedral and had it entered in a gospel-book, so that the witness of the shire should not be forgotten.[10]

The Normans found many things in old English land tenures that had a familiar look. They too had written diplomas recording gifts of land, and they quickly took over the writ-charter, changing the language to Latin and applying it far more widely. Their charters, however, were purely records of grants; when land changed hands a new charter was given to the new recipient. And the distinction between patrimony and acquisitions was far more clearly established in their customs; this may have resulted from the greater emphasis on tenure in the duchy. Though the duke did not exercise royal power, his effective authority was remarkable. Smaller and more compact than England, Normandy allowed a high degree of ducal control; and the duke was heir both to Carolingian traditions of government and to the personal authority of the Scandinavian war leader.[11] Ducal authority, combined with the emergence of lineages of which the greatest were blood relations of the duke, led to a strengthening of a hierarchy of tenure in the holding of land. Lordship advanced rapidly in Normandy; holders of family patrimonies were drawn into vassalage when they commended themselves and their land to a lord. The rights of lords and kinsmen survived together in the customs known as parage. These were not recorded in writing until the first Norman customary was compiled at the very end of the twelfth century.[12] But the narratives and charters that describe conditions in Normandy before the conquest of England show the customs already taking shape. The gifts of the family of Giroie to the abbey of Saint-Evroult reveal a typical division of property. Giroie's eldest surviving son, William, inherited the main patrimony and had authority of some kind over his younger brothers. Robert, the next son, received lands round Saint-Céneri acquired by his father. One son became a monk; others died young, though one of them held half a village under William, and his illegitimate children later consented to its transfer to William's son. Four daughters were dowered and married well. Complex as the family rights were, it is clear that the bulk of the inheritance, divided into patrimony and acquisitions, passed to the two eldest sons, though the other members of the family all had rights to some provision out of it. The lands of the family of Tosny were divided between sons and daughters in a similar

---

[10] Bishop and Chaplais, pp. ix–xiii; DB, i. 177b; *EHD*, i. 556.

[11] Yver, *1 Normanni*, 299–366; Bates, *Normandy*, ch. 4; Musset, 'Gouvernés et gouvernants', pp. 439–68.

[12] R. Génestal, *Le parage normand* (Caen, 1911); for Norman customs in general see J. Yver, *Égalité entre héritiers et exclusion des enfants dotés* (Paris, 1966).

way.[13] Custom favoured the eldest son, but not to the exclusion of the others. Subdivision was not allowed to proceed so far that the way of life of the main branch or branches of the family was threatened, or the lord was deprived of any service due to him.

The life of Herluin, founder and first abbot of Bec, illustrates how a vassal's possessions might be divided between his share of the family patrimony and lands held more precariously by the gift of a lord. Herluin was a knight of Count Gilbert of Brionne, but even after he had withdrawn from Gilbert's service he could command a force of twenty knights of his own. All forms of land-holding were, however, becoming tenures; in eleventh-century Normandy the term alod was applied to land held by hereditary right, and did not imply full possession.[14] The foundation charters of Bec, drafted in and soon after 1034, show that Herluin's patrimony was shared by his two brothers, over whom Herluin exercised some authority as an elder brother did in developed parage custom; but Count Gilbert of Brionne also had some rights over all three as his vassals, and his consent was necessary before the brothers could transfer the services and customs that they owed him for their alods to the new monastery.[15]

So lordship was powerful; but feudal tenures could emerge only slowly, against a background of patrimonial rights rooted so deeply that even the duke of Normandy could not flout them with impunity. When William the Conqueror founded his great abbey of St Stephen at Caen he built it on land that had formed the patrimony of a townsman named Arthur, whom he failed to compensate. In a dramatic scene many years later, Arthur's son Ascelin interupted the funeral of King William in the abbey church by demanding compensation for the land taken from his family; and this was paid without demur by the assembled lords and bishops before the funeral could proceed.[16] It is a measure of the tenacity of patrimonial rights, in spite of the great advance of lordship in Normandy. And it bears some resemblance to conditions in England; there too, as innumerable charters show, family claims had to be satisfied before a new church could be founded in their patrimony.

The circumstances of the conquest put a greater emphasis on lordship, for the Normans insisted on a renegotiation, real or assumed, of existing rights. But they also claimed to preserve the customs of the kingdom. There was no attempt to produce any new code of laws, such as the codes that had followed the earlier Danish settlements, in order to integrate the

---

[13] Fauroux, no. 122; Orderic, ii. 22–41; Musset, *Francia* (1977), 45–80.

[14] R. Carabie, *La propriété foncière dans le très ancien droit normand* (Caen, 1943), pp. 236–9.

[15] Fauroux, no. 98.

[16] Orderic, iv. 106–7.

customs of different peoples. Indeed there was no need for one. In the first place, the number of Norman settlers was relatively small, and confined in the main to the upper ranks of society: the magnates and their vassals and knights, and the higher clergy. They were accustomed to settle their differences in the court of their lord, whether count or duke. The great land pleas show how William felt his way into the workings of the existing shire courts in pleas concerning Norman vassals of English churches; at times, when knights replaced thegns, he left them to work out their obligations with their new lords.[17] As Normans replaced English in church offices a balance had to be struck between the relations of lord and vassal, to which the Normans were accustomed, and the traditional rights and legal privileges of the English churches. Difficult problems were carried, as in Normandy, to the court of the duke, now king. If they were widespread enough to produce a general ruling, the king issued writs to local officers presiding over the shire courts, much as he had issued synodal decrees to his vicomtes in Normandy. The difference was partly in the nature of the problems to be settled, and even more in the process of enforcement through local assemblies of a kind that did not exist in Normandy; but the initial process of debate, agreement and promulgation in the central court was very similar. The position of the church, influenced in both Normandy and England by the rapid development of canon law and the strengthening of the ecclesiastical hierarchy, was another factor.

The general ordinances and writs issued by William I and his sons show the areas where emergency measures were necessary, and where adjustment caused most stress. One emergency measure to protect the king's followers left lasting traces; a fine was imposed on any hundred where a Norman was found murdered and his assassin escaped; this later became the *murdrum* fine collected for unsolved murders of all free men.[18] One area of stress was the relationship between the older communal courts and the newer honorial courts that were gradually working their way into the social structure. Private jurisdiction had existed before the conquest, as numerous grants of sake and soke show. But above the manorial level, where the evidence is particularly obscure, rights were probably exercised in the courts of shire and hundred whenever the grants implied more than a grant of the profits of justice. Norman lords, on the other hand, were accustomed to hold courts for their vassals. Like all early courts, these dealt with a variety of business, not all of which was judicial; they were gatherings where knights did homage to their lords, grants were made and witnessed, and matters of common interest

---

[17] E. Miller, *The Abbey and Bishopric of Ely* (Cambridge, 1951), pp. 51–2.
[18] Stubbs, *Charters*, p. 98; Liebermann, i. 487.

were discussed. Whatever the overriding rights of the ducal court in many matters, questions involving the failure of a vassal to perform the duty owed to his lord could most easily be decided in the place where he had entered into his obligations.

Honorial courts made their appearance in England immediately after the conquest. The existence of English communal courts, in some of which the holders of judicial liberties were already exercising delegated jurisdiction, was bound to lead to confusion. Great franchises such as the eight-and-a-half hundreds of Bury St Edmunds, or the triple hundred of Oswaldslaw, where the bishop of Worcester claimed by ancient custom 'all the revenues of jurisdiction and all customs therein, pertaining to his demesne, and the king's service and his own, so that no sheriff can have any claim there', were well established before the conquest.[19] These great ecclesiastical lords soon began to hold courts for the vassals they enfeoffed; and although the business and procedures of honorial courts, largely concerned with the obligations arising from homage, differed from those of the hundred courts, where breaches of the peace were handled, it was not difficult for lords to confuse the jurisdiction they exercised in the various courts over which they presided. Some business must have been settled in courts that ought never to have handled it, in spite of the declared intentions of the new rulers.

One of the aims professed by William I was to allow the different peoples under his rule to keep their own customs as far as possible. He made use of the established shire courts in the process of settling conflicting claims to property in the aftermath of conquest. He respected traditional methods of proof, allowing Normans and other Frenchmen to defend themselves through trial by battle, to which they were accustomed, while Englishmen were offered the choice of compurgation or the ordeal; or at least the right to substitute a champion if battle could not be avoided.[20] In dealing with the numerous complaints of unjust dispossession and spoliation that reached his ears from many of the great churches, he sent small commissions of magnates to hold special sessions, sometimes joint sessions, of the shires where the property lay. This type of procedure was gaining ground all over Europe; ambulatory courts were kept in touch with local assemblies by the use of such commissioners. William's sons employed them in a variety of ways to settle complaints and enforce the observance of law.

In property disputes the concern of William Rufus and Henry I was less with the wholesale dispossessions that had troubled their father's reign than with the conflict of rights resulting from the development of

[19] Dyer, *Lords and Peasants*, p. 35; Harmer, *Writs*, pp. 145–8; for rulings on ecclesiastical jurisdiction and the slave trade, see below, pp. 188, 193–4.

[20] Liebermann, i. 487; *EHD*, ii. 399–400.

more defined feudal tenure. Writs from the early years of Henry I show him grappling with numerous complaints from abbots whose military tenants failed in one way or another to recognize their lordship, or whose farmers treated the manors in their charge as family estates to be transmitted to their heirs. Some knights enfeoffed on the land of the abbey of Abingdon refused to do homage or perform their due service to the new abbot, Faritius, appointed in 1100 after a three-year vacancy. In 1101 William Mauduit, the king's chamberlain, who held a manor near Abingdon, refused to do service or send a knight in his place when the army was called out to resist the invading forces of Robert Curthose; he was condemned by a judgement in the shire court in the presence of royal justiciars to lose his land, and recover it only if he undertook to do homage and perform the service for one knight on the same conditions as the other vassals of the abbey.[21] Jocelin de Riparia was ordered to perform the service due from his fee as his brothers had done in the time of Abbot Aldhelm, under pain of distraint by the abbot. In 1105 Robert Mauduit was commanded in similar terms to do the service to Abbot Faritius that his predecessor, William Mauduit, had done. All the barons of the abbey were ordered to keep the king's guard at Windsor as in the time of Abbot Rainald, and as Faritius had directed; the king added a note of stern rebuke because they did not obey the abbot's command as they ought to do.[22]

These writs are typical of many; other abbots had similar problems. Tenants and vassals were, it seems, refusing to recognize either their own obligations to a new abbot or the competence of his court. Many of the king's writs explicitly referred a case to the court of an abbot, and demanded respect for the court's jurisdiction. Jocelin de Riparia was ordered to go to the court of the abbot of Abingdon, and to no other place, if he wished to pursue a claim to land at Hill in Warwickshire. Hugh son of Thurstan was to be constrained by the same abbot's court to perform certain non-military services (the repair of bridges and deer-fences) due from the land he held.[23] After Robert of Staverton, who claimed to hold Charwelton in fee farm of the abbot of Thorney, had complained to the king that the abbot had disseised him, Henry ordered Hugh de Bocland, the sheriff, and two others to accompany him to the abbot's court to hear whether right had been done; the court made a judgement in favour of Thorney.[24] Other pleas were referred to the shire or hundred. Out of the tangle of jurisdictions emerged a general definition of the spheres of competence of different courts. Henry's writ of

---

[21] Bigelow, pp. 75–6; *Chron. Abingdon*, ii. 128.

[22] *Regesta*, ii. 553, 697, 725.

[23] *Regesta*, ii. 654, 789.

[24] Stenton, *English Justice*, pp. 138–9; van Caenegem, *Writs*, no. 7.

1108, addressed to the bishop, sheriff and barons of Worcestershire, emphasized his right to summon special meetings of the shire court if the royal interest required it, but otherwise ordered that shire and hundred courts should meet at the same places and at the same terms as in the days of King Edward. Land pleas between the king's own tenants-in-chief should be heard in the king's court, and between vassals of different lords in the shire court.[25] Numerous individual writs had already made it clear that vassals of the same lord should, in the first instance, claim their right in the court of their lord.

Towards the middle of the reign an anonymous ecclesiastic, probably a minor official of some kind, with considerable experience of the law, began to put together a compilation of the laws and customs of the time.[26] His work, never quite completed, goes by the name of the *Leges Henrici primi*. Once regarded as primarily an antiquarian work, it is now recognized as one of the most precious guides to the changing customs of the English courts in the early twelfth century. Accepting the diversity of custom, the writer described the triple division of England into Wessex, Mercia and the Danelaw, and mentioned other local variations; but he also emphasized the 'formidable authority of the royal majesty'.[27] The king, however respectful of traditions, had more to do than merely hold the ring. The writer quoted Anglo-Saxon codes freely, because many of the regulations were still relevant to the practice of the courts; some clauses show how the provisions of the codes were being adapted to the conditions of the Norman settlement. Pronouncements as recent as Henry I's writ on the holding of shire and hundred courts were included. His treatment of private courts faithfully reflects what royal writs and monastic chronicles show to have been the rights baronial courts were entitled to enjoy at that date.

He stated categorically that every lord might summon his man, even a man residing in a distant manor of the honour, to his court, and impose justice on him there. Judgement was given by the peers of the honour: the free vassals of equal standing, though agreements by consensus were always possible in any court. Failure to answer a summons or to comply with a ruling of the court could be punished by a series of penalties, ranging from distraint by chattels or sequestration to confiscation of the vassal's land. The *Leges* included a statement that a lord might seize the land of any man who refused to perform his obligations after a lawful summons.[28] In one case settled between 1113 and 1127 Abbot Robert of

[25] Liebermann, i. 524; *Regesta*, ii. 892; cf. *Leges Henrici*, 7. 1 (pp. 98–9).
[26] *Leges Henrici*, pp. 37–44.
[27] *Leges Henrici*, 6.1, 2, 2a (pp. 96–7).
[28] *Leges Henrici*, 31.7; 43. 4, 5 (pp. 134–5, 152–3).

Thorney disseised a tenant who was unjustly holding lands, broke up his houses, and stubbed up his holt.[29] These are the rights that Henry I had forced on the notice of unwilling vassals from the early years of his reign, and they continued to be exercised throughout the century.

Our knowledge of the early proceedings of these feudal courts comes only from charters, or any chronicle entries kept for private information, and these are very rare indeed. Judgement was by memory of the suitors, who were both judges and witnesses; the visible ceremony was the essential part of any transaction. Witness lists to charters show that the suitors included men from the lower ranks of the free tenants no less than the leading vassals, together with the lord's family and household officers. Tenants were put in seisin of land by the transfer of an object; it might be a piece of turf, a rod, a knife, a book, a piece of horse's harness, or whatever was convenient. A charter of Roger of Mowbray recorded the surrender by his tenant, Reginald Puher, of land in Middlethorpe, which Roger then transferred to the abbey of Whitby by handing over the same staff that he had received from Reginald.[30] The ceremonies performed were similar to those in the shire court, with the suitors of the honour court substituted for the witness of the shire. Robert of Yaxley, the nephew of Abbot Gunter of Thorney, who had unjustly occupied land in Sibson and Yaxley belonging to the abbey, restored it to the next abbot 'by the rod of Odo Revel which is laid up in the treasury of the church'. This restoration took place in the shire court at Huntingdon; but afterwards Robert and his son William for good measure 'restored and quitclaimed the same land upon the high altar by the gospels', and swore on the same gospels to keep the agreement. Robert's son William repeated his renunciation in the abbot's court at Yaxley.[31]

The courts of lay barons met at a convenient centre of the honour; those of great monasteries sometimes met in the abbey's precincts. Since the court was the repository of custom it had a part to play in approving the surrender of family property, or the relaxation of customary dues. In 1133 the court of the abbot of Peterborough witnessed and approved a family agreement to transfer the church of Castor to the abbey. The case is an interesting one, since it involved a family where the elder son, Richard, elected to become a priest, and by arrangement his younger brother William was granted the family fee. Richard held the church at Castor, which was part of the patrimony; he wished to become a monk at Peterborough and give his church to the abbey. Since his kindred had an interest his brother William had to be persuaded to renounce his rights.

[29] Stenton, *English Justice*, p. 141.
[30] Greenway, *Mowbray Charters*, pp. lvi–lviii; nos 109, 290.
[31] Stenton, *English Justice*, pp. 141–5.

The transaction took place in a full court held in the abbot's chamber, before the barons of the honour. Two royal representatives, William of Aubigny and Richard Basset, were also present; they had probably come to hand over the temporalities to a new abbot, since this was the court when Martin of Bec, newly elected, took the homage of his men.[32]

Martin's installation may explain the holding of this particular court at the abbey; some of the courts were held at a convenient centre such as Castor. Various witness lists show that the court might comprise a miscellaneous assemblage of household officials, members of the honorial baronage, knights, and holders of serjeanties.[33]

After a decision had been reached in a feudal court one of the lord's household officials, frequently his steward, could be called upon to enforce it. A writ of Gilbert fitz Richard of Clare, ordering a tenant to restore tithes he had been withholding from the priory of Stoke-by-Clare, ended with the words, 'If you fail to do this, let Adam my steward do it quickly, that I hear no complaint for lack of right.'[34] Baronial stewards, like powerful royal officials, at times abused their trust and used their position to enrich themselves; but if charged they were answerable in the lord's court. The great honour courts could be effective by the standards of the day, and they played an important part in keeping order and shaping custom in the first century after the conquest.

They exercised, in Milsom's definition, both disciplinary and pro- prietary jurisdiction. The first arose from the bond of homage; the tenant had received a tenement for which he owed services that might be military, financial or ministerial, and incidental dues.[35] Any breach of contract might be followed by distraint and forfeiture; the court might be asked to define the customs to which the tenant had bound himself, but the matter was one between lord and man, within the competence of the court. None of the developments of jurisdiction during the twelfth century weakened this fundamental right of the lord, first described in the *Leges Henrici primi*. In the reign of Henry II the rights remained unchanged. Glanvill then asserted, with much greater precision arising from the legal experience of almost a century, that any lord might 'lawfully bring his man to trial and distrain him to come to court by judgment of his court; and unless he can clear himself against the lord by swearing as the court shall direct, the whole of the fee which he holds of that lord shall be at the lord's mercy.'[36] And even without a command of the king or his justices, a lord might distrain his man to come to his court

[32] King, *Peterborough*, pp. 30–2.
[33] King, *Peterborough*, p. 30.
[34] *Stoke-by-Clare Cartulary*, ii. 236, no. 345; Stenton, *English Feudalism*, pp. 81–2.
[35] Milsom, *Legal Framework*, ch. 1.
[36] Glanvill, ix. 1 (p. 105).

to answer a complaint that he was withholding service. Glanvill was repeating as a general rule what Henry I had hammered home in his executive writs.

Proprietary jurisdiction, on the other hand, dealt with the question of who ought to have a tenement, and this might involve someone outside the fee.[37] The question was one of right, not seisin. In settling the matter customs of inheritance were important, and they were changing. Feudal needs, both military and financial, were beginning to make themselves felt, but family interests still had a place. At the beginning of the twelfth century the son of a former vassal could only plead a claim deriving from the grant made to his father. By the end of that century he was more likely to demand a right, though his success would depend on the rules of hereditary descent accepted by the court. The change is charted in the changing language. Early records speak only of a man being seised of property; later ones say that he claimed or recovered seisin. So an abstract right was created from repeated legal actions.[38] And abstract rights, if violated by the lord, were enforceable in the king's court.

In the course of the century the feudal courts did much to help the slow movement of feudal custom towards the greater standardization that ultimately forced them out of business. The lords who presided over them were themselves vassals of a greater lord, the king, and they met in his court. His officials appeared from time to time in their courts when royal business was involved. The lords themselves sometimes acted as royal justices. Cases that were outside the competence of individual honours were heard in the shire courts, where knights were among the regular suitors. Household officials moved between royal and private service. Ralph of Hastings, for example, served as steward to Queen Eleanor before being invested with the stewardship of the abbey of Bury St Edmunds in 1155; some ten years later his nephew William of Hastings, one of King Henry's stewards, succeeded him in the now virtually hereditary stewardship of Bury.[39] Men moved between the households of Henry II's brother William and his son, the young Henry, and their households were connected at many points with the king's court.[40]

A lord's court, capable though it was of dealing with much of the everyday business of any honour was not an enclosed and self-sufficient world. Many cases lay outside its competence because the litigants held of different lords; and some of its decisions could be challenged on the

---

[37] Milsom, *Legal Framework*, ch. 3.

[38] S. F. C. Milsom, 'F. W. Maitland', *Proceedings of the British Academy*, 66 (1980), 278.

[39] Douglas, *Feudal Documents*, p. cxxxviii, and nos 87, 88.

[40] F. M. Stenton, *Facsimiles of Early Charters* (Northants. Record Society, 4, 1930), p. 25.

grounds of the interpretation of custom. For some customs of inheritance were slow to become fixed; and some feudal incidents varied throughout the period. Exactly how much military service, or what financial aids, could legitimately be exacted depended on changing circumstances. Sometimes, however, even early in the century, direct intervention came from the king, in consultation with his vassals. If a recurrent problem seemed to demand a general rule, this was formulated after discussion in the king's court. Such decisions have left few direct traces; they appear· only through very rare references in charters, and through the effects of their application in the courts. Customs of inheritance in particular were under pressure from the process of subinfeudation and the changing relations of men to the lords who received their homage, as vassalage gradually merged into the holding of hereditary fiefs by military tenure. Whereas parage and many other inheritance customs favoured the division of property, the practical needs of military tenure encouraged the descent of property to a single male heir. And family interests, which on the whole preferred certainty of descent, even to a minor, to a freer choice of heirs within the kindred, which was dangerously open to pressure from a lord, helped to ensure the final triumph of the principle of primogeniture.

However, if a man had several daughters and no sons the descent was uncertain. Division between daughters was customary, and it had the advantage of making better provision for all the members of a family, and providing more heiresses to attract good marriages. Towards the end of Henry I's reign a general decision was reached about the partition of fees among heiresses. It is known only through a chance reference in a charter of Binham priory to a certain *statutum decretum*. Agnes, the younger daughter of Walter de Valognes, granted land to the priory in the court of the abbot of St Albans; she was known by the witnesses to be Walter's heir 'in respect of this land according to the *statutum decretum* that where there is no son the daughters divide their father's land by the spindles, nor can the elder take from the younger her half of the inheritance without violence and injury.'[41] *Statutum* on its own then simply implied something that had been appointed; *decretum* gave it the force of a decision that had been promulgated, and the reference was clearly to a ruling made in the king's court, after consultation and by general agreement. The decision meant that traditional customs were to be preserved when daughters inherited, even though military tenure was developing to the advantage of the single male heir.

If any general decree fixed the rule for male heirs its date is unknown; perhaps none was necessary. Certainly custom had become settled by the

---

[41] Stenton, *English Feudalism*, pp. 38–40; for further discussion see Holt, forthcoming in *TRHS* (1985).

later years of Henry II's reign. One case heard between 1162 and 1166 shows that the rule was not yet quite rigid. An agreement in the court of William, earl Ferrars, between Henry son of Fulcher and his younger brother Sewall arranged for the succession of Sewall to the father's two baronies, with the consent of the elder brother.[42] This did not, as Stenton thought, 'cut straight across all the customs of inheritance accepted by feudal society'; it was a somewhat late example of a type of arrangement that had once been acceptable. But by the end of the century primogeniture had become established as a normal rule. In 1199 a suit was brought by Walter, the great-grandson of Bernard 'le Franceis', claiming one hide of land with appurtenances from his uncle Ralph. Bernard had lived and died in the reign of Henry I; on his death his younger son was declared his heir by consent of the lord's court because of the insufficiency of the elder son. This was perfetly acceptable at the time, and on the death of the tenant his son Ralph was put in seisin. But in 1199 Walter, the grandson of the elder son, won his case against his uncle; the king's court ruled that, as the heir of the body of the elder son, he had the greater right.[43] The rule was then so firmly established that a court could retrospectively change the descent of an inheritance.

A few years earlier, probably between 1187 and 1189, an anonymous writer put together the treatise on the laws and customs of England that is generally known as 'Glanvill'. The author was probably either Ranulf Glanvill, the justiciar, or Geoffrey fitz Peter, an experienced justice and sheriff of Northampton, unless he was a lesser royal clerk employed about the court.[44] Whoever wrote it, he was a practical man with experience of the royal courts, some slight acquaintance with Roman law, and a smattering of canon law. The treatise is the earliest English customary, a few years ahead of the Norman *Très ancien coutumier*. It described customs in the process of becoming fixed, but still very fluid; some variations were indicated. But the writer tried to formulate some general rules, and to apply a few principles of Roman jurisprudence to somewhat recalcitrant material. As far as inheritance went, he was most positive on military tenures. The rule of inheritance 'according to the law of England' was, he stated unequivocally, that if a knight or tenant of a military fee died, the eldest son succeeded to his father in everything. This general rule did not exclude the right of the father to make some provision for a younger son, with the consent of the heir, during his lifetime.[45] Daughters inherited only if there were no sons, and then the

[42] Stenton, *English Feudalism*, pp. 51–4, 263–4.

[43] Milsom, *Legal Framework*, pp. 181–2; *Rotuli Curiae Regis*, i. 253, 360.

[44] Glanvill, pp. xxx–xl.

[45] *Le Très Ancien Coutumier de Normandie*, ed. E.-J. Tardif (Coutumiers de Normandie, 1881–3); Glanvill, vii. 3 (p. 75); vii. 1 (p. 72).

inheritance was to be divided between them.[46] Lineal descendants were preferred to collaterals, but there was still some doubt about the right of a younger son against the heir of a deceased elder son; this was the *casus regis*, which was to become of crucial importance in the reign of John. The age of majority was twenty-one. As for reliefs, he considered 100s. a reasonable relief for a knight's fee; for baronies he could give no certain figure 'because the chief baronies in making satisfaction to the lord king for their reliefs are at his mercy and pleasure, and the same is true of serjeanties.'[47] Richard fitz Nigel said the same in the *Dialogue of the Exchequer*: the heir to a barony must make his own terms, whereas the holder of a knight's fee should pay 100s. for a whole fee, or proportionately less for a fraction of one.[48] These customs, which were being applied by the justices and the barons of the Exchequer, are beginning to have the familiar look of conventional feudal tenure as it was known in the later middle ages. What must never be forgotten is that nobody could have written so positively even half a century earlier, and a number of the customs described are very different from those that Henry I had promised to respect when he issued his coronation charter.

Procedure too had changed, under pressure of accumulating business. The writs, which were one of the principal instruments for exercising royal authority, had originally been executive. The king ordered an individual or individuals to obey a specific command. Sometimes, however, he used a writ with a judicial intention, by ordering an enquiry to be carried out or commanding that right should be done in respect of some alleged injury. He might specify the court where the matter should be settled. Sometimes he named a second or even a third person who was to take action if the recipient failed to do so. A typical writ of Henry I ordered Jordan de Sackvill to do full right to the abbey of Abingdon concerning the land he had taken from it; 'and unless you do so (*nisi feceris*) Walter Giffard is to do it, and if he does not, Hugh de Bocland is to do it, so that I hear no more complaint for lack of right.'[49] Some writs directed that if the lord failed to act, the sheriff should do so, with a justiciar as the third agent. Although the king frequently tried to force cases of vassals failing in their services back into the lord's court for final settlement there, cases of default of right, which frequently involved the lord himself, were more likely to be brought before the sheriff, or one of the king's justiciars in the shire court. One writ of Henry I ordered the bishop of London to do full right to the abbot of Westminster concerning the armed men who broke into his church at Werrington at night, with

[46] Glanvill, vii. 3 (p. 76).
[47] Glanvill, ix. 4 (p. 108).
[48] *Dialogus de Scaccario*, pp. 96, 121.
[49] *Regesta*, ii. 974; van Caenegem, *Writs*, no. 36.

the proviso that 'unless you do it, my barons of the exchequer shall have it done'; an exceptionally early reference to the judicial work of the barons of the exchequer.[50]

Throughout the century the initiative that brought the great majority of land pleas into the king's court came from the tenants themselves. The king did not go out to capture jurisdiction, profitable though it was; his intervention was actively sought through complaints of lack of right that arose spontaneously. So great was the tenurial complexity of some regions that a powerful abbey could hold of a simple knight, and so be summoned to the court of the honour to which the knight belonged. The king's own abbey of Battle held land of the descendants of Ingelran 'beacon-rider', subtenants of the count of Eu; when the abbot complained of being unjustly disseised of the land Henry II ordered the count of Eu to do full right, with the warning that unless he did so the sheriff of Sussex would act. It was only after the count had failed to get the tenant into court and the sheriff had taken no action that the case was settled before the justiciar, Richard de Lucy, in the king's court at Clarendon.[51]

Most cases coming into the king's court, held wherever the king happened to be, carry traces of unsuccessful efforts to reach a settlement in a lower court of some kind. A prolonged dispute between the abbots of Thorney and Peterborough was settled in Thorney's favour in Henry I's court at Brampton, a favourite hunting lodge. It concerned four fishermen from Farcet, claimed by both abbots. Abbot Robert of Thorney was able to prove that they were bound to come to his hallmoot at Stanground, pay head-tax, and give him twelve days' harvest work in August. Since on this occasion the sheriff of Huntingdon and Ralph fitz Baldric testified that eighteen men of the hundred had sworn to this by order of Ralph Basset, who was then 'justiciar of England', some earlier proceedings must have taken place before a royal justice in the shire court. The monks of Thorney took the precaution of preserving among their archives an informal record of how the four fishermen had afterwards come to the hallmoot and recognized that they held their land of the abbot for the services he claimed.[52] Here both litigants were prominent ecclesiastical tenants-in-chief, but the ramifications of the case extended through shire and hundred to the hallmoot, and no feudal court was directly involved.

However, the method of issuing writs on receiving complaints was cumbrous, and if the unsuccessful party was influential enough to win the king's ear he might secure a second writ, countermanding the first. This

---

[50] *Regesta*, ii. 1538; van Caenegem, *Writs*, no. 13.

[51] *Battle Chronicle*, pp. 118–19, 210–19; E. Searle, 'The abbey of the conquerors', *Anglo-Norman Studies*, 2 (1980), 160–2.

[52] See the unpublished 'Red Book of Thorney', CUL MS Add. 3021, ff. 418v–419r.

might happen more than once, particularly if the dispute was spun out over several reigns. In the course of protracted legal proceedings over Marcham church between the abbey of Abingdon and Simon the king's dispenser (who was succeeded by his son Thurstan), the case began c.1120 and was finally settled in the reign of Henry II, after royal executive writs had been twice countermanded by later writs. Here, if the abbey's chronicler is to be believed, influence and bribery played a part; but the matter was particularly sensitive since it involved a claim by a lay farmer to hold a very wealthy parish church by hereditary right; and it was not finally settled until it came to the king's court at Clarendon.[53]

Out of hundreds of royal writs issued to meet the needs of particular suitors some common forms emerged. The *nisi feceris* clause was sufficiently familiar to be imitated by the lords of great honours in conducting their own business. It still did not provide for the failure of the second agent to act; and in time a new writ was devised, which ran, 'Render the land in X to Y or come and plead in my court.' By a single order it either settled the case or initiated a judicial process, and so made a decisive advance in the development of originating judicial writs. The earliest known examples come from the reign of Stephen; an indication that even in that troubled time the royal administration continued to function actively, perhaps even creatively, in at least a part of the kingdom.[54] But there was then only a trickle of writs compared with the full flood of judicial writs that became formalized in the reign of Henry II.

The most important of the early originating writs were those that dealt with disseisin and with the establishment of right, particularly in claims of inheritance. The procedures were settled in the king's court by decrees known as assizes. Royal writs set in motion certain defined judicial actions; a sheriff was ordered to ascertain the truth of an allegation by means of a sworn inquisition. Sworn statements by jurors were already an integral part of normal legal proceedings in many regions; the assizes set up the machinery for impanelling a jury to give true answers to precise questions, and ordered the demandant to be present in court at the same time. One of the earliest assizes was *novel disseisin*, promulgated c.1166 and arising out of the numerous complaints of tenants that they had been unlawfully disseised of land and rights. Although disseisin had frequently taken place in Stephen's reign, large-scale acts of violence were not the principal factor in producing the assize. Many of the early assizes were brought by small tenants, very often against their lord who had distrained them for services they did not acknowledge and had confiscated their land. Sometimes the complaint was of exclusion from a lawful

---

[53] *Chron. Abingdon*, ii. 166–8, 184–7, 223, 226.
[54] Van Caenegem, *Writs*, no. 45; *Regesta*, iii. 692.

inheritance. This gave rise to the assize of *mort d'ancestor*, whereby the sheriff was ordered to summon twelve free and lawful men of the neighbourhood of the vill to be before the king or his justices on a given day, and recognize under oath whether the father of the demandant was seised 'in his demesne as of his fee' of the land in question on the day he died, and whether the plaintiff was the next heir.[55] Its importance is that it implied an abstract right reaching back into the past; and this, with the procedure initiated by the writ of right, was bound ultimately to undermine the jurisdiction of the baronial courts.[56] Much of this development lay in the future but, a century after the Norman conquest, England was entering a significant phase in the development of the common law.

Another aspect of this development was the emergence of the general eyre in the reign of Henry II. Earlier Norman kings had sent out justices with *ad hoc* commissions, and Henry I had frequently appointed both local justiciars and justices with slightly wider commissions to hear pleas in several counties. These experiments prepared the way for Henry II's appointment of justices *ad omnia placita* to go out on circuit to enforce the Assize of Clarendon and hear other pleas in 1166. They replaced the local justiciars; and their appointment was a symptom of the great increase in royal judicial activity.[57]

Procedures were changing slowly. In the first century after the conquest witness remained paramount; but written records gradually gained in importance. A claimant who could produce neither was ruled to have lost his case. In 1081 Bishop Herfast's attempt to secure control over the abbey of Bury failed in the king's court on all counts: he was unable to produce either documents or witnesses in support of his claim, and Herman the archdeacon, in recording the miracles of St Edmund, asserted that he stammered in his speech through the intervention of the saint and so demonstrated the illegality of his claim, since a mistake in a formal oath might render it invalid.[58] Baronial courts used the same methods. The court of the abbot of Thorney rejected Robert of Staverton's claim to hold Charwelton of the abbot in fee-farm because he failed to produce either charter or witness to prove it.[59] Sworn inquisition remained the most common form of proof; an inquisition taken in the king's court or before royal justices sent into a lower court and recorded was recognized as a satisfactory way of establishing a right. Thorney's

---

[55] Glanvill, xiii. 3 (p. 150).

[56] Milsom, *Historical Foundations*, pp. 128–9.

[57] William T. Reedy, Jr, 'The Origins of the General Eyre in the Reign of Henry I', *Speculum*, 41 (1966), 688–724.

[58] *Memorials of St Edmunds Abbey*, ed. T. Arnold (RS, 1890–6), i. 60–7; Harmer, *Writs*, pp. 141–5.

[59] Stenton, *English Justice*, pp. 138–9.

claim to the four fishermen of Farcet was recognized in this way. But the record of a court decision was still far more likely to be oral than written. If charters were produced during a case they might be read aloud to impress the facts on those present. The sworn inquisition held its own and became an integral part of the royal assizes. Sometimes when charters were produced they were vaguely worded, and their validity could be challenged. As rights became more sharply defined proofs were required for tenures that had long been taken for granted. This gave an incentive to forge records, or to insert clauses in genuine charters to guarantee freedom from jurisdictions that had not been exercised at the time the charters were granted. Churches in particular had ancient rights to which they could show no title; their efforts to find proof often led to lengthy litigation.

Charters of lay enfeoffment, rare in the eleventh century, became increasingly common from the early years of the twelfth. Gifts to monasteries were among the earliest to be recorded in writing in both charters and histories of the foundation and endowment of a house. From about the second quarter of the twelfth century more and more monasteries preserved informal records of transactions in their own courts, and of cases that involved them in the royal courts. Narratives had no legal standing, but they provided abbots, obedientiaries responsible for supervising estates, and administrative officers with practical information about how to defend their rights. They became sources for later chronicles. Records of suits in the court of Abbot Martin of Peterborough survive in a later cartulary. Henry of Blois, who became abbot of Glastonbury in 1125, left a short account of his successful attempts to restore the dilapidated estates of the abbey, which Adam of Domerham incorporated in his *History of Glastonbury* in the following century. Details of Thorney's cases which go far beyond the bare bones of charters and writs must have been written down long before they were copied into the still unpublished *Gesta abbatum* in the Red Book. In writing his *Gesta abbatum* of the abbey of St Albans, Matthew Paris made use of a roll compiled by Adam, cellarer from about 1141, which was rich in details of cases from the time of Abbot Robert (1151–66). Adam's duties as cellarer had given him a leading part in the law suits relating to land.[60] The chronicles of Battle and Abingdon, written in the reign of Henry II, gave particularly full details of law suits from the middle years of the century. 'We have determined', wrote the Battle chronicler, 'to pass down to our successors some cases as examples.'[61]

[60] J. D. Martin, *The Cartularies and Registers of Peterborough Abbey* (Northants. Record Society, 28, 1978), pp. xiii, 15–16; CUL MS Add. 3021, ff. 414v–61v; Adam of Domerham, pp. 304–15; R. Vaughan, *Matthew Paris* (Cambridge, 1958), pp. 182–4.

[61] *Battle Chronicle*, pp. 210–11.

Jocelyn of Brakelond also knew the value of detailed accounts of court proceedings. The rare lay cartularies and family histories like the Hotot cartulary, which survive from the thirteenth century, are mostly concerned with details of tenures and slightly later law suits, from the time when proceedings had become more formalized, and literacy had penetrated a little more deeply into society. The Hotot cartulary opens with a brief account of the descent of the family lands from the period immediately following the conquest, which was probably based on oral tradition for the first hundred years; litigation is recorded from the reign of Richard I.[62]

The Battle chronicle is particularly rich in details of procedure. Abbot Walter de Lucy (1139–71) was a brother of the chief justice, Richard de Lucy, who heard a number of their pleas. Charters figure prominently in the proceedings; even their forged charters claiming exemption from the bishop of Chichester's authority were never effectively challenged, though the bishop evidently had misgivings and complained unsuccessfully that they were contrary to the privileges of the church of Chichester. In the case between the abbot of Battle and Gilbert de Balliol, lord of an estate given to the abbey by Ingelran 'beacon-rider', which finally came to the king's court, the abbot defended his claim by producing charters of Gilbert's predecessors granting the land. Gilbert complained that they lacked seals; he assured Richard de Lucy that he himself had a seal, but the great man swept aside the objection with the comment, 'It was not the custom in the past for every petty knight to have a seal.' Gilbert's attempts to challenge the confirmation of Henry I fared no better, and the king himself intervened to say that 'if by a like charter and confirmation the monks could show this sort of right to this very Clarendon which I dearly love, there would be no way for me to deny that it should be given up to them completely.'[63]

Charters were not always accepted, however. Later in Henry II's reign, in a case before the king's court, the monks of Bury failed to break the hold of the Cockfield family on Semer and Groton, even when they produced a charter of Robert of Cockfield renouncing his claim to the manors. In Jocelyn of Brakelond's words, 'Our charter was read in public, but in vain ... The knights having been sworn said that they knew nothing about our charter or our private agreements, but that they believed that Adam, his father and his grandfather, had for a hundred years back held the manors in fee farm, one after the other.' In another case of conflicting claims to rights of jurisdiction, which came before the

---

[62] *A Northamptonshire Miscellany*, ed. E. J. King (Northants. Record Society, 32, 1983), pp. 3–58.

[63] *Battle Chronicle*, pp. 214–17.

king in person, deadlock was reached; the abbot of Bury and archbishop of Canterbury produced contradictory charters of King Edward. The abbot then offered to place himself upon the verdict of the counties of Norfolk and Suffolk; the archbishop refused to stand by their testimony because most of the men had a great love for St Edmund and were under the abbey's jurisdiction. Finally the king stormed out of the room, saying, 'Let him take who can!' and the matter remained unjudged for a number of years.[64]

Deadlock was sometimes resolved by compromise, or by the duel, which remained a valid form of proof throughout the period. By the end of the twelfth century it had become more unusual for duels to be fought to a finish; proceedings were opened, and then the parties reached a compromise. But the older forms of proof, such as the duel and compurgation, played an important part in earlier twelfth-century proceedings. Glanvill had something to say about them, alongside the newer procedure by possessory assize. Either battle or witnesses could be offered to prove the validity of a charter, in addition to more objective proofs such as comparison of the seal with others of accepted authenticity.[65] The assizes were gradually introducing a speedier and more final method of settling cases, but given the tangle of older customs and the possibility of legal delays and illegal pressures, it is not surprising that compromise remained a very common and popular method of bringing a dispute to an end, even before the introduction of the final concord towards the end of the century.[66]

The years before Glanvill wrote were a time of increasing definition of tenures and rights. His treatise contained the forms of many writs, and some rules of inheritance, particularly of military fees. But even his positive statements sometimes expressed only what a group of leading justices thought desirable, and there were many areas where custom was still varied and flexible. For some non-military tenures he was able to formulate only a few tentative guide-lines. Socage tenure had its own customs. The land was partible among heirs; in some places the oldest son, in others the youngest, had the chief holding with the house; and where there were no sons exactly the same rules applied to daughters. Minors were in the wardship of the 'procheyn amy': the nearest relative who could not inherit. Probably because lords had no interest in prolonging wardship, minors came of age when they were fifteen, and were capable of managing an agricultural tenement, whereas the heirs to military fees did not inherit until they were twenty-one. The son of a

[64] Jocelyn of Brakelond, pp. 123–4, 50–2.

[65] Introduction to the Curia Regis Rolls, ed. C. T. Flower (Selden Society, 62 (1943)), pp. 1, 113–22.

[66] On the final concord see Clanchy, pp. 48–9; and for the importance of consensus, Reynolds, Kingdoms and Communities, pp. 23–34.

burgage tenant, according to Glanvill, was of full age when he could count money carefully, measure cloth, and generally do his father's business.[67] These non-military tenures preserved many characteristics of the older customs of inheritance in both England and Normandy; like them they showed some variations of custom according to region within the broad framework of established family right.

Local variations persisted most of all in the unfree tenures that were the business of the manorial courts. The royal courts, after a period of hesitation, rejected them entirely from their sphere of competence. This decision brought the practical difficulty of defining villein tenure; but it also permitted peasant customs of inheritance to survive in all their variations for centuries after free tenures were forced into more general moulds. The military tenures in particular, as Milsom wrote, brought with them a logic which was to generate anachronisms throughout English history.[68] The anachronisms were not confined to the sphere of law; they emerged in the seventeenth century in interpretations of history, and proved equally persistent. The myth of the 'Norman yoke' treated the tenures, which were archaic by that date, as oppressive impositions brought by the Normans, to be contrasted with the original freedom of the English. Yet as common law began to emerge in the twelfth century it was neither rigid nor archaic. It was an evolving, practical, and on the whole effective response to the needs of society. And it was sufficiently mature to resist any wholesale application of Roman law when a knowledge of that law became sufficiently widespread to be influential. When Englishmen trained in the practice of the English courts studied in the schools of Bologna in the mid-twelfth century, and became familiar with the principles of Roman law, they received as Heinrich Brunner put it, the inoculation which enabled them to withstand a full-scale reception of Roman law later.[69] Glanvill's treatise owed much to contemporary legal theory in its ability to distinguish between civil and criminal pleas, or between the king's pleas and the sheriff's pleas. But the substance of the treatise was the fruit of long practical experience in the work of the courts. It is certainly arguable that if there had been no Norman conquest there would have been no common law. For it could not have developed as it did without, on the one hand, the feudal courts of the invading Normans, the strong principles of tenure established by the circumstances of the conquest, and the executive power of the Norman kings; and, on the other, the unifying authority of English kingship, the older courts of shire and hundred, and the effective Anglo-Saxon instrument of the writ.

[67] Glanvill, vii. 3, 9 (pp. 75–6, 82).
[68] Milsom, *Historical Foundations*, p. 20.
[69] Cited P. Stein, 'Vacarius and the Civil Law', *Church and Government*, p. 119.

7

Serfdom and Villeinage: the Manorial Courts

Large areas of judicial activity remained outside the common law. The royal forests had their own laws, enforced by special forest eyres, and were directly subject to the king's authority.[1] Privileged jurisdictions existed, and were taking clearer legal shape; Durham and Chester in time became immunities where the king's writ did not run. Tenures with special privileges within the competence of the royal courts were slowly defined. A separate assize, now lost, was ordained for the convenience of burgage tenants in cases of *mort d'ancestor*. Sokemen of the ancient demesne were allowed to sue in the king's courts by the little writ of right; these were customary tenants who had been settled on any royal demesnes at the time of Domesday Book, regardless of whether the land had since been alienated.[2] Many other customary tenures were, after a period of hesitant sifting, deemed to be unfree and rejected by the royal courts. The customs of one region only, the gavelkind of Kent, won lasting recognition by the royal justices.[3]

Many gavelkind customs seem to be survivals from the type of custom that was widespread at an earlier date in England. The chief peculiarities of the tenure included partible inheritance between male heirs, a widow's dower of half rather than a third of the land, and wardship not by the lord but by the 'procheyn amy'. Moreover tenure by gavelkind was assumed to exist unless a different form of tenure, such as knight service or serjeanty, was proved. Gavelkind even applied to lands recently reclaimed from the marsh or inned from the sea, whereas elsewhere it was more usual for such lands to be let for money rents or on terms prescribed by the lord, and not to enjoy the common rights attached to the standard tenements. Of particular interest too are the provisions for changing gavel land to frank fee. This could be done by reversion to the

[1] For the forests see Young, *The Royal Forests*.
[2] Glanvill, xii. 3 (p. 137); xiii. 11 (p. 155); Miller and Hatcher, pp. 118–19; Hilton, *Stoneleigh*, pp. 100–8; Pollock and Maitland, i. 393–4.
[3] N. Neilson, 'Custom and the common law in Kent', *Harvard Law Review*, 38 (1924–5), 482–98.

lord through escheat or failure of services, or by charter. Initially a royal charter was necessary; but King John granted Archbishop Hubert Walter and his successors the right of changing gavel land to frank fee.[4] This charter is reminiscent of the early Anglo-Saxon landbooks, when the king's intervention was necessary to change the status of land. Outside Kent certain customs of inheritance could be changed on individual manors with the consent of lord, kindred and local community; such changes were made from time to time piecemeal in the manor courts.[5] By contrast the gavelkind customs of Kent, resistant but not impervious to change, preserve many characteristics of older customs; they give some indication of the way custom, changeable only by powerful intervention, may have spread into newly cultivated and settled lands at an earlier period.

From the end of the twelfth century the royal justices sent most pleas relating to customary unfree tenures outside Kent (where there was no villeinage) to the manorial courts. These were the guardians and repositories of local custom. The right to hold a court did not merely derive from tenure; unlike the honorial courts, hallmoots were older than the conquest. Maitland suggested that they were derived from a principle that 'men of a certain rank have certain jurisdictional powers.'[6] There were also basic agricultural requirements, such as the regulation of common rights, or the apportionment of meadow land, which, together with the election of manorial officials, would have called for regular meetings of the customary tenants of at least a quasi-judicial nature. The hallmoot appears in close association with the Domesday manor, whether that protean word was applied to a large scattered estate with many hamlets over which a lord had rights of soke, or to a nucleated village, or to a part of a village divided between several lords. As tenure gained in importance after the conquest the right of a lord to hold a court for his tenants, in which they could be invested with their lands and distrained for failure to perform their services, must have emphasized the judicial side of the hallmoot's work. Scattered references in the *Leges Henrici primi* testify to the ubiquity of hallmoots, and indicate something of the business transacted there.

If the farmer of a manor had done homage to a lord as a fee farmer would do any dispute would be settled in the honorial court; but if the farmer had not done homage the settlement would be in the manor court.[7] This implies that normally the court witnessed the handing over

---

[4] F. R. H. Du Boulay, 'Gavelkind and the knight's fee in medieval Kent', *EHR*, 77 (1962), 510 n. 5.

[5] See for example M. Morgan, *The English Lands of the Abbey of Bec* (Oxford, 1968), p. 71.

[6] Maitland, *Domesday Book*, p. 81.

[7] *Leges Henrici*, 56. 1, 2 (pp. 174–5).

of a manor to a farmer for a term of years, and witnessed also the terms of the oral contract. Even when, later in the twelfth century, written farm contracts began to appear on some of the better organized great estates they probably merely supplemented and recorded the ceremony witnessed in the manor court. And when the farmer returned the manor to his lord at the end of his term, enquiry was made of the herdsmen and other manorial servants about the numbers of stock, the state of cultivation, and whether the value had decreased in any way. Manorial custumals written in Henry I's reign contain information relevant to the fixing of the farm, and probably arose out of testimony in the courts. The *Leges Henrici primi* name the reeve as the normal presiding officer. This is too sweeping; the more elastic reference in a Thorney case to 'the abbot or his officer' would be a safer generalization.[8] At a later date the presiding officer might be a bailiff or estate steward, and there must have been some variation even in the early twelfth century on great estates with a hierarchy of servants. An important meeting of the manor court would have called for the presence of one of the higher estate officials. Enquiries into manorial customs and detailed services owed by tenants of different types became common from the early years of Henry II. On some estates the information, partly provided by the tenants themselves, was confirmed by the sworn testimony of juries drawn from a cross-section of the peasantry.[9] Such information must have been given to the itinerant officials of larger estates in special meetings of the manorial courts.

There were both legal and economic reasons for these enquiries. From the angle of the law, both tenure and status were liable to be called in question. Although the assizes of *mort d'ancestor* and *novel disseisin* have at times been regarded as simply a remedy for the disorders of Stephen's reign, they were made necessary as much by the normal process of distraint and disseisin in seignorial courts at every level. As long as tenurial obligations remained traditional and not clearly defined, peasants no less than knights might be distrained for failure to perform services that seemed to them excessive and unjust. The fragmentation of holdings within families, and a market in land that was already active, meant that the same individual might hold a number of small tenements by different services. The same knight could hold various properties divided between military tenure and socage or, in Kent, gavelkind. Holdings combining villein, burgage and military tenures occurred on some estates.[10] A

---

[8] Cf. Chibnall, *Charters and Custumals of Caen*, pp. xxxi–xxxii; *Leges Henrici*, 20,1a (pp. 122–3); 'The Red Book of Thorney', CUL MS Add. 3021, f. 418v.

[9] R. Lennard, 'Early manorial juries', *EHR*, 77 (1962), 511–18.

[10] See for Worcester, *The Red Book of Worcester*, ed. M. Hollings (Worcs. Historical Society, 4, 1950), p. 412; for Shaftesbury see the unpublished Shaftesbury cartulary, BL MS Harleian, ff. 61–2. I owe this reference to Dr Ann Williams.

villager with a free holding might also have land in a standard villein tenement.

Naturally there was confusion about obligations. As Milsom has shown, 'the overwhelming majority of all early assizes seem to be brought in respect of peasant holdings.' Glanvill's specimen writs in a number of petty assizes are framed in terms of a virgate or a carucate of land, which was the standard holding of a prosperous peasant family.[11] Many sworn recognitions were uncertain at first what criteria to use to determine whether a tenement was free or not. Once the king's courts had decided to exclude villein tenures on the grounds that holders had never been legally seised of their tenements, and the true holders were the lords, they had to find a definition of villein tenure. Various criteria were tried, none wholly satisfactory because of the variations in local custom. The common law definition emerged only in the thirteenth century. In the reign of Henry II the royal justices were still in the early stages of sorting out the cases they were prepared to consider. When finally they rejected cases involving villein tenure, anyone claiming to hold a tenement in villeinage had to sue for his customary right in the court of his lord; but he still had a customary right, protected by that court.[12]

Even more difficult than the question of free or unfree tenure was that of freedom of status. The origins of serfdom differed from those of villeinage, and the common practice of using the terms 'serfs' and 'villeins' as interchangeable has added confusion to a complex subject. At the time of the Norman conquest personal servitude was widespread in England. More than 25,000 slaves (*servi*) were enumerated in Domesday Book. Men had been enslaved through war, capture in raids, sale by their families in time of need, and as a punishment for serious crimes. Individual manumissions were frequent, and the church, which at first had confined itself to insisting that slaves and free men were equal before God, gradually set its face more firmly against some forms of slavery. The synod of Chelsea in 816 laid down that on the death of a bishop every Englishman enslaved in his days was to be set free. Manumissions in wills became common. The will of Alfwold, bishop of Crediton, which freed all whom he had bought himself on every episcopal estate, was typical of a bishop's will; and many laymen freed at least their household slaves.[13] How far manumissions kept pace with fresh enslavements is uncertain; it may be true that slavery was declining by the middle of the eleventh century, under pressure from economic change no less than ecclesiastical opposition. Even so, the Norman conquest was the first conquest that did

---

[11] Milsom, *Legal Framework*, p. 24; Glanvill, xiii. 3, 27, 29 (pp. 150, 165, 166).

[12] For a full account see Paul R. Hyams, *King, Lords and Peasants in Medieval England* (Oxford, 1980).

[13] *Councils and Ecclesiastical Documents*, ed. A. W. Hadden and W. Stubbs (Oxford, 1869–78), iii. 583; *Councils and Synods*, i. 386.

not lead to an increase in the number of slaves. Between 1066 and 1086 the number of *servi* declined in some places.[14] William I was ready to give secular support to recent ecclesiastical canons which forbade the enslavement of Christians and attacked the slave trade; and Henry I took the same line. The 1102 Council of London still found it necessary to repeat that no one should practice the infamous trade, hitherto widespread in England, whereby men were sold like brute beasts. But prohibition of the slave trade did not affect the status of the thousands of men previously enslaved; nor indeed did it prevent individuals from voluntarily surrendering their liberty. The *Leges Henrici primi* described the ceremony in hallmoot or hundred court whereby a man could become a slave; and no doubt in times of famine or personal hardship some men were still driven by necessity to this desperate expedient.[15] Twelfth- and even thirteenth-century charters contain evidence of private sales of serfs. The trend, however, was away from slavery towards servile tenure.

There were different degrees of freedom and unfreedom. Most of the Domesday *servi* were household serfs or farm workers; many were ploughmen. But the large class of cottagers who held a few acres and worked several days on their lord's demesne included many of servile origin. Sometimes called *bubulci* they helped to perform the ploughing work of the former household serfs. They were in a similar position to the hutted slaves of the later Roman empire. Many were still of servile status, but the cottar class of mixed origins included falconers and craftsmen and the children of free peasants established on small assarts. In the village community intermarriage between free and unfree was frequent. Many small-holders must have spent their whole lives in ignorance of their exact legal status unless the question arose in a plea. Commendation blurred the dividing line still further, since it might bind a man and his land to a lord and involved humble sokemen no less than men of higher status. 'It shall be known separately, for all persons, of what status they are to be reckoned, whether free or servile', wrote the compiler of the *Leges Henrici primi*; but in practice this probably meant only that powerful lords were not to claim their men sometimes as slaves and sometimes as free men according to their convenience, as they had been known to do in the past. It proved sometimes almost beyond the wit of juries faced with conflicting evidence to determine how a particular individual ought to be classed.[16]

[14] Miller and Hatcher, p. 24.

[15] *Vita Wulfstani*, p. 43; *Councils and Synods*, i. 678; *Leges Henrici*, 78.2 (p. 243); A. L. Poole, *Obligations of Society in the Twelfth and Thirteenth centuries* (Oxford, 1946), pp. 18–20.

[16] *Leges Henrici*, 78. 2a, 2b (pp. 242–4); Helen Cam, *Liberties and Communities in Medieval England* (Cambridge, 1944), ch. 8.

Various writs issued by the first Norman kings show the royal courts grappling with the problem of servile status in cases which arose in the normal course of business. From at least the reign of William Rufus the king had to take notice of claims that certain men belonged with their chattels to a lord who brought a petition for their return. No doubt money was paid for the king's intervention, and he replied by issuing a writ of a type that ultimately developed into the common law writ of naifty. In origin the writs were purely executive; they ordered a sheriff or other officer to restore to a petitioner men who had run away. The terms used were *homines* or *fugitivi*, not *servi*; they may have referred either to former slaves or men who were bound to the soil but personally free. Sometimes chattels were included with the men, which suggests servile status; though the tenants of Ranulf Flambard who fled with their money from the lands of the bishoric of Durham to escape from paying fines he demanded from them were not necessarily servile. Sometimes, however, the lord definitely alleged that the fugitives were his serfs, while the men countered with a claim to be free; in other cases a new lord claimed that they were serfs and had been lawfully purchased by him. These cases led to a judicial enquiry to determine the status of the fugitives. Early cases involved the production of kinsmen on both sides, but the extent of intermarriage between persons of different status made the process unsatisfactory, and in time the courts fell back on the far from satisfactory expedient of treating certain obligations, such as the payment of merchet to marry a daughter or the performance of week work, as proofs of servility.[17]

In the early twelfth century tenants of all kinds, including the highest magnates, could be transferred from one lord to another. There were appropriate ceremonies for important vassals who had consented to a change of homage.[18] Humble peasants probably attended the next manor court of their new lord and paid their head tax or other dues to him. Charters record numerous gifts to churches that included both land and the men settled on it. Gifts of tithes were very often accompanied by the gift of a peasant to collect the tithe sheaves. The language of charters making grants of men was often ambiguous because the need for greater precision had not yet become apparent. Some granted the homage and *sequela* of a particular peasant; and although in time homage would be taken to imply a free man and *sequela* as a term for his descendants would be a sign of servility the confusion persisted well into the thirteenth century.[19] Exact status became significant chiefly in times of

---

[17] Van Caenegem, *Writs*, pp. 336–43, 467–77; Hatcher, *Past and Present* (1981), 3–39.
[18] Cf. Orderic, vi. 58–9.
[19] Lennard, *Rural England*, pp. 360–1; Hyams, *King, Lords and Peasants*, pp. 12–13; *Stoke-by-Clare Cartulary*, nos 66 (i. 48), 508 (ii. 331–2).

economic crisis and change. Lords recorded in their courts the duties of their peasants with steadily increasing precision, and that sufficed for most everyday business.

When the writers of treatises pronounced on the legal rights of the unfree their words were often out of touch with reality. Phrases taken from Roman law were applied to conditions where they were inappropriate. Richard fitz Nigel asserted in the *Dialogue of the Exchequer* that a lord had absolute right over both the land and the chattels of his serfs, using the Roman legal term *ascripticii*. Glanvill, in explaining how a man of unfree status might be freed with money offered by another person, stated that he could not himself purchase his freedom because all his money and chattels were the property of his lord. But even the Anglo-Saxon slaves had been allowed limited rights to some chattels. A law of Alfred prescribed that the four Wednesdays in the four Ember weeks were 'to be given to all slaves, to sell to whomsoever they please anything of what anyone has given them in God's name, or of what they can earn in any of their leisure moments'.[20] And the clergy, anxious to secure the soul's part in any legacy, pressed the moral right even of the unfree to offer something to secure prayers for their soul. There were undoubtedly cases in the later middle ages when the harshest possible interpretation was put on the inability of the serf to own anything; but the more liberal and confused tradition was one of the elements that broke down servitude in England at a relatively early date. There was also a limited amount of social mobility. Glanvill discussed the position of a former serf who had become a knight after being freed.[21] He was a practical man, and one cannot assume that the possibility was purely hypothetical.

However, the fact that Glanvill used the term *villanagium* to describe the condition of the men he sometimes called *nativi* is a sign of the confused thinking on unfree status that then prevailed. The courts were beginning to send cases of villein tenure (*villanagium*) back to the lords' courts on the grounds that land held in this way belonged to the lords. Yet the men brought before the courts by writs of naifty were not necessarily villeins, and a hundred years earlier the villeins had been substantial villagers quite distinct from the *servi* and clearly distinguishable at law by their higher wergilds. Glanvill even claimed in describing how men became naifs (*nativi*) that if a free man married a wife who was a naif and lived on a villein tenement 'so long as he is bound in this way by the villein tenure he loses, as a naif, all legal rights.' This is muddled thinking indeed, for it fails to distinguish tenure from status, and the

---

[20] *Dialogus de Scaccario*, pp. 56, 101; Glanvill, v. 5 (pp. 57–8); *Councils and Synods*, i. 34–5.

[21] Glanvill, v. 5, 6 (pp. 57–8).

courts had to recognize that many free men were holding some of their lands by villein tenure. Glanvill's confusion is one example of how, in Maitland's words, 'new theories could not master all the ancient facts.'[22]

A hundred years of Norman rule had the effect of eliminating slavery in England, or at least hastening its elimination. But as the serfs who, in 1086, had made up some nine or ten per cent of the total population, were absorbed into the peasantry the legal status of the great class of villeins (some 45 per cent of the population) was depressed.[23] Villein tenure slowly became a matter for the lord's court only. Whether the manorial courts protected or exploited customary tenants is a question on which historians have held opposing views, depending partly on the dates and regions on which they have relied for evidence. The most satisfactory solution so far is that proposed by J. Hatcher: where there was a shortage of men the advantage lay with the lord, who could usually find some means of oppression in the custom of the manor; where there was a shortage of land rather than labour the custom of the manor was respected and the peasantry had security of tenure.[24] In the first part of the twelfth century, as opportunities for assarting and expansion into the waste increased, there was probably a shortage of men. Temporarily villein status was depressed. In time the ancient facts proved too strong for the new theories, but it took two centuries for copyhold tenure to emerge, and another two for it to be recognized as falling within the scope of the common law. In the meantime the lord's court remained the normal court for the great mass of the peasantry to attend in order to receive or surrender their holdings, or make family settlements. For convenience many of these courts began to imitate the procedures of the common law courts. Villein tenants were far from being rightless; but there was no appeal for them from an unjust decision in the court of the manor to the court of the king. It was a potentially dangerous situation, until the inconsistencies that survived the changes of the eleventh and twelfth centuries brought copyhold tenure back into the common law courts in the sixteenth. Among the peasantry the men of Kent, with their protected gavelkind tenure, came best out of the legal turmoil of the twelfth century.

---

[22] Maitland, *Domesday Book*, p. 83.

[23] The figure of nearly 10 per cent is suggested by Miller and Hatcher, p. 22.

[24] Hatcher, *Past and Present* (1981), 21–6.

8

Canon Law and the Church Courts

The period from the pontificate of Leo IX (1049–54) to that of Alexander III (1159–81) was one of the great formative periods in the history of canon law. A series of church councils from the Council of Rheims in 1049 to the Third Lateran Council in 1179 promulgated reforming decrees that spread slowly through the western church. At the same time canonists were attempting to introduce some kind of order into the mass of ecclesiastical laws and customs that had accumulated through the centuries, and to resolve their apparent contradictions. Of the numerous earlier collections the *Panormia* of Ivo of Chartres was one of the most popular; and the *Decretum* of Gratian, which was published in Bologna *c.*1140, proved to be the most enduring.[1] Among the papal decretal letters answering enquiries many of those of Alexander III were to find a permanent place in the codes of canon law. But that was a later development; in the twelfth century many of the classical tenets of the law were still in the process of being formulated in the light of practical experience and custom, with some assistance from the definitions of Roman jurisprudence.

An essential part of this development was the liberation of the church from secular control and the strengthening of the hierarchy. This meant reinforcing the authority of the bishop in his diocese as well as that of the pope in the whole church. In Normandy and England immediately after the conquest bishops and archbishops certainly occupied a much more prominent place in the eyes of reformers than the distant pope, though his ultimate authority in spiritual matters was fully recognized in principle, and papal legates visited the realm from time to time. In Normandy church reform owed its impetus to the duke. William himself promulgated and to some extent enforced the Truce of God; he also summoned

---

[1] Among the fundamental works on the development of canon law are, P. Fournier and G. Le Bras, *Histoire des collections canoniques en Occident depuis les Fausses Décrétales jusqu'au Décret de Gratien* (Paris, 1931–2); S. Kuttner, *Repertorium der Kanonistik (1140–1234); Studi e testi,* 71 (Vatican City, 1937, reprinted 1973).

and presided over the provincial councils that promulgated the reforming decrees of the 1049 council of Rheims against simony and clerical marriage.[2] In England the picture was somewhat different. In spite of a close traditional bond between the church of Canterbury and Rome, going back to the mission of Augustine and the foundation of the see, the most recent reforms had made no impact. Among other causes the irregular position of Stigand was a real, if temporary, barrier to reform.[3] So it fell to William to initiate a new phase of church reform in England no less than Normandy. In 1070 he approved the holding of a council in which two papal legates participated. Their presence ensured that the removal of Stigand from Canterbury would not be challenged, and that the appointment of Lanfranc as his sucessor was of unquestionable legality. Lanfranc presided over the council of London in 1075, and played a leading part in the enforcement of earlier reforms, and in the introduction of some canon law texts into England.[4] The book he brought with him was a version of Pseudo-Isidore, the most popular collection of early papal decrees, authentic and forged. If it was soon to seem old fashioned, it was initially of great practical use in resolving the kind of questions that came before the courts, such as the authority of a metropolitan over the bishops of his province, or the legality of investigating charges against a bishop while he was deprived of liberty and property. Lanfranc himself made a distinction between the position of Odo of Bayeux as bishop and as earl, and imprisoned him as earl. In seizing the estates of William, bishop of Durham, before bringing him to trial for treason in 1088 he distinguished the vassal from the bishop.[5] This was a first step in the complex process of disentangling the spiritual and secular functions of the princes of the church.

The need to distinguish spiritualities and temporalities extended to every level of society, and it was only partially solved by the slow separation of ecclesiastical and lay courts. Whatever the purpose of William I's ordinance on the church cases, it certainly did not aim at such a separation.[6] It was phrased rather in terms of defining jurisdictions, insisting on the settlement of spiritual matters in accordance with canon law. Although it demanded the holding of the ordeal by hot iron under episcopal supervision at the bishop's seat or some place appointed by

[2] R. Foreville, 'The synod of the province of Rouen', *Church and Government*, pp. 19–39.

[3] Barlow, *English Church 1000–1066*, ch. 7; Brooks, *Church of Canterbury*, pp. 296–310.

[4] *Councils and Synods*, i. 565–616; Gibson, *Lanfranc*, pp. 138–40; Z. N. Brooke, *The English Church and the Papacy* (Cambridge, 1931), pp. 57–83.

[5] *Letters of Lanfranc*, nos 7, 47 (pp. 62–3, 152–3); Orderic, iv. pp. xxvii–xxx, 42–3; Gibson, *Lanfranc*, pp. 160–1.

[6] *Councils and Synods*, i. 620–4.

him, and this effectively took it out of the shire courts, it did not interfere with the holding of the ordeal of water for lesser crimes in numerous local courts. Bishops and archdeacons were forbidden to hold episcopal pleas only in the hundred courts; the shire courts continued to provide a venue for business of all kinds. In this, as in so much, William preserved the older traditions of the realm in so far as they were compatible with new developments. The Anglo-Saxon law codes contained provisions dealing with the payment of ecclesiastical dues, the condition of churches, and the status of the clergy; they respected the force of ecclesiastical regulations for some of the crimes of the clergy and sins of the laity. Cnut's code stated that for a grave crime a priest was to forfeit his orders and go on a distant pilgrimage, and that for lesser crimes 'ecclesiastical amends are always to be diligently demanded according to the instruction in books of penance, and secular amends according to the secular law.' Before the conquest it was a matter of convenience to hold many kinds of pleas in the same assembly, where sheriff and bishop presided and priests as well as lay witnesses were present.[7] The practice changed very slowly; the *Leges Henrici primi* listed bishops among those who ought to attend the shire court, and included a clause that the 'due rights of the Christian faith' were to be dealt with first, before the pleas of the crown and the causes of individuals. The treatise distinguished procedures rather than courts, stating that 'all causes have their own methods of legal procedure.' The section on ecclesiastical pleas belonging to the king was largely concerned with the division of pecuniary penalties.[8]

However, episcopal synods were ancient institutions; and as the amount of ecclesiastical business coming before prelates and archdeacons increased separate courts were established and slowly widened their competence. Judicial work regularly arose in the course of a synod or chapter. A bishop's competence was imperfectly defined; since he was also a great feudatory part of the work of his court touched on secular business. Archdeacons gradually took over routine diocesan business, at first as the bishop's deputies, but in time in their own right.[9] In this formative period there were more complaints of infringement of rights by another ecclesiastic than by the lay power. But there were some areas of overlapping jurisdiction where the difficulty of separating spiritualities from temporalities gradually created rights that would in time have to be defined. One such area was the holding of churches, tithes, and all ecclesiastical dues and property.

[7] II Cnut, 41, 38. 2 (*EHD*, i. 424–5); Barlow, *English Church 1066–1154*, p. 152.

[8] *Leges Henrici*, 7. 2, 3 (pp. 98–101) and p. 315; 57. 8b, 9, 9a (pp. 178–9).

[9] Barlow, *English Church 1066–1154*, pp. 135–7, 154–5; Brett, *The English Church*, pp. 150–61.

The Anglo-Saxon law codes distinguished between three types of church; the old minster, usually the mother church of an extensive parish served by several priests, a thegn's church with a graveyard, and a field chapel without a graveyard. Minster churches might be very well endowed with several hides of land; the families who provided the clerks to serve them usually regarded their portions as part of the family inheritance. The thegns who built and endowed the smaller churches with a ploughland or two expected to appoint a priest and to derive some profits from the church.[10] In the eleventh century it was not uncommon for churches to be bought and sold, given in pledge, divided, or let out at farm. In spite of the attacks of reformers on the proprietary church, the Normans still accepted it as part of the social order. They were prepared to concede that laymen should not hold tithes; but they continued to give tithes to monasteries, who treated them as monastic property. It became normal for any lord to be able to dispose freely of two-thirds of his demesne tithes to a religious house, with the permission of the bishop.[11] Besides the revenues derived from parish churches, patrons expected to enjoy the right of presenting the incumbents. All these things made up the advowson of churches at the beginning of the twelfth century, and litigation about possession of advowsons normally fell within the sphere of seignorial or royal courts. It was only when advowson was redefined in the course of the century that canonists were able effectively to bring some of the spiritual elements in church property within the acknowledged competence of the church courts. It had to be made clear that the presentation of a clerk to the bishop for admission to a church was not the same as the enfeoffment of a lay vassal.[12]

Bishops were responsible for inducting new incumbents and for the consecration of new churches and chapels. These duties involved enquiries into the parochial status of the churches, whether they were canonically vacant, and whether an alleged patron was competent to present. So bishops were drawn into investigations that might, if an advowson was contested, either be settled by compromise or give rise to a legal process involving the bishop. Archbishop Theobald was drawn by appeal into a number of such cases. Between 1156 and 1161 there was a conflict about Hinton church, which Ernald of Devizes claimed had been wrongly taken from him by Reginald of Dunstanville, earl of Cornwall, for his own clerk, Osbert. At first a compromise was arranged whereby the church was restored to Ernald while the question of right was settled judicially. The earl then complained that he had been disseised of the church by 'a certain ruffian'; Ernald maintained that he held it justly by

---

[10] II and III Edgar. 1, 2 (*EHD*, i. 395); Lennard, *Rural England*, pp. 306–32.
[11] Giles Constable, *Monastic Tithes* (Cambridge, 1964), pp. 83–110.
[12] See Yver, *BSAN* (1965), 189–283; Cheney, *Roger of Worcester*, pp. 95–6.

the authority of Bishop Jocelyn of Salisbury with the consent of the patron. When the earl obtained a royal writ ordering the archbishop to restore the church to Osbert, Ernald complained that no one dared to appear against the powerful earl, and he therefore appealed to the archbishop. Osbert finally decided that the church was not worth the expense, and withdrew from the suit and the appeal. Another case came to Theobald from the diocese of Norwich, where Richard of Drayton and Alexander his brother appealed from a decision in the archdeacon's court, whereby the archdeacon 'under pretext of the king's command and after the semblance of a trial, attempted to deprive Alexander of the advowson of St Andrew of Ringstead in order to transfer it to Ralph Lestrange'. Ralph and the archdeacon were prepared to prove their case with witnesses and documents.[13] Bishops were properly concerned with the spiritual business of admission and induction to benefices; the royal courts succeeded in tightening their hold on cases of advowson only after the meaning of advowson had been more narrowly defined. Even then many disputes continued to be settled extra-judicially during the bishop's enquiries into whether a church was truly vacant, and who had the right of presentation.[14]

Some of the archbishop's increased business resulted from appeals that came to him as metropolitan. But William of Corbeil and Theobald both acted at times as papal legates, and it was becoming normal for an archbishop of Canterbury to look to the pope for this special status. In the twelfth century the appellate jurisdiction of the pope developed throughout western Europe 'from an inchoate state to a more advanced one'. Canon law, in contrast to the civil law with which it was often studied, allowed direct appeal to the pope at a relatively early stage of proceedings. Litigants did not have to wait for judgement, or take their case step by step through the hierarchy. The archbishop was frequently invoked, possibly in his capacity as legate, to prevent an inferior court from proceeding with a case, and to protect the property of a litigant from sequestration. By the end of the century a well-defined system of tuitorial appeal had been established; appeals were made to Rome and for the tuition of Canterbury in the time of Archbishop Hubert Walter, but the roots of the system went back for half a century. In one capacity or another Theobald was probably concerned with some fifty appeals to Rome.[15]

Recourse to Rome was made easier by the practice of appointing judges delegate. Cases were delegated by papal mandate for settlement in

---

[13] *Letters of John of Salisbury*, i. 162–3, 123–4; van Caenegem, *Writs*, p. 284 n.2.

[14] Sayers, *Papal Judges Delegate*, p. 184; *Select Canterbury Cases*, pp. 76–7.

[15] Sayers, *Papal Judges Delegate*, pp. 3, 96–7; *Letters of John of Salisbury*, i. p. xxxii.

the provinces where they originated. Like the early royal writs, the early papal mandates were protean in form, but under Lucius II (1144–5) and Eugenius III (1145–53) a common form began to be used.[16] The circumstances in which appeals might be undertaken were as yet imperfectly understood, and it was still possible for one lay litigant, in a suit being heard by the bishop of Lichfield as papal judge delegate, to appeal from the bishop's court to the archbishop, without understanding that appeal in such a case could be made only to the pope himself.[17] The case is symptomatic of the slow penetration of canon law through the imperfectly organized hierarchy of the lower courts, and through them into society in general. England was not alone in this. Even if the disorders of Stephen's reign increased recourse to the church courts in borderline cases where the litigants despaired of any effective action from the secular authorities, the growing volume of appeals owed far more to general changes in the western church than to any local political uncertainties. The English bishops such as Gilbert Foliot, Bartholomew of Exeter, Hilary of Chichester and Roger of Worcester were all 'men of Europe, familiar with the papacy in action'.[18] Studies at Paris, attendance at papal councils and experience as papal advocates had familiarized them with the broad movements in the church. By the end of the pontificate of Alexander III procedures were being systematized and applied throughout western Europe.

Apart from property cases – an area of jurisdiction that was particularly contentious – lay and ecclesiastical jurisdictions overlapped in cases that had a penitential or pastoral side, or concerned the persons of clerks. Two main categories where the church was recognized as having a special competence were matrimonial and testamentary cases. Courts had frequently to decide on the legitimacy of marriages, and to determine the consequences, civil and ecclesiastical, of bastardy. This sensitive subject was particularly difficult because canonists were hotly debating the question of what made a valid marriage, and different views prevailed even after Alexander III attempted to give a general ruling. Marriage was, in origin, a civil contract. Vacarius likened the handing over of a woman to the transfer of property in Roman law. This view did not prevail among theologians, who saw it as a sacrament, or canonists, who fought a long and ultimately successful battle to introduce an element of consent. Consent was bound to be potential dynamite in a world where the disposal of heiresses was of crucial importance to lords and kindred

---

[16] Adrian Morey, *Bartholomew of Exeter, Bishop and Canonist* (Cambridge, 1937), pp. 44–78; Sayers, *Papal Judges Delegate*, ch. 1.

[17] *Letters of John of Salisbury*, i. 93; Sayers, *Papal Judges Delegate*, p. 44.

[18] Knowles, *Episcopal Colleagues*, pp. 51–2.

alike, and often it was more theoretical than real. Nevertheless if the validity of a marriage was challenged, the form in which consent was given might decide the outcome.

In the early twelfth century one prevailing view was expressed by Gratian: whatever promises had been given, the marriage was not fully legal unless it had been consummated.[19] This was challenged by the theory of some canonists, favoured by Eugenius III, that consent was all that was necessary, even if the parties never lived together. A slightly subtler view, propounded by the Paris doctors, ultimately found favour with Alexander III: an espousal was made valid only by *verba de praesenti* ('I take you'), not *verba de futuro* ('I will take you'). There were dangers in this interpretation, since it recognized the validity of clandestine marriages; lay men and women were strongly encouraged to exchange their vows publicly and formally before a priest at the church door for greater security. The priest could then dictate the ritual words, and there would be witnesses to the truth of what had been said. One witness in a case of *c.*1200, when asked whether he knew by what words it was customary to contract matrimony, replied that he did not know very well; though he had married a wife that very year he did not know by what words he had contracted with her.[20] It is unlikely that ordinary men and women were any better informed in the middle of the century.

Indeed the maximum uncertainty prevailed at that time, since the law was changing. Litigation might be lengthy and expensive as the notorious Anstey case, which dragged on from 1158 to 1163, illustrates.[21] It was a case of a disputed inheritance, depending on whether William de Sackville, who had been contracted to Albereda de Tresgoz but had never lived with her, was free to marry Adelicia de Vere, with whom he later contracted marriage and who was the mother of his children. His nephew, Richard of Anstey, successfully claimed to be his heir, on the grounds that the first marriage was lawful and could not be annulled, and therefore the children of the second marriage were illegitimate. At a slightly earlier date, when Gratian's views were in favour, he would probably have lost his case; but it went to the papal court at a time when Alexander III had just come down on the side of the Paris doctors, and had not yet pronounced the children of annulled marriages to be legitimate. The case was both costly and worth winning; within a very few years Richard of Anstey was able to pay off debts of over £340 for legal expenses out of the estate. Litigation began and ended in the king's court,

[19] See *Select Canterbury Cases*, pp. *81–8*; Georges Duby, *Medieval Marriage* (Baltimore, Md., 1978), pp. 62–81.

[20] *Select Canterbury Cases*, pp. 25–7, 23.

[21] For details of the case see P. M. Barnes, 'The Anstey Case', *Early Medieval Miscellany*, pp. 1–24.

but the intermediate stages were settled in the papal court, under the protection of the archbishop of Canterbury. A letter drafted by John of Salisbury neatly summed up the king's attitude: 'Since matrimony is annulled or confirmed in accordance with ecclesiastical law, the court of our catholic sovereign, Henry II, decreed that the case should return for judgment to an ecclesiastical court, where the question of marriage might be duly determined in accordance with canon law, which the clergy know, whereas the common people do not.'[22] Once the validity of the marriage was settled, the case returned to the king's court for the final settlement of the question of inheritance. This practical division of labour between two jurisdictions was in line with accepted traditions.

In testamentary cases too the church courts had a recognized place.[23] Wills were oral, made before witnesses, but they might for convenience be recorded. Most Anglo-Saxon wills fell into two classes: *post obit*, which could be made at any time and might be changed, and *verba novissima*, or final death-bed bequests. Priests were likely to be present at a death-bed to hear a final confession and administer extreme unction; they frequently appeared among the witnesses, and encouraged the penitent to leave some goods as alms for the soul's part. There was far greater freedom of devise for chattels than for real estate; most land could be disposed of by will only with the consent of kindred and lord, and this remained a very important limitation. Churchmen had, at first, no particular responsibility as executors. One problem was to ensure the carrying out of a donor's wishes; in Anglo-Saxon England the heriot owed to a lord on the death of a tenant was often enlarged to propitiate him and ensure his protection of the estate. But in the twelfth century the view slowly gained ground that legacies should be sought before an ecclesiastical judge. A letter of Gilbert Foliot as abbot of Gloucester to his bishop, Robert Bethune, asked for support in carrying out the bequests of Gunni of Stanton, a clerk who had taken the monastic habit on his death-bed. He had left the corn in his house to his servants, and had divided the remainder of his goods between the abbey of Gloucester and the cathedral of Hereford.[24] Some canonists were reluctant to concede that bishops should be involved in the execution of testaments; but a few Anglo-Norman canonists put responsibility squarely on the bishop. Glanvill, though uncertain about the respective duties of heirs and executors, took the same general view: if a dispute arose about the execution of a will it should be settled in an ecclesiastical court.[25] At the same time, the royal courts were becoming increasingly hostile to the bequest of land. As a

---

[22] *Letters of John of Salisbury*, i. 227–37, no. 131.
[23] The subject is fully treated by Sheehan, *The Will*.
[24] Morey and Brooke, *Letters of Gilbert Foliot*, pp. 49–50.
[25] Glanvill, vii. 5, 8 (pp. 79–81, 186); *Select Canterbury Cases*, pp. 88–9.

result of feudal pressures, the secular courts were also defining and limiting the rights of married women and the rights of villeins.[26] But within the sphere allowed to testamentary disposition, the church courts kept alive legal practices derived from sources different from those that were slowly building up the common law. The insistence on the soul's part preserved some residual property rights over chattels, even for the members of society whose rights were, in theory, most severely curtailed.

A third area in which spiritual and temporal jurisdiction overlapped related to persons. Laymen were subject to ecclesiastical authority when their offence was a serious sin leading to excommunication. But in a legal system whose sanctions depended on the enforcement of oaths it was not always easy to distinguish crime from sin, or perjury from sacrilege. Usury was a sin, but the lay courts claimed cases of debt. Jews were in a special position; they could take usury from Christians without violating any penitential code, and as aliens they came under different controls when charges were brought against them. In 1144 the Jews of Norwich were accused in the synod of Bishop Everard of murdering a boy; but in obedience to the sheriff they did not answer the formal summons to the synod, and the bishop took no action. The sheriff was doing his duty in protecting them; as aliens they came directly under the jurisdiction of the king.[27]

The greatest difficulties arose from the position of the clergy. Cases of married clerks were entirely the business of the church courts, except when the Norman kings expressed their willingness to help in enforcing the canonical prohibition of marriage; and clerks who married, held property and lived in a secular way were liable to be treated as laymen.[28] Clerks recognized as such came under the jurisdiction of their ecclesiastical superiors for all offences; the problem was whether a clerk guilty of murder or some other grave crime that led to his being deprived of his orders should then undergo further punishment. As long as bishops were present to handle ecclesiastical pleas in the shire courts the question may rarely have arisen. The same court could have pronounced a further layman's penalty for the unfrocked offender without the obviously double judgement involved by separate proceedings in a different court. It was also uncertain whether a clerk ought to appear first in the king's court for his status to be established. By the early years of Henry II's reign this was a contentious area of jurisdiction; the little surviving evidence of

---

[26] See Glanvill, vii. 5 (pp. 79–80) for the rights allowed a married woman in practice.

[27] *Select Canterbury Cases*, p. 96; Glanvill, x. 12 (pp. 126, 191–2). For the position of Jews see *Dialogus de Scaccario*, pp. 99–100; Barlow, *English Church 1066–1154*, pp. 154–5. The case of St William of Norwich is discussed in detail by Gavin I. Langmuir, 'Thomas of Monmouth: Detector of Ritual Murder', *Speculum*, 59 (1984), 820–46.

[28] *Leges Henrici*, 57. 9 (p. 178).

actual cases suggests that practice varied. Becket made the question of the double judgement an issue of principle, but it is far from certain that many clerks had been dragged through two courts. When the king, in consultation with his learned advisers, attempted to find an acceptable formula for procedure in cases involving criminous clerks they arrived at a compromise solution that did not exactly describe previous practice.[29]

Some of the procedures adopted in ecclesiastical cases were well established and traditional; others were more innovatory. Canon law allowed considerable influence to local custom; and similar experiments might arise in secular and ecclesiastical courts. The older procedure for bringing offenders before the courts, going back at least to Carolingian times, was communal accusation by a group of sworn members of the parish, the synodal witnesses. The 1108 primatial council held by Anselm at London, which was particularly concerned with clerical marriage, spelled out procedures for stamping out the abuse. Anyone charged by synodal witnesses with violating the council's decrees should purge himself with the oaths of six reliable witnesses if he were a priest, five if a deacon, and four if a subdeacon. The later legatine council held at Westminster in 1127 put the duty of seeking out offenders firmly on the archdeacons and other responsible officials.[30] This is a clear reference to an alternative, newer procedure: prosecution on the initiative of individual ecclesiastical officials by virtue of their office. It had certainly been practised in the late eleventh century: the growing influence of the archdeacon and his regular exercise of much of the petty disciplinary jurisdiction of the bishop helped to extend its use and abuse. It could be an instrument both of reform and of oppression. No doubt it contributed to the bad reputation of archdeacons: John of Salisbury coined the apt word 'ambisinistrous' to describe them. Henry II attacked the practice on several occasions early in his reign, and in the Constitutions of Clarendon forbade the accusation of lay persons except by reputable witnesses in the presence of the bishop; he also offered the assistance of the sheriff, who might summon a jury of twelve lawful men of the neighbourhood to make a sworn statement before the bishop when powerful offenders were involved.[31] The clause is interesting, as van Caenegem has shown, in offering a form of procedure that had a long future in secular courts. But in spite of the king's opposition, *ex officio*

---

[29] For the most recent discussions of the very complicated question of criminous clerks and Clause 3 of the Constitutions of Clarendon, see *Councils and Synods*, i. 848–52, 857–62; Smalley, *Becket and the Schools*, ch. 5; Charles Duggan, *Canon Law in Medieval England* (London, 1982), ch. 10.

[30] R. van Caenegem, 'Public prosecution of crime in twelfth-century England', *Church and Government*, pp. 61–70; *Councils and Synods*, i. 694–703, 743–9.

[31] *Councils and Synods*, i. 863, 880.

proceedings continued to have a place in later church courts. Similar procedures of impleading by a royal justice in the secular courts, which had been widely applied in the early years of the century in both Normandy and England, proved equally unpopular. Minor officials like Robert *Malarteis,* who was said to accuse men whenever he could in order to bring cases before the royal justices, were as heartily disliked as were the archdeacons.[32] Though Henry II had little success in controlling procedures in the church courts, he was able to put an end to the practice in his own courts. The Assize of Clarendon in 1166 firmly established prosecution by means of indicting juries as the normal method of initiating criminal proceedings before lay judges.

The clergy and the church courts played their part in establishing methods of proof. Since both the judicial duel and the ordeal were appeals to the judgement of God the presence of priests was necessary in both. The clergy were becoming increasingly unwilling to participate in either. Robert Pullen, who wrote a theological textbook *c.*1142–4, stated his opinion that ordeals should be banished from the church of God. Some twenty years later a monk called Senatus, who drew up a kind of penitential for Roger, bishop of Worcester, treated the duel as an occasion for imposing penance on two angry men, both victor and vanquished. Not until 1215, however, was there any general decree against clerks in major orders taking part in the ceremony of the ordeal.[33] Custom was too strong, and alternative forms of proof were too defective for the practice of the courts to catch up with the views of the most educated theologians and canonists without a very long time lag.

In cases involving spiritual property or unlawful alienation some of the proofs offered in church courts were much the same as those available in the royal courts. Litigants might produce witnesses or documents in support of their claims. In taking up an appeal from the diocese of Norwich, Archbishop Theobald explained that the appellant was prepared to produce both.[34] Bishop Roger of Worcester sought the advice of Alexander III about a case in which an abbot was accused by his convent of making grants out of the convent's property. The pope cautiously advised the bishop to use his own judgement, taking into account the size of the grant and local custom, 'always provided that custom does not clearly run counter to the canons'. On the question of the validity of charters after the death of the witnesses named in them he was almost

[32] Orderic, iii. 348–9.

[33] Barlow, *English Church 1066–1154,* pp. 159–64; J. W. Baldwin, 'The intellectual preparation for the canon of 1215 against ordeals', *Speculum,* 36 (1961), 613–36; Cheney, *Roger of Worcester,* pp. 61–4.

[34] See above, p. 196.

equally cautious; he did not think that they had any validity unless they had been drawn up by a notary (a provision that would rarely have applied in England at that date, when there were no licensed notaries) or had an authentic seal by which they could be tested.[35] In the later practice of the courts witnesses continued to play a predominant part, and even seemed at times to be preferred to charters. This may have been because of a procedure pioneered by the church courts during the twelfth century and later to be widely and advantageously adopted, namely the systematic cross-examination of witnesses.

Detailed records of cases survive only from about 1200; but procedures were then running so smoothly as a matter of routine that they must have gone back for several decades. Instead of merely depending on the reliability and number of the witnesses produced by the opposing parties, who might be swearing to contradictory statements, the presiding officers asked them searching questions. If the validity of a marriage was in question they might be asked, 'When exactly did the marriage take place? Morning or afternoon? Where? Was the weather wet or fine? What words were used? Who was present? What were they wearing?' (a question on which the women were usually better informed than the men) and so forth. Although the earliest records do not reveal how the evidence collected in this way was handled, and often do not tell the outcome of the case, they provided material that must often have helped the judges to reach a fair settlement.[36] They show a rational approach to legal judgements, even if up to the middle of the twelfth century, in spite of promising new developments, many formal procedures in courts of all kinds were still customary and archaic.

In the early years of Henry II's reign, up to the time of his quarrel with Archbishop Thomas Becket, the everyday relations of secular and ecclesiastical courts were on the whole harmonious, as in the Anstey case. There were, however, a number of very dangerous areas, where ancient custom ran contrary to new canon law, and on several occasions a clash was averted only by concession and compromise. One danger area was that of appeals to Rome, for the king expected them to take place only with his permission, and not at all if they seemed contrary to his interests. When Hilary, bishop of Chichester, pressed his rights as bishop against privileges of exemption claimed by the abbot of Battle, which the abbot defended with forged royal charters in the king's court, he was prepared to tell the king initially that it was impossible for any layman, even for a king, to give ecclesiastical privileges and exemptions to churches.[37] But

---

[35] Cheney, *Roger of Worcester*, pp. 178–9.
[36] For details of cases see *Select Canterbury Cases*, pp. 1–3, 18–24, *et passim*.
[37] *Battle Chronicle*, pp. 186–207.

he was not prepared to face the king's mounting anger when it transpired that he had procured a letter from the pope without royal permission. Henry took him aside for a quiet talk, and he withdrew his charges. 'Is it correct', the king then asked openly, 'that you have done and said this not under compulsion, but voluntarily?' 'It is true', replied the bishop. 'I have done and said this voluntarily, on the compulsion of right reason.' Becket proved less complaisant, and friction increased. The position of criminous clerks was another very difficult subject; the king wished their status to be decided in his court, just as he wished cases of advowson to come to his court so that a decision could be reached there about whether it involved lay fee or spiritualities only. His determination to treat advowson as a form of secular property was contrary to the developing law of the church. And he steadfastly resisted any attempt to excommunicate any minister of his without his consent. Matters came to a head in the council of Clarendon in January, 1164.[38]

The constitutions issued at Clarendon are a landmark in the history of Anglo-Norman government. When Henry II ordered in his court at Clarendon that a record should be made of some of the customs and liberties and prerogatives of his ancestors, in particular of his grandfather, King Henry I, he was following precedent up to a point, but thereafter departing radically from it. His great-grandfather William I had presided over a Norman assembly at Lillebonne in 1080, and had issued a series of canons defining the liberties and customs which king and bishops traditionally enjoyed in Normandy. Copies of the canons were made by some or all of the bishops who attended, and they were used as a working guide for the bishops' courts. They were never challenged; and indeed the king offered a remedy by promising to restore any rights which any bishop or layman was able to prove in the king's court that he was entitled to enjoy by long tenure or ducal grant.[39] Henry II offered no such remedy; and eighty years had radically altered the relations of secular and ecclesiastical courts. In looking back to the reign of Henry I he was attempting to ignore the changes brought about by the refinement of canon law and the growth of a system of appeals to Rome, no less than by any temporary lapses of royal vigilance during Stephen's reign. Moreover some of the customs recorded appear to have been less what had been done in the past than what the king thought ought to be done; others, such as the correct procedures in elections of bishops and abbots, were tolerated anomalies, which earlier popes like Paschal II and Innocent II had allowed to continue in order to avoid a struggle with the

---

[38] *Councils and Synods*, i. 852–93, provides an excellent analysis and bibliography, together with the text of the Constitutions.

[39] Orderic, iii. 24–35.

king of England when they already had a schism and a war with the Emperor on their hands. One at least, the celebrated Clause 3 on criminous clerks, was carefully drafted after long discussion, and attempted to reach a compromise satisfactory to all in a particularly difficult area of overlapping jurisdiction.

What was most unusual, however, was the fashion in which the constitutions were promulgated. They were recorded in the form of a chirograph or charter, which the bishops were required to seal. In spite of the statement in one manuscript of Fitz Stephen's *Life of Becket* that the bishops complied, the overwhelming weight of evidence is against this; they would not go beyond verbal consent, to which some added a proviso saving their order.[40] Becket himself insisted that the approval of the pope should be obtained; and Alexander III refused to confirm the Constitutions. The king, however, had three copies made: one for each of the two archbishops and one to be kept in the royal archives. It is the first known example of the recording in this way of customs issued in the king's court.

The earliest written records preserved in the treasury were financial. Geld rolls, Domesday Book, the early Pipe Rolls and records relating to the royal manors were among the archives accumulating there. The scribes in the royal chancery may well have kept copies of the forms of writs for their own convenience, as the scribes in episcopal chanceries kept copies and drafts of some of the letters sent out by the bishops. But these were formularies and letter books in the making rather than legal records. Charters were sent to beneficiaries, and the responsibility for proving their authenticity rested with the recipients, not with the king. The record of court proceedings still rested on the oaths and memories of witnesses, supported sometimes with private documents. We are still some decades away from the keeping of the *curia regis* rolls and chancery enrolments. The development of the tripartite chirograph recording the settlement or final concord that brought private disputes to an end belongs to the time when Hubert Walter was active as chief justiciar (1193–8); one copy went to each of the litigants and the third, the 'foot of the fine', was placed in the Treasury as a record.[41] The preservation of the third chirograph of the Constitutions of Clarendon was a stage in the development of this form of record keeping. But it was particularly unusual in that a written, official series of canons or constitutions was being preserved in the royal archives.

The development of law in twelfth-century England was largely the work of the courts, guided and controlled by an increasing number of

[40] Cheney, 'William Fitz Stephen', p. 149.
[41] Clanchy, p. 48.

royal administrative directives. Even the most literate court in western Europe, the papal court, was only beginning to preserve a permanent record of the canons of church councils in the twelfth century. Canons were promulgated by being read out at the close of a council; copies of the canons of the 1095 council of Clermont, for instance, which were carried away all over Europe, differed in content and detail according to the interests of the participants.[42] The early royal ordinances or constitutions were issued as instructions to sheriffs, bishops and others, and were either lost or preserved in private (mostly ecclesiastical) archives. Their chance survival was due to chroniclers or to officials like the compiler of the *Leges Henrici primi*, who tried to put together a working collection of customs and laws. From about 1164 Henry II devoted more and more attention to clarifying and defining, in a series of great assizes, the work of government. His assizes dealt with the punishment of crimes, the position of the sheriffs, the laws of the forest and the boroughs. Some have been lost; those that survive are known to us because of their preservation in chronicles. Monasteries often received official documents; but in the late twelfth century a new type of historian, the royal clerk, was appearing alongside the monk chroniclers and archdeacons. Roger of Howden in particular made it his business to include in the two chronicles he wrote copies of any royal assizes he could find; and he added interpretations and explanations from his own experience in the royal court and as a justice of the forest.[43] But his work belongs to the later years of the reign, and was in any case an unofficial record. The king's wish to keep an official record of the Constitutions of Clarendon was before Howden's time and, as far as we know, it stands alone. A few years later, in 1169, supplementary clauses further sharpening and defining the original clauses and giving details for their enforcement were issued in a more conventional way: three different versions have survived.[44] They were adapted to the recipients, most probably the sheriff of Kent, the royal justices, and the bishop of London; they were the products of adminsitrative activity, whereas the original constitutions were intended to be a permanent written record.

This novelty may explain the reaction of some contemporaries to the Constitutions of Clarendon. When Becket's supporter, Nicholas of Mont St Jacques, Rouen, told Henry II's mother, the Empress Matilda, that some of them were contrary to the Christian faith and almost all to the

[42] For details of the various versions see Robert Somerville, *The Councils of Urban II*, vol. i, *Decreta Claromontensia, Annuarium Historiae Conciliorum*, Supplementum i (Amsterdam, 1972).

[43] J. C. Holt, 'The Assizes of Henry II: the Texts', *The Study of Medieval Records*, ed. D. A. Bullough and R. L. Storey (Oxford, 1971), pp. 85–106.

[44] *Councils and Synods*, i. 926–39.

liberty of the church, and that she and her son were in danger of eternal damnation, she asked to see them.[45] He procured a copy and reported her response:

> This woman is of the race of tyrants, and she approved some of them, such as the clause forbidding the excommunication of the king's justices and ministers without his permission ... But she condemned others. And what particularly displeased her was that they had been put in writing, and that the bishops had been forced to swear to observe them; that had never been done by any of their predecessors.

She thought that it would be enough for all to promise to observe the ancient customs of the kingdom, on the understanding that the secular justices would not take away the liberty of the church, and the bishops would not abuse their liberties. She pleased Nicholas by commenting shrewdly that much trouble arose because bishops ordained clerks before they had a title to any church, so that poverty drove them to crime; and they were not restrained by fear of losing a church since they had none, or of being committed to the bishop's prison, since the bishop would rather allow them to go unpunished than have the trouble and expense of guarding and feeding them. Yet some wealthy clerks had as many as six or seven churches, in flat contravention of the sacred canons. The old Empress expressed the traditional views of the first Norman rulers: respect for ancient customs and liberties, a keen sense of the value of moral reform in the church, and a reluctance to come to grips with the new problems raised by the interlocking of two increasingly centralized systems of jurisdiction and the immanent question of sovereignty. Her son had a keener appreciation of some of the changes; and when he had the Constitutions of Clarendon recorded and preserved he was taking one step at least towards legislative rather than purely executive action in an increasingly literate society. It was one sign of a change in law and government that has been characterized as the 'Angevin leap'.[46]

---

[45] *Materials for the History of Thomas Becket* (RS), v. (ed. J. C. Robertson), 148–50.
[46] Stenton, *English Justice*, ch. 2.

9

Normans and English

The history of England from the conquest to Magna Carta has been described as 'the amalgamation of two nations, the *Franci* and the *Anglici*' into a single country, which was 'ruled by an English king, lived under a common law, and spoke one language'.[1] Much was achieved even in the first hundred years. The assimilation of the last wave of invaders in a multi-racial society took very little longer than the assimilation of the previous Danish invaders. There were differences because the Normans and their allies came as a dominant aristocracy, both lay and ecclesiastical, and established themselves through the length and breadth of the country. They spoke a widely current language, which was to persist far longer than any Scandinavian tongue as a vernacular spoken at court and in government. But after the first decade it began to be clear that they were far more than an army of occupation, provoking all the hatred and hostility that such armies have to face in any age. They had come to stay and had a common interest in the prosperity of the land they occupied. They appreciated from the first the arts of government that contributed to the wealth of its rulers. Within a generation they were beginning to cherish its traditions and venerate its saints alongside their own.

The Norman or Frankish element in the population was relatively small. No figures exist, but in 1086 the newcomers were probably much less numerous than the 25,000 slaves at the other end of the social scale. They had, however, effectively ousted all the earls and great tenants-in-chief;[2] the aristocratic element in old English society survived principally through the marriages of its womenfolk to Norman lords. For many new barons this strengthened their hereditary claim to the lands they acquired; and as Normans moved into Welsh lands some of them likewise married into the families of native Welsh princes. In England survival without

[1] R. C. van Caenegem, *The Birth of the Common Law* (Cambridge, 1973), pp. 4–5.
[2] F. M. Stenton, 'English families and the Norman Conquest', *TRHS*, 4th ser., 26 (1944), 1–12; Clark, *Speculum* (1978), 223–51.

diminished wealth was easier for the lesser thegns, for the moneyers in
the large towns, and for certain skilled craftsmen. Those who prospered
became in time possible marriage partners for the daughters of great
Norman families, but this took longer to achieve. It was the great-
grandson of Deorman, the London moneyer, not his son as Douglas
believed, who married a kinswoman of Gilbert of Clare.[3] As long as the
canonical prohibition of clerical marriage was ignored by many of the
higher clergy, Norman bishops like Roger of Salisbury frequently took
English women as their wives and concubines. Richard, the son of Nigel
bishop of Ely, was himself of mixed blood. When he wrote in the
Dialogue of the Exchequer that 'nowadays, when English and Normans
live close together and marry and give in marriage to each other, the
nations are so mixed that it can scarcely be decided (I mean in the case of
freemen) who is of English birth and who of Norman', he was describing
the upper segment of society that he himself knew.[4] The Norman element
was certainly strengthened by further immigration of knights and clergy
during the twelfth century; studies of individual honours such as Holderness and Leicester have shown that many lords established the sons of
their Norman vassals on their English estates as subinfeudation proceeded in the twelfth century. But English-born knights too appear,
particularly in the north and in the Welsh marches; and some younger
sons of Norman families found it more profitable to seek their fortune in
Scotland.[5]

English priests could sometimes rise to high office in the church and in
great households. Ailred, the son of the last of a line of 'learned,
respectable and conscientious' married priests of Hexham, was brought
up at the court of King David of Scotland, and for a time performed the
duties of steward; he might have been promoted to the bishopric of
St Andrews if he had not entered the Cistercian order where he rose to
be abbot of Rievaulx.[6] There is no evidence for mass migration at the
peasant level, apart from the settlements round Carlisle, which were
probably of peasants from England, and the colonies of Flemings who
were deliberately planted in Pembrokeshire. The Norman element in the
population remained relatively small, if powerful, and was gradually
diluted by intermarriage. How many Normans actually slipped down the
social scale into the peasantry, or left children of mixed blood among the

---

[3] Nightingale, *Numismatic Chronicle* (1982), 38–9, correcting Douglas, *Domesday Monachorum,* pp. 62–3.

[4] Roger's concubine, called Matilda of Ramsbury in an interpolation in Orderic, vi. 533n, may have been English; for intermarriage see *Dialogus de Scaccario,* p. 53.

[5] English, *Holderness,* ch. 4; David Crouch, *The Beaumont Twins* (forthcoming); for Scotland, G. W. S. Barrow, *The Anglo-Norman Era in Scottish History* (Oxford, 1980), ch. 1.

[6] Powicke, *Life of Ailred,* pp. xxxiv–xlii.

serfs during the first century is a matter for conjecture. Richard fitz Nigel and the justices collecting murder fines assumed that the unfree would be English; this may have been a convenient legal fiction. In 1066 the Normans found thousands of unfree men and women in the country; they brought no serfs with them. The assumption was therefore plausible whether it was true or not. Twelfth-century cases of alleged naifty revealed many unions of free and unfree parents; some of the free may have been Normans. But the majority of the English too were free in status, in spite of the growing legal concept of villeinage. And as fashions for names such as William, Richard or Henry spread to all classes, Christian names ceased to be a reliable guide to racial origins.

Assimilation of culture and tradition advanced rapidly. Even before the end of the eleventh century the cavalier attitude to the unfamiliar English saints expressed by Picot, sheriff of Cambridgeshire and invader of the lands of Ely, had disappeared. Norman abbots and bishops identified themselves with the interests and traditions of the churches they came to rule. Lanfranc learned from Anselm to respect the saints of England, and Anselm actively promoted their cult. Geoffrey, abbot of Crowland, helped to foster a local cult of the executed Earl Waltheof.[7] Hagiography became a thriving branch of historical writing in the English abbeys; new lives of English saints were written, and new collections of miracles assembled.

Historical writing too, with its emphasis on lineage, stretched back into the English no less than the Norman past. Orderic Vitalis at Saint-Evroult in Normandy, and William of Malmesbury in England, were both of mixed blood, alert to the traditions of both peoples. Many Anglo-Norman chronicles included genealogies of English kings. Henry I's marriage with the granddaughter of Edward Atheling was a master-stroke of policy; it provided a link with the line of Cerdic to strengthen the claim of the Conqueror to be the legitimate successor to the crown of England. Norman magnates who put down roots in England as well as Normandy liked to feel themselves heirs to the races settled in both lands. When, shortly before 1140, Gaimar wrote his *Estoire des Engleis* for Constance, the wife of a minor Lincolnshire lord, Ralph fitz Gilbert, he treated old English history as a part of the Norman heritage.[8] The Englishman, Ailred of Rievaulx, was equally ready to enter the minds of the Norman barons when he described the battle of the Standard, prefacing it with a rhetorical speech by Walter Espec on the valiant deeds of the Normans in regions as far away as Sicily, Apulia and Calabria. Yet

[7] *Liber Eliensis*, pp. 210–22; B.J. Levy, 'Waltheof "earl" de Huntingdon et de Northampton', *Cahiers de civilisation médiévale*, 18 (1975), 183–96.

[8] G. Gaimar, *L'Estoire des Engleis*, ed. A. Bell (Anglo-Norman Text Society, xiv–xvi, 1960).

when he addressed his *Genealogy of the Kings of England* to the multi-racial future king, Henry II, it was the Saxon side of Henry's very mixed ancestry that he stressed: 'You, greatest of men, are the son of the most glorious Empress Matilda, whose mother was the most excellent and Christian queen of the English, the daughter of the most blessed Margaret queen of Scots ... whose father was Edward son of Edmund, son of Ethelred', and so on back to the noble King Alfred.[9] Geoffrey of Monmouth plunged into legend in his determination to invest the kings of England with a genealogy older and more distinguished than that of the Frankish rulers descended from Charlemagne. Most of these historians wrote in Latin; but Gaimar and after him Wace and other historian poets pleased their patrons in French. The *Anglo-Saxon Chronicle*, attenuated and kept up only at Peterborough, came to an end early in Stephen's reign; and no one after this date recreated the old English past in the old English tongue. Anglo-Norman French had taken over as the language of the court.

There is little direct evidence of the languages spoken at different levels of society in the early years of Norman rule. After a year or two Latin gradually replaced Old English as the language of royal writs; and though some bilingual charters were still written in local monastic scriptoria early in the twelfth century, the vernacular was rapidly ousted by Latin as the language of written instruments of government.[10] Since, however, most royal and seignorial business was transacted orally, it was possible for magnates and administrators at all levels to carry on their daily duties in one or other of the current vernaculars. Naturally all the magnates were French speaking; there was no place for spoken English in Normandy, where attendance at court and the administration of their own scattered estates frequently took them. The fact that Normandy and later Anjou and other continental provinces were an integral part of the Anglo-Norman realm throughout the twelfth century ensured that French would establish itself so firmly as the language of the court and of oral legal business that it passed into the written government records of the later Middle Ages. Some knowledge of Latin as well as French was desirable for the laity at the highest levels of government, even if they never formally studied grammar or learned to construe Latin, and were therefore described by chroniclers as illiterate. In Normandy the younger sons of counts might be educated and trained, like Henry of Blois, for high office in the church; and the ducal house gave more than a merely military training to its elder sons as well.

[9] *Relatio de Standardo*, in *Chronicles of the Reigns of Stephen, Henry II and Richard I*, ed. R. Howlett (RS, 1884–9), iii. 181–99; Powicke, *Life of Ailred*, p. xliii; *Historiae Anglicanae Scriptores* x, ed. R. Twysden (London, 1652), col. 347.

[10] Bishop and Chaplais, p. xiii; Clanchy, pp. 12–17.

All the children of William the Conqueror, including his daughters, appear to have been well educated by contemporary standards. Robert Curthose was schooled by tutors who are described as grammarians. William Rufus (and possibly Henry also) was brought up under Lanfranc's direction. Henry, as the fourth son, may originally have been intended for the church, and his court had a reputation for culture.[11] Robert, earl of Gloucester, Henry's eldest bastard son, was said by Geoffrey of Monmouth to have been 'educated in the liberal arts'; and William of Malmesbury, welcoming him as a literary patron, praised his love of letters.[12] Henry's daughter, the Empress Matilda, was literate enough for the needs of government, which sometimes weighed on royal ladies with the duties of acting as regent and supervising their own households. When in 1164 Nicholas of Mont St Jacques took the Constitutions of Clarendon to her in the hope of winning her support for Becket's resistance, she asked him to read them to her in Latin and explain them in French.[13] Henry's wife, Matilda, educated by her aunt Christina in the convents of Romsey and Wilton, could read Latin. She kept her own court at Westminster when her husband was in Normandy, and according to William of Malmesbury attracted to it poets and musicians, many from overseas.[14] A monk named Benedeiz, who wrote a *Voyage de St Brendan* first in Latin and then in French, dedicated his work to her. It is the earliest surviving example of literary Anglo-Norman, written in a somewhat archaic and eclectic language, with some words of occitan or Italian origin alongside a dialect of north-western France. Benedeiz's younger contemporary, Philippe de Thaon, had three English queens as patrons: Matilda herself, Henry's second wife Adeliza of Louvain, and lastly Eleanor of Aquitaine. His works show the varied interests of the educated, French-speaking laity; he wrote a vernacular *Bestiary*, a *Computus* and two *Lapidaries*, as well as a *Livre de Sibylle* dedicated to the Empress Matilda.[15]

Even if Anglo-Norman literature was spreading from the royal to the baronial courts such as that of Ralph fitz Gilbert, the great mass of the population remained English speaking. Bilingualism spread wherever it was needed for everyday business, or for the advancement of the able and ambitious. In the baronial class most men, women and children picked

---

[11] David, *Robert Curthose*, p. 6; M. D. Legge, 'L'influence littéraire de la cour d'Henri Beauclerc', *Mélanges offerts à Rita Lejeune* (Gembloux, 1969), i. 679–87.

[12] Geoffrey of Monmouth, *Historia regum*, ed. A. Griscom (London and New York, 1929), pp. 219–20; Malmesbury, *GR*, ii. 356.

[13] *Materials for the History of Thomas Becket* (RS) v. (ed. J. C. Robertson), 148–9.

[14] Clanchy, p. 217; Malmesbury, *GR*, ii. 493–5.

[15] M. D. Legge, 'Les origines de l'anglo-normand littéraire', *Revue de linguistique romane*, 31 (1967), 44–54.

up enough colloquial English to run their households and supervise their estates. Learning began from their English nurses, but they were soon fostered in other households where they mixed with French-speaking knights and ladies.[16] Some of those who presided in the local courts where English was spoken may have mastered the language thoroughly; others relied on interpreters. In the church a noble priest of English birth who rose to high office needed to be trilingual. Ailred of Rievaulx certainly spoke French at King David's court and was fluent in Latin; but on his death-bed it was the English language he had spoken in childhood that came naturally to his lips in the words recorded by Walter Daniel, 'Festinate, for crist luve.'[17] Many of the lower clergy spoke only English. One of the miracles recorded in the life of Wulfric of Haselby describes how he cured a deaf and dumb boy, who immediately began to speak in French and English. The parish priest who witnessed the miracle complained bitterly that a stranger from far away, who would have been grateful for the gift of speech in a single language, had been granted the use of two, whereas he himself, who had served Wulfric devotedly for many years, had never been given the knowledge of French, and had to stand silent whenever he went to the bishop or archdeacon. Clearly in the west of England at that date the higher clergy conducted their business with each other in French. Though local dialects may have compounded the difficulty of communication, French was the surest language for advancement in the early twelfth-century church. This was only natural, since it was the *lingua franca* of the greatest schools in northern Europe, and in all areas of Norman or French settlement, from Jerusalem to Aragón.

We do not know how many of the parish priests were bilingual. The majority of the lower clergy may have been of pre-conquest stock, but many churches were in the gift of Norman lords who treated them as family livings for their sons. If a substantial number of the parish clergy were linguistically out of touch with their flocks, this may explain why so many of the hermits like Wulfric, who ministered to the needs of the 'submerged majority', came from the non-Norman strata of society.[18] Another hermit was the Norfolk-born St Godric, who settled in a hermitage at Finchale about 1110. A contemporary *Life* describes his earlier career as pedlar and merchant, trading in Flanders, Denmark and Scotland. In these occupations the English language evidently sufficed; he remained English-speaking all his life. If those who came to consult him

---

[16] M. D. Legge, 'Anglo-Norman as a spoken language', *Anglo-Norman Studies*, 2 (1980 for 1979), 109; Clark, *Speculum* (1978), 230.

[17] Powicke, *Life of Ailred*, p. 60.

[18] Ian Short, 'On bilingualism in Anglo-Norman England', *Romance Philology*, 33 (1979–80), 467–79; Holdsworth, 'Christina of Markyate', pp. 202–3.

in his hermitage spoke French he used an interpreter. A self-taught layman, he could understand Latin; but when on several occasions he spoke fluent French it was regarded as miraculous.[19]

Godric has an additional interest for us as the author of some of the earliest-known Middle English verse; he composed hymns to the Virgin Mary and to St Nicholas.[20] English, so widely spoken, was the language of popular devotion, and a prelate who wished to preach to his flock had to do so in a dialect they could understand. There must have been more English hymns like those of Godric, and many more sermons than have survived. Jocelyn of Brakelond said, in speaking of the preaching of Abbot Samson, that he 'read English perfectly'; and the abbot advised a new prior, whose ability to preach in chapter was questioned by the monks, to learn by heart the sermons of others if need be, adding that in many churches sermons were preached before the convent 'in French or better still in English'.[21] But English, even if spoken informally in some monasteries, scarcely emerged as a written, literary language until the thirteenth century; whereas Anglo-Norman French was important both in the literature of the court and as a spoken vernacular throughout the twelfth.

In the first half century after the conquest, Anglo-Norman and Latin together gradually ousted Old English as a literary language. Changes in monastic libraries, however, show far more than a change in language. There was a shift in interest and in monastic culture. Before 1066 the library of Christ Church, Canterbury, contained 'the books that formed the "Anglo-Saxon curriculum", that is the works that served for the instruction and regular annual reading of English monks'. For the most part they were books for moral and religious teaching, like the *Distichs* of Cato, the biblical poems of Juvencus and Arator, or Aldhelm's *De Virginitate*: books typical of the interests in tenth-century continental monasteries like Fleury, which had contributed to the English monastic revival in the time of Dunstan. Many had Old English glosses and some were written entirely in Old English.[22] Both Canterbury and other churches had substantial collections of poetry, both pagan and Christian. But there were few of the great patristic works, apart from Gregory the Great's *Liber pastoralis*. In spite of the flourishing cults of English saints the lives of many were still unwritten; and history was represented chiefly

---

[19] Short, 'Bilingualism'; *Vita S. Godrici*, ed. J. Stevenson, Surtees Society, 20 (1847), pp. 179–80, 203–4, 206–7.

[20] *The Oxford Dictionary of Saints*, ed. D. H. Farmer (Oxford, 1978), p. 175.

[21] Jocelyn of Brakelond, pp. 40, 128.

[22] Brooks, *Church of Canterbury*, pp. 266–70; M. Lapidge, 'The study of Latin texts in late Anglo-Saxon England: (1) the evidence of Latin glosses', *Latin and the Vernacular Languages in Early Medieval Britain*, ed. N. P. Brooks (Leicester, 1982), 99–140.

by vernacular chronicles or short Latin annals. Canterbury was not alone in having no copy of Bede's *Ecclesiastical History*; even the clerks of Durham, who had his bones, appear not to have possessed one.

The Norman abbots and bishops lost no time in filling the libraries of abbeys and cathedral priories with copies of the books regarded as essential reading in Norman monasteries.[23] Gundulf at Rochester, Ernulf at Christ Church and later Rochester, Godfrey at Malmesbury, and William of Saint-Calais at Durham were conspicuously active in the work. Pride of place, after biblical commentaries and homilies, went to the works of the Fathers, particularly Augustine, Jerome, Ambrose and Gregory the Great. Historical writings were not neglected: first of all the standard histories of Eusebius, Josephus and Bede; and later histories of particular peoples, such as Paul the Deacon's *History of the Lombards*, and William of Jumièges's *Gesta Normannorum ducum*, as well as collections of church canons. Carolingian writers still had their place, but the emphasis had changed. Within a generation or two interests became more diversified; when William of Malmesbury pursued his studies and continued the work of collecting books for his monastic library, the range of books – biblical, patristic, classical, Old English, Carolingian and contemporary – was wide enough for him to become one of the best read men in twelfth-century England. Bury St Edmunds developed an active scriptorium under Abbot Baldwin, but did not build up its basic collection of standard patristic works until after his death. In the twelfth century it collected more varied and contemporary works, including some of Anselm's writings and the *De sacramentis* of Ivo of Chartres, as well as a rich selection of classical texts.[24]

Book production changed slowly, as older scribes died and new styles were introduced. The best products of an English scriptorium such as Canterbury before 1066 were written in a graceful English Caroline minuscule, with beautifully decorated initial letters; the illustrations were often finely executed. The new volumes copied under Norman influence were often splendidly produced, matching in quality the grandiose new churches being constructed at the same time. The earlier volumes gave less attention to illustration, though the Norman scriptoria such as that at Mont Saint-Michel had a tradition of historiated initials and author

[23] N. R. Ker, *English Manuscripts in the Century after the Norman Conquest* (Oxford, 1960), pp. 8–10, 22–5; R. A. B. Mynors, *Durham Cathedral Manuscripts to the End of the Twelfth Century* (Oxford, 1939), pp. 33–45; K. Waller, 'Rochester Cathedral library; an English book collection based on Norman models', in Foreville, *Les mutations socio-culturelles*, pp. 237–50.

[24] R. M. Thompson, 'The reading of William of Malmesbury', *Revue bénédictine*, 85 (1975), 362–402; R. M. Thompson, 'The library of Bury St Edmunds Abbey in the eleventh and twelfth centuries', *Speculum*, 47 (1972), 619–45.

portraits. But within a generation Anglo-Norman scribes had begun to combine English and Norman styles to produce a new romanesque style of remarkable richness and variety. Such works as the great Bible, illuminated by Master Hugo in about 1135 for Bury St Edmunds, or the slightly later Winchester Bible, show how tradition could be combined with innovation to revitalize both English and Norman art.[25] At a humbler level, the script and spelling of names in such works as the *Liber vitae* of Thorney show how Old English orthography persisted into the mid-twelfth century, and was gradually modified as Norman clerks and English monks adapted each other's usages to their own traditions.[26]

Nowhere is the complexity of the relationship between Norman, Anglo-Saxon and early Anglo-Norman traditions more apparent than in architecture and the fine arts. The effect of the conquest was to produce an immediate upsurge of building, as new castles, cathedrals and monasteries sprang up all over the country. 'In every village, town and city', wrote William of Malmesbury, 'you may see churches and monasteries rising in a new style of architecture.'[27] Continuous employment and higher remuneration led to increased professionalism in the work of masons, who perfected techniques of shaping ashlar blocks and overcame problems of construction. The best quarries were exploited for building materials; Caen stone, brought by sea for the building of Lanfranc's new cathedral of Canterbury, was also in great demand elsewhere. The grandiose scale of the planning stemmed from the patrons; the execution was in the hands of master masons, some of whom were of continental origin with experience in Normandy; the sculpture and metal work came from the hands of craftsmen working in local workshops. Some were Normans, especially when the simpler sculpted capitals were mass-produced in larger workshops; but many were either English or immigrants trained locally in English techniques. Post-conquest buildings were constructed in a developing Anglo-Norman, not an imported Norman, romanesque style. And although the initial impulse to early romanesque came from Normandy, there had been exchanges of ideas and mutual borrowings even before the conquest.[28]

An early romanesque style appeared in Normandy in the second quarter of the eleventh century, in such buildings as the great abbey

[25] Brooks, *Church of Canterbury*, pp. 270–5; J. J. G. Alexander, 'Manuscripts', in *English Romanesque Art 1066–1200* (Catalogue of the Exhibition at the Hayward Gallery, 1984), pp. 83–4; and in general see R. M. Thompson, 'England and the twelfth-century Renaissance', *Past and Present*, 101 (1983), 3–21.

[26] C. Clark, 'L'Angleterre anglo-normande et ses ambivalences socio-culturelles: un coup d'oeil de philologue', in Foreville, *Les mutations socio-culturelles*, pp. 99–110.

[27] Malmesbury, *GR*, ii. 306.

[28] *English Romanesque Art 1066–1200* contains a detailed bibliography and excellent introductory essays. Important modern studies include Zarnecki, *Proceedings of the British*

church at Bernay. It drew its inspiration from many sources, particularly Italy (and beyond Italy from Byzantine influences), the valley of the Loire, and even Mozarabic Spain. One characteristic was the architectural quality of the sculpture; 'not made in the workshops of craftsmen, but in the mason's yard on the building site', and therefore monumental rather than decorative.[29] In England craftsmen often worked in many media; they carved stone and ivory, painted murals, illuminated manuscripts and modelled and engraved metals. Motifs were copied from one medium to another; manuscript illustrations reappear on stone capitals or in the designs of silversmiths. Sculpture tended to be a form of engraving on stone; figures like the lions flanking the arch in St Benet's church in Cambridge are, in Zarnecki's words, 'superimposed, as a brooch is pinned to a dress'. Even before 1066 Norman romanesque was penetrating England; Edward the Confessor's plan for his new abbey at Westminster was derived from the great abbey church at Jumièges, begun some years earlier; but the building of the two churches continued simultaneously, and Jumièges may in its turn have been influenced by Westminster.[30] Robert of Champart, archbishop of Canterbury and previously abbot of Jumièges, gave his Norman abbey English manuscripts, which included a magnificent illuminated Sacramentary; and the low relief ornamentation on some of the capitals at Jumièges is certainly copied from motifs in Anglo-Saxon manuscript illustration. The fusion of two different stylistic traditions to form a new Anglo-Norman romanesque was to continue after the conquest.

The great churches constructed by Norman patrons in England in the last three decades of the eleventh century were probably designed to equal the most imposing continental churches. In particular Winchester cathedral, with its royal associations, may have been intended by Bishop Walchelin to rival in scale the basilica of St Peter in Rome. When Lanfranc came to Canterbury in 1070, immediately after arranging the building of the abbey church of St Stephen at Caen, one of his first tasks was to rebuild the cathedral church, destroyed by fire three years previously. Owing much to Caen, it was planned on a larger scale and was completed in Lanfranc's lifetime. The new church of St Augustine's at Canterbury, begun about three years later owed in turn much to Christ

---

Academy (1966), 87–104; Richard Gem, 'The romanesque cathedral of Winchester', British Archaeological Association Conference Transactions, 6 (1983), 1–12; R. Gem, 'The significance of the eleventh-century rebuilding of Christ Church and St Augustine's Canterbury', (British Archaeological Association Conference, 5 (1982)), 1–19; W. Oakeshott, The Two Winchester Bibles (Oxford, 1981).

[29] Zarnecki, Proceedings of the British Academy (1966), p. 96.

[30] R. Gem, 'English Romanesque Architecture', in English Romanesque Art 1066–1200, pp. 27–36.

Church cathedral, but introduced some new features, notably in the plan of the crypt with its ambulatory. This became a prototype for imitation at Worcester, Bury St Edmunds, and elsewhere.

Some of the Norman prelates respected older liturgical practices in planning their new churches. Such features as the western extensions and aisled eastern transepts at Winchester and Ely helped to provide subsidiary altars both for the 'secret places of prayer' prescribed in the *Regularis Concordia* which had been adopted during the tenth-century reforms, and for the veneration of local saints.[31] Master masons for their part often introduced themes derived from the craft tradition in which they had been trained. The influence of the new style evolving in England was soon felt in Normandy, where the flat Anglo-Saxon decorative sculpture of the kind introduced at Ely, or in a humbler setting at the little church of Water Stratford, soon found favour. One capital in the church of Saint-Georges-de-Boscherville appears to have been directly copied from a capital at Steyning in Sussex. There were new advances too in structure and design in the twelfth century. Durham cathedral, begun in 1093 and completed about 1130, was innovatory in its successful attempts to cover the whole of a large building – nave, aisles and transepts – with ribbed stone vaults. This technical achievement was soon adopted elsewhere, either by imitation or by independent experiment, and was to revolutionize late romanesque architecture.

As with institutional development, architectural change shows the fruitful amalgamation of different traditions, each one already eclectic in its content, under the stimulus of sudden and violent change. Recent European movements, more deeply felt in Normandy, combined with earlier European and insular traditions existing in England to produce something that was neither Anglo-Saxon nor Norman, but truly Anglo-Norman. This would not have been possible without the skills fostered in both countries. Some earlier writers have regarded the Norman conquest as an artistic disaster; but far from destroying native English skills it provided a new milieu in which they were able to be exercised in new ways. The work of such a man as Master Hugo, who worked at Bury St Edmunds in the second quarter of the twelfth century, painting the great Bible, casting the bronze doors of the abbey, carving a wooden crucifix, and possibly also painting murals and carving in stone, is a measure of the artistic achievement, strongly influenced by English traditions, that was possible in this age.[32]

---

[31] A. W. Klukas, 'The continuity of Anglo-Saxon liturgical tradition', in Foreville, *Les mutations socio-culturelles*, pp. 111–23.

[32] Cf. G. Zarnecki, 'General Introduction', *English Romanesque Art 1066–1200*, pp. 15–24. The Bury Bible is in Corpus Christi College, Cambridge, MS 2.

Epilogue

When Henry, duke of Normandy, count of Anjou, and duke of Aquitaine, added the kingdom of England to his dominions in 1154 he brought it into a much wider framework of government than that of the earlier Anglo-Norman realm welded together by William I and his sons. But this did not affect its society and institutions as profoundly as the Norman conquest of 1066 had done. One reason for this was that the three-tiered structure of Angevin government necessitated a great deal of local autonomy.[1] The king with his chamber, chancery and other household officials, travelled ceaselessly throughout the whole of his dominions, dealing with whatever business required his personal attention wherever he happened to be. Below him local justiciars, seneschals and treasurers exercised his delegated authority. The frequent absences of Henry I in Normandy had hastened the emergence of a type of viceregent; the more extensive travels of Henry II necessitated the appointment of a justiciar and other great officers of state to carry on business in his absence. And below them the local administration of sheriff and reeve continued to function as local custom required.

Within the realm of England some local variations resulted from the conditions of Norman settlement in a land of diverse customs. Lords in the marches of Wales and the north of England enjoyed exceptional judicial privileges. These originated partly in the authority that William I and his sons had given to men such as Hugh of Avranches and Roger of Montgomery to enable them to push the frontiers forwards; and partly in the different administrative structure of the northern counties with their long history of separatism. Yet even in regions of exceptional privilege the framework of royal control had been established in the first century of Norman rule. The king was in a position to claim at a later date that any lord entitled to hold pleas of the crown did so through a grant of privilege that was revocable if abused; the royal forests everywhere were

---

[1] Le Patourel, *Feudal Empires*, ch. 8, p. 298.

under the jurisdiction of the king, and his justices held the forest pleas.[2] By 1166 the limits of effective government had been established, extending to the Scottish border and including south Wales, with some claim to lordship and ecclesiastical authority in north Wales too. However independent the marcher lords might seem to be, then or later, they were bound to the royal authority, and a twitch upon the string would in the end bring them back to order. The Anglo-Norman realm had been established as an effective unit of government; and in spite of local variations it had too the beginnings of a common law.

A second reason for its greater resistance to fundamental change was that a hundred years of assimilation had produced a society which in its social structure no less than in its art and culture was truly Anglo-Norman. The cross-Channel interests of the aristocracy that had made it impossible for Stephen to hold England indefinitely once he had lost Normandy remained strong; but the knightly class was firmly entrenched in England. Descendants of vassals and household knights had secured English estates and held them for several generations. Some great Norman families, like Tosny, though still cherishing their Norman patrimonies, were gradually devoting more and more of their time and resources to their English honours.[3] Their piety more rarely extended to the monasteries founded on their Norman patrimonies; they had established new patrimonies in England, founded their own monasteries, and chosen them for their places of burial. Many of the new abbeys and priories were either independent houses of Augustinian or Premonstratensian canons, or dependencies of the great orders of Cluny and Citeaux, rather than cells of the Norman abbeys favoured by the first generation of settlers. As the interests of the lower ranks of landed vassals and subvassals became focused in England, and their military obligations became convertible into cash payments, their transformation from fighting knights into knights of the shire began. In 1166 they still made up a knightly rather than a gentry class; but the new duties of serving on commissions and grand juries were very soon to be laid upon them, and they were becoming settled and established. They had taken the first step on the long road that led eventually to the eighteenth-century knights of the shire who 'had never shot anything but woodcocks'.[4]

There was less room for further colonization, and the relatively few Poitevin captains who found their way to landed fortunes in England by royal favour under Henry II's sons mostly did so as the husbands of unwilling heiresses. And conditions affecting marriage alliances had

---

[2] Davies, TRHS (1979), 41–61; J. C. Holt, The Northerners (Oxford, 1961), p. 197–200.

[3] Musset, Francia (1978), 45–80.

[4] Horace Walpole, Letters, cited R. W. Ketton-Cremer, Norfolk Portraits (London, 1944), p. 152.

changed since the first Norman settlement. Matilda of Laigle had not complained of disparagement when she was married to Nigel of Aubigny, and Sibyl of Montgomery had accepted Robert fitz Haimo without apparent demur; though both husbands were relatively poor household knights they belonged to the same Norman race and were of comparable social standing.[5] The new resentment was due in part to social change; but it resulted too from rejection of the Poitevins as aliens. When Normandy was finally lost fifty years after Henry II's accession there was resentment, disturbance and rebellion; but the severance was not as unacceptable as it had seemed to be in Stephen's reign. Even by 1166 the shape of the future realm of England in law, institutions and social structure was beginning to be visible behind the broader framework of the old Anglo-Norman realm and the new Angevin 'Empire'.

[5] See R. A. Brown, 'The status of the Norman knight', *War and Government in the Middle Ages: Essays in honour of J. O. Prestwich*, ed. J. Gillingham and J. C. Holt (Boydell, 1984), pp. 18–32.

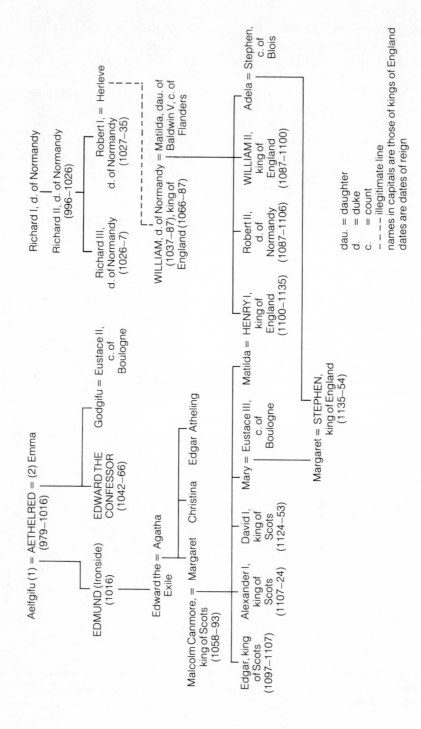

APPENDIX 1 Claimants to the English Throne, 1066–1100

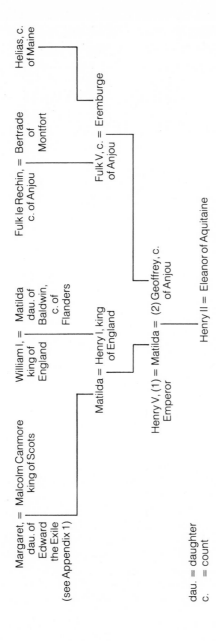

APPENDIX 2 The Ancestors of Henry II (*simplified*)

dau. = daughter
c.   = count

Bibliography of Abbreviated Titles

This bibliography includes only works that are cited more than once. Where a reference has been greatly abbreviated and might not be easily recognizable, the shortened form is given before the full reference. Abbreviated references to series and journals are included.

Adam of Domerham, *Historia de rebus gestis glastoniensibus*, ed. T. Hearne, 2 vols, Oxford, 1727.

Anderson, A. O. (ed.), *Scottish Annals from English Chroniclers*, London, 1908.

Anglo-Norman Studies: *Proceedings of the Battle Conference on Anglo-Norman Studies*, ed. R. Allen Brown, 1–4 (1979–82), continued from 1983 as *Anglo-Norman Studies*.

Anselm, *Opera*: *S. Anselmi Opera Omnia*, ed. F. S. Schmitt, 6 vols, Edinburgh, 1938–61.

ASC: *The Anglo-Saxon Chronicle*, ed. and trans. D. Whitelock, D. C. Douglas and S. I. Tucker, London, 1961 (citations are by version (A–E) and year).

Aston, T. H. 'The origins of the manor in England', *Social Relations and Ideas*, pp. 1–43.

Barlow, Frank, *Edward the Confessor*, London, 1970.

—— *The English Church 1000–1066*, 2nd edn, London and New York, 1979.

—— *The English Church 1066–1154*, London and New York, 1979.

—— *William Rufus*, London, 1983.

Barrow, G. W. S., *The Kingdom of the Scots*, London, 1973.

Bates, David R., *Normandy before 1066*, London and New York, 1982.

—— 'The character and career of Odo, Bishop of Bayeux', *Speculum*, 50 (1975), 1–20.

—— 'The land pleas of William I's reign', *BIHR*, 51 (1978), 1–19.

Battle Chronicle: *The Chronicle of Battle Abbey*, ed. Eleanor Searle (OMT), Oxford, 1980.

Bayeux Tapestry: *The Bayeux Tapestry*, ed. Frank Stenton et al., London, 1959.

Biddle, Martin (ed.), *Winchester in the Early Middle Ages*, Oxford, 1976.

Bigelow, M. M., *Placita Anglo-Normannica*, London, 1879.

BIHR: *Bulletin of the Institute of Historical Research*.

Bishop, T. A. M. and Chaplais, P., *Facsimiles of English Royal Writs to A.D. 1100*, Oxford, 1957.

Bisson, Thomas N., *Conservation of Coinage*, Oxford, 1979.

BL: British Library.

Brett, Martin, *The English Church under Henry I*, Oxford, 1970.

Brooke, Christopher, *London 800–1216: The Shaping of a City*, London, 1975.

Brooks, Nicholas, *The Early History of the Church of Canterbury*, Leicester, 1984.

Brown, R. Allen, *The Norman Conquest* (Documents of Medieval History, 5), London, 1984.

—— *The Normans and the Norman Conquest*, London, 1969.

Brown, R. A., Colvin, H. M. and Taylor, A. J., *The King's Works*, vol. 1, London, 1963.

Brut y Tywysogyon, or The Chronicle of the Princes (Red Book of Hergest version), ed. Thomas Jones, Cardiff, 1955.

BSAN: Bulletin de la Société des Antiquaires de Normandie.

Campbell, James (ed.), *The Anglo-Saxons*, Oxford, 1982.

Carmen: The Carmen de Hastingae Proelio of Guy Bishop of Amiens, ed. C. Morton and H. Muntz (OMT), Oxford, 1972.

Chaplais, P., 'Une charte originale de Guillaume le Conquérant', *L'Abbaye bénédictine de Fécamp*, 2 vols, Fécamp, 1959–60, 93–104.

Cheney, M. G., *Roger, Bishop of Worcester 1164–1179*, Oxford, 1980.

—— 'William Fitz Stephen and his Life of Archbishop Thomas', *Church and Government*, p. 149.

Chibnall, Marjorie (ed.), *Charters and Custumals of the Abbey of Holy Trinity Caen*, British Academy, Records of Social and Economic History, new ser., 5, 1982.

—— *The World of Orderic Vitalis*, Oxford, 1984.

Chronica Rogeri de Hoveden, ed. W. Stubbs, 4 vols, RS, 1868–71.

Chronicles of the Reigns of Stephen, Henry II and Richard I, ed. Richard Howlett, 4 vols, RS, 1884–9.

Chronicon abbatiae de Evesham, ed. W. D. Macray, RS, 1863.

Chronicon monasterii de Abingdon, ed. Joseph Stevenson, 2 vols, RS, 1958.

Church and Government: Church and Government in the Middle Ages, Essays presented to C. R. Cheney, ed. Christopher Brooke et al., Cambridge, 1976.

Clanchy, M. T., *From Memory to Written Record*, London, 1979.

Clark, C., 'Battle *c*.1100', *Anglo-Norman Studies*, 2 (1980), 21–41.

—— '"This ecclesiastical adventurer": Henry of Saint-Jean d'Angély', *EHR*, 84 (1969), 548–60.

—— 'Women's names . . .', *Speculum*, 53 (1978), 223–51.

Clay, Charles (ed.), *Early Yorkshire Families*, Yorkshire Archaeological Society, Record Series 135, 1973.

CNRS: Centre national de la recherche scientifique.

Complete Peerage: The Complete Peerage of England, Scotland, Ireland, Great Britain and the United Kingdom, by G. E. C. [okayne] new edn, 13 vols in 14, 1910–59.

Constable, G., *Monastic Tithes from their Origins to the Twelfth Century*, Cambridge, 1964.

Councils and Synods: Councils and Synods with other Documents relating to the

English Church, vol. 1, ed. D. Whitelock, M. Brett and C. N. L. Brooke, Oxford, 1981.

CUL: Cambridge University Library.

David, C. W., *Robert Curthose, Duke of Normandy* (Harvard Historical Studies), Cambridge, Mass., 1920.

Davies, R. R., 'Kings, lords and liberties in the March of Wales, 1066–1272', *TRHS*, 5th ser., 29, 1979, 41–62.

Davis, R. H. C., *King Stephen*, London, 1967.

—— 'The Treaty between William earl of Gloucester and Roger earl of Hereford', *Early Medieval Miscellany*, 139–46.

—— 'William of Jumièges, Robert Curthose and the Norman Succession', *EHR*, 95 (1980), 597–606.

DB: Domesday Book, 4 vols, Record Commission, 1783–1816.

Dialogus de Scaccario: Richard fitz Nigel, *Dialogus de Scaccario*, ed. Charles Johnson, with corrections by F. E. L. Carter and D. E. Greenway (OMT), Oxford, 1983.

Diceto: *Radulfi de Diceto opera historica*, ed. W. Stubbs, RS, 1876.

Dolley, Michael, *The Norman Conquest and the English Coinage*, London, 1966.

Douglas, D. C. (ed.), *Feudal Documents from the Abbey of Bury St Edmunds*, British Academy, Records of Social and Economic History, 8, 1932.

—— (ed.), *The Domesday Monachorum of Christ Church Canterbury*, London, 1944.

—— *William the Conqueror*, London, 1964.

Dyer, Christopher, *Lords and Peasants in a Changing Society*, Cambridge, 1980.

Eadmer, *HN: Eadmeri historia novorum in Anglia*, ed. M. Rule, RS, 1884.

Eadmer, *Vita Anselmi: The Life of St Anselm by Eadmer*, ed. R. W. Southern (OMT), Oxford, 1972.

Early Medieval Miscellany: A Medieval Miscellany for Doris Mary Stenton, ed. P. M. Barnes and C. F. Slade, PRS, new ser., 36, 1962.

Edwards, Kathleen, *The English Secular Cathedrals in the Middle Ages*, Manchester, 1949.

EHD: English Historical Documents, vol. 1 (*c.*500–1042), ed. D. Whitelock; vol. 2 (1042–1189), ed. D. C. Douglas and G. W. Greenaway, London, 1953–5.

EHR: English Historical Review.

English, Barbara, *The Lords of Holderness*, Oxford, 1979.

English Romanesque Art 1066–1200, Catalogue of the Exhibition at the Hayward Gallery, 1984, Arts Council of Great Britain, London, 1984.

EYC: Early Yorkshire Charters, vols 1–3, ed. W. Farrer; vols 4–12, ed. C. T. Clay (Yorks. Archaeological Society), 1914–65.

Eyton, R. W., *Antiquities of Shropshire*, 12 vols, London, 1854–60.

Fauroux: *Recueil des actes des ducs de Normandie de 911 à 1066*, ed. Marie Fauroux, Mémoires de la Société des Antiquaires de Normandie, 36, Caen, 1961.

Finberg, H. P. R., *Tavistock Abbey*, Cambridge, 1951.

Foreville, R. (ed.), *Les mutations socio-culturelles au tournant des xie–xiie siècles* (CNRS), Paris, 1984.

—— 'The synod of the province of Rouen in the eleventh and twelfth centuries', *Church and Government*, 19–40.

Fowler, G. H., *Bedfordshire in 1086*, Quarto memoirs of the Bedfordshire Historical Record Society, 1922.

Freeman, E. A., *The History of the Norman Conquest of England*, 6 vols, Oxford, 1867–79.

FW: Florence of Worcester, *Chronicon ex chronicis*, ed. B. Thorpe, 2 vols, English Historical Society, London, 1848–9.

Galbraith, V. H., *Domesday Book: Its Place in Administrative History*, Oxford, 1974.

—— *The Making of Domesday Book*, Oxford, 1961.

—— 'Notes on the career of Samson, bishop of Worcester', *EHR*, 82 (1967), 86–101.

—— and Tait, James (eds), *Herefordshire Domesday*, PRS, 1950.

Gervase of Canterbury, *Historical Works*, ed. W. Stubbs, 2 vols, RS, 1879–80.

Gesta abbatum monasterii sancti Albani, ed. H. T. Riley, 3 vols, RS, 1867–9.

Gesta Stephani, ed. K. R. Potter, revised R. H. C. Davis, (OMT), Oxford, 1976.

Gibson, Margaret, *Lanfranc of Bec*, Oxford, 1978.

Giraldi Cambrensis Opera, ed. J. S. Brewer et al., 7 vols, RS, 1861–91.

Glanvill: *The Treatise on the Laws and Customs of England commonly called Glanvill*, ed. G. D. G. Hall (NMT), London and Edinburgh, 1965.

Green, J. A., '"Praeclarum et Magnificum Antiquitatis Monumentum": the earliest surviving Pipe Roll', *BIHR*, 55 (1982), 1–17.

—— 'The last century of Danegeld', *EHR*, 96 (1981), 241–58.

Greenway, D. E., *Charters of the Honour of Mowbray 1107–1191*, British Academy, Records of Social and Economic History, new ser., 1, 1972.

Harmer, F. E., *Anglo-Saxon Writs*, Manchester, 1952.

Harvey, Barbara, *Westminster Abbey and its Estates in the Middle Ages*, Oxford, 1977.

Harvey, S. P. J., 'The extent and profitability of demesne agriculture in England in the later eleventh century', *Social Relations and Ideas*, pp. 45–72.

Haskins, C. H., *Norman Institutions* (Harvard Historical Studies), Cambridge, Mass., 1925.

Hatcher, John, 'English serfdom and villeinage: towards a reassessment', *Past and Present*, 90 (1981), 3–39.

Henry of Huntingdon, *Historia Anglorum*, ed. T. Arnold, RS, 1879.

Herefordshire Domesday, see Galbraith and Tait.

Hill, J. W. F., *Medieval Lincoln*, Cambridge, 1948.

Hilton, R. H. (ed.), *The Stoneleigh Leger Book*, Dugdale Society, 24, 1960.

Holdsworth, C. H., 'Christina of Markyate', *Medieval Women*, ed. Derek Baker, Studies in Church History, Subsidia 1, Oxford, 1978.

Hollister, C. Warren, '"Magnates and *Curiales*" in early Norman England', *Viator*, 8 (1977), 63–82.

—— *The Military Organization of Norman England*, Oxford, 1965.

—— 'The misfortunes of the Mandevilles', *History*, 58 (1973), 18–28.

—— 'The origins of the English treasury', *EHR*, 93 (1978), 262–75.

—— and Baldwin, J. W., 'The rise of administrative kingship: Henry I and Philip Augustus', *American Historical Review*, 83 (1978), 867–905.

—— and Keefe, T. K., 'The making of the Angevin Empire', *Journal of British Studies*, 12 (1973), 1–25.

Holt, J. C., 'Feudal Society and the Family in Medieval England', *TRHS*, 5th ser., 32 (1982), 193–212; 33 (1983), 193–220; 34 (1984), 1–26; 35 (1985), forthcoming.

—— 'Politics and property in early medieval England', *Past and Present*, 57 (1972), 3–52.

—— 'The introduction of knight service in England', *Anglo-Norman Studies*, 6 (1984 for 1983), 89–106.

Howell, M. E., *Regalian Right in Medieval England*, London, 1962.

Hyams, P. R., *King, Lords and Peasants in Medieval England*, Oxford, 1980.

Jocelyn of Brakelond: *The Chronicle of Jocelyn of Brakelond*, ed. H. E. Butler (NMT), Edinburgh and London, 1949.

John of Salisbury, *Historia Pontificalis*, ed. M. Chibnall (NMT), Edinburgh and London, 1956.

John of Worcester: *The Chronicle of John of Worcester 1118–1140*, ed. J. R. H. Weaver, Oxford, 1908.

Jordan Fantosme's Chronicle, ed. R. C. Johnston, Oxford, 1981.

Kapelle, W. E., *The Norman Conquest of the North*, London, 1979.

Kealey, E. J., *Roger of Salisbury*, Berkeley and London, 1972.

King, Edmund, 'The Anarchy of King Stephen's Reign', *TRHS*, 5th ser., 34 (1984), 133–54.

—— *Peterborough Abbey 1086–1310*, Cambridge, 1973.

Knowles, David, *The Episcopal Colleagues of Archbishop Thomas Becket*, Cambridge, 1951.

—— *The Monastic Order in England*, 2nd edn, Cambridge, 1962.

Leges Henrici primi, ed. L. J. Downer, Oxford, 1972.

Lemarignier, J.-F., *Recherches sur l'hommage en marche et les frontières féo-dales*, Lille, 1945.

Le Neve, John, *Fasti Ecclesiae Anglicanae 1066–1300*, compiled by D. E. Greenway, 3 vols, London, 1968–77.

Lennard, Reginald, *Rural England 1086–1135*, Oxford, 1959.

Le Patourel, John, *Feudal Empires, Norman and Plantagenet*, London, 1984.

—— 'The Norman colonization of Britain', *I Normanni e la loro espansione in Europa nell'alto medioevo*, Centro Italiano di Studi sull'Alto Medioevo, Settimana 16, Spoleto, 1969, 409–38.

—— *The Norman Empire*, Oxford, 1976.

—— 'The reports of the trial on Penenden Heath', *Studies in Medieval History presented to F. M. Powicke*, ed. R. W. Hunt et al., Oxford, 1948, 15–26.

(The) Letters of John of Salisbury, vol. 1, ed. W. J. Millor and H. E. Butler, revised C. N. L. Brooke (NMT), 1955; vol. 2, ed. W. J. Millor and C. N. L. Brooke (OMT), Oxford, 1979.

(The) Letters of Lanfranc, ed. H. Clover and M. Gibson (OMT), Oxford, 1979.

Liber Eliensis, ed. E. O. Blake, Camden 3rd ser., 92, 1962.

Liebermann, F. (ed.), *Die Gesetze der Angelsachsen*, 3 vols, Halle a. S., 1903–16.

Lloyd, J. E., *A History of Wales from the Earliest Times*, 3rd edn, 2 vols, London, 1939.

Maitland, F. W., *Domesday Book and Beyond*, Cambridge, 1907.

Malmesbury, *GP: Willelmi Malmesbiriensis de gestis pontificum Anglorum libri quinque*, ed. N. E. S. A. Hamilton, RS, 1870.

Malmesbury, *GR*: William of Malmesbury, *De gestis regum Anglorum*, ed. W. Stubbs, 2 vols, RS, 1887–9.

Malmesbury, *HN: The Historia Novella by William of Malmesbury*, ed. K. R. Potter (NMT), Edinburgh and London, 1955.

Map, Walter, see Walter.

Mason, J. F. A., 'Roger de Montgomery and his sons (1067–1102)', *TRHS*, 5th ser., 13, 1963, 1–28.

—— *William the First and the Sussex Rapes*, Historical Association, Hastings, 1966.

Migne, *PL: Patrologiae cursus completus series latina*, ed. J. P. Migne, 221 vols, Paris, 1844–64.

Miller, Edward and Hatcher, John, *Medieval England: Rural Society and Economic Change 1086–1348*, London and New York, 1978.

Milsom, S. F. C., *Historical Foundations of the Common Law*, 2nd edn, London, 1981.

—— *The Legal Framework of English Feudalism*, Cambridge, 1976.

Morey, Adrian and Brooke, C. N. L., *Gilbert Foliot and his Letters*, Cambridge, 1965.

—— and Brooke, C. N. L. (eds), *The Letters and Charters of Gilbert Foliot*, Cambridge, 1967.

Musset, L., 'Aux origines d'une classe dirigéante: Les Tosny', *Francia*, 5 (1978 for 1977), 45–80.

—— 'Gouvernés et gouvernants dans le monde scandinave et dans le monde normand', *Gouvernés et gouvernants*, 2, Recueils de la Société Jean Bodin, 23, Brussels, 1968.

—— (ed.), *Les actes de Guillaume le Conquérant et de la reine Mathilde pour les abbayes caennaises*, Mémoires de la Société des Antiquaires de Normandie, 37, Caen, 1967.

Nightingale, Pamela, 'Some London moneyers in the eleventh and twelfth centuries', *The Numismatic Chronicle*, 142 (1982), 34–50.

NMT: Nelson's Medieval Texts.

OMT: Oxford Medieval Texts.

Orderic: *The Ecclesiastical History of Orderic Vitalis*, ed. Marjorie Chibnall (OMT), Oxford, 1969–80.

Pollock, F. and Maitland, F. W., *The History of English Law before the time of Edward I*, 2nd edn, with an introduction by S. F. C. Milsom, Cambridge, 1968.

Poole, A. L., *From Domesday Book to Magna Carta 1087–1216*, Oxford, 1951.

Poole, R. L., *The Exchequer in the Twelfth Century*, Oxford, 1912.

Powicke, F. M. (ed.), *The Life of Ailred of Rievaulx by Walter Daniel* (OMT), Oxford, 1978.

PR 31 H.I: Magnus Rotulus Scaccarii 31 Henry I, ed. J. Hunter, Record Commission, 1833.

Prestwich, J. O., 'The military household of the Norman Kings', *EHR*, 96 (1981), 1–37.

PRS: Pipe Roll Society.

Rees, Una (ed.), *The Cartulary of Shrewsbury Abbey*, 2 vols, Aberystwyth, 1975.

Regesta: *Regesta regum Anglo-Normannorum*, vol. 1, ed. H. W. C. Davis; vol. 2, ed. C. Johnson and H. A. Cronne; vols 3 and 4, ed. H. A. Cronne and R. H. C. Davis, Oxford, 1913–69.

Reynolds, Susan, *An Introduction to the History of Medieval Towns*, Oxford, 1977.

—— *Kingdoms and Communities in Western Europe 900–1300*, Oxford, 1984.

—— 'The rulers of London in the twelfth century', *History*, 57 (1972), 337–57.

Richter, Michael, *Giraldus Cambrensis*, Aberystwyth, 1972.

Robert of Torigni, *Chronicles of the Reigns of Stephen, Henry II and Richard I* (RS), 4.

Round, J. H., *Feudal England*, London, 1909.

RS: Rolls Series (Chronicles and Memorials of Great Britain and Ireland during the Middle Ages).

Rowlands, I. A., 'Aspects of the Norman settlement in Dyfed', *Anglo-Norman Studies*, 3 (1981 for 1980).

Saltman, A., *Theobald Archbishop of Canterbury*, London, 1956.

Sayers, J. E., *Papal Judges Delegate in the Province of Canterbury 1198–1254*, Oxford, 1971.

Select Canterbury Cases: *Select Cases from the Ecclesiastical Courts of the Province of Canterbury c.1200–1301*, ed. Norma Adams and Charles Donahue, Selden Society, 95, 1981 for 1977–8.

Sheehan, M. M., *The Will in Medieval England*, Toronto, 1963.

Simeon of Durham: *Symeonis monachi opera omnia*, 2 vols, ed. Thomas Arnold, RS, 1882–5.

Smalley, Beryl, *The Becket Conflict and the Schools*, Oxford, 1973.

Social Relations and Ideas, Essays in honour of R. H. Hilton, ed. T. H. Aston et al., Cambridge, 1983.

Southern, R. W., *Medieval Humanism and other Studies*, Oxford, 1970.

—— *St Anselm and his Biographer*, Cambridge, 1963.

Stenton, Doris M., *English Justice between the Norman Conquest and the Great Charter 1066–1215*, London, 1965.

Stenton, F. M., *Anglo-Saxon England*, 3rd edn, Oxford, 1971.

—— (ed.), *Documents illustrating the Social and Economic History of the Danelaw*, British Academy, Records of Social and Economic History, 5, 1920.

—— *The First Century of English Feudalism 1066–1166*, 2nd edn, Oxford, 1961.

—— *The Latin Charters of the Anglo-Saxon Period*, Oxford, 1955.

Stoke-by-Clare Cartulary, ed. C. Harper-Bill and R. Mortimer, Suffolk Records Society, Suffolk Charters, 3 vols, 1982–4.

Stubbs, William, *Select Charters*, 9th edn, Oxford, 1929.

Tillmann, H., *Die päpstlichen Legaten in England*, Bonn, 1926.

TRHS: *Transactions of the Royal Historical Society*.

van Caenegem, R. C. (ed.), *Royal Writs in England from the Conquest to Glanvill*, Selden Society, 77, 1959.

VCH: *The Victoria History of the Counties of England.*

Vita Herluini, ed. J. Armitage Robinson, in *Gilbert Crispin, Abbot of Westminster*, Cambridge, 1911, 87–110.

(The) 'Vita Wulfstani' of William of Malmesbury, ed. R. R. Darlington, Camden 3rd ser., 40, 1928.

Voss, Lena, *Henrich von Blois*, Berlin, 1932.

Walter Map, *De nugis curialium*, ed. M. R. James, revised C. N. L. Brooke and Roger Mynors (OMT), Oxford, 1983.

Warren, W. L., *Henry II*, London, 1973.

Whitelock, Dorothy (ed.), *Anglo-Saxon Wills*, Cambridge, 1930.

Wightman, W. E., *The Lacy Family in England and Normandy 1066–1194*, Oxford, 1966.

William of Jumièges, *Gesta Normannorum Ducum*, ed. J. Marx, Société de l'Histoire de Normandie, Rouen, 1914.

William of Malmesbury, see Malmesbury.

William of Newburgh, *Historia rerum Anglicarum, Chronicles of the Reigns of Stephen, Henry II and Richard I*, RS, vol. 1.

William of Poitiers: Guillaume de Poitiers, *Histoire de Guillaume le Conquérant*, ed. R. Foreville, Les Classiques de l'Histoire de France au Moyen Âge, Paris, 1952.

Worcester Cartulary: The Cartulary of Worcester Priory, ed. R. R. Darlington, PRS, 1968.

Young, C. R., *The Royal Forests of Medieval England*, Leicester, 1979.

Yver, Jean, 'Autour de l'absence d'avouerie en Normandie', *BSAN*, 57 (1965), 189–283.

—— 'Les premières institutions du duché de Normandie', *I Normanni e la loro espansione in Europa nell'alto medioevo*, Centro Italiano di Studi sull'Alto Medioevo, Settimana 16, Spoleto, 1969, 299–366.

Zarnecki, G., '1066 and architectural sculpture', *Proceedings of the British Academy*, 52 (1966), 87–104; reprinted, *Studies in Romanesque Sculpture*, London, 1979.

Index